W. Simpson.

The Northern Muse

The
Northern Muse

An Anthology of Scots Vernacular Poetry

Arranged by
John Buchan

Thomas Nelson and Sons, Ltd.

London, Edinburgh, and New York

(Printed in Great Britain.)

First Impression, October 1924

TO

LORD ROSEBERY

IN MEMORY OF THE GREEN BOUNDS OF
TWEEDDALE AND LOTHIAN

v

CONTENTS

Contents

(2,470)

Contents

ix

BOOK III

CHAGRIN D'AMOUR

BOOK IV

THE HEARTH

BOOK V

THE OPEN ROAD

BOOK VI

KING AND COMMONWEAL

Contents

BOOK VII

The Human Comedy

Contents

BOOK VIII

BACCHANALIA

BOOK IX

CHARACTERS

Contents   xiii

BOOK X

LITERATURE

BOOK XI

SPORT

BOOK XII

NATURE

xiv   Contents

Contents

BOOK XIV
ENCHANTMENTS

BOOK XV
LACRIMAE RERUM

Contents

Contents

BOOK XVIII

DIVINE PHILOSOPHY

BOOK XVIII

Divine Philosophy

INTRODUCTION

I HAVE made this little anthology with no other purpose than to please myself. It contains the things which, as a lover of Scots verse, I turn to most often and desire to have in a compact form. Since there is no motive of instruction, I have felt myself at liberty to arrange it, not chronologically, but according to subject, and boldly to mingle old and new. Many Scots poems have a vogue altogether independent of their poetic merit ; these I have neglected, and have confined my choice to pieces which in varying degree seem to me to be literature, from a bottle song just redeemed from doggerel by some quaintness of fancy to the high flights of Burns and Dunbar. If it is complained that much has been omitted which was worthy of inclusion, the reply must be that the book is not a *Corpus Poeticum Boreale*, but a selection, and a selection governed by personal tastes.

The Ballads have been sparingly used, for they are accessible in many editions. I have not scrupled to print a single verse or a group of verses from a poem, or to omit a passage where it seemed desirable ; the notes in the Commentary will show where the complete text may be found. The fantastic spelling of the older pieces has in certain cases been very slightly modified. With a little practice there is no difficulty in under-

standing the " makars," even Gawain Douglas, provid-
ing they be read aloud.   There is a glossary at the foot
of each page to vernacular words and idioms, and to
those accustomed to one dialect only, let me repeat the
advice to read aloud.   " Aberdeen-awa " looks difficult
to, say, a Lothian eye, but it is simple enough to a
Lothian ear.

The compiler of such an anthology as this makes by
implication a claim of merit for his exhibits.   It is only
by an effort that I can force myself to judge these with
any pretence to impartiality.   The sweet old airs to which
the lyrics go have been in my ear since childhood.   The
speech with its rich and vigorous idiom is so linked to
memories that no other tongue can ever seem to me so
expressive.   But since everybody has not this happy
obsession, I propose briefly to set forth what seems to
me to be the reasonable claim which can be made for the
Scots vernacular and its literature.

I

The Teutonic speech of Northern England was brought
into Scotland by the first Anglian settlers, and acquired
throughout the succeeding centuries certain minor but
clearly marked peculiarities.   When Scots literature begins, towards the close of the fourteenth century, it is
written in a tongue substantially the same as the Northern dialect of Early English, which was the speech
current north of the Humber.   Gradually a literary
language was formed, akin to, but not the same as, the
spoken tongue, and this literary language was influenced
by Chaucer and the poets of the South.   But presently
the Midland dialect became the only literary language
in England, and the Northern dialect drew further away

from it and followed a path of its own. The early Scots writers, like Barbour and Wyntoun, wrote what was virtually Northern English. The *Kingis Quair* of James I., though written originally in Southern English, was northernized by the copyists; Henryson's language was little affected by the south; then, as the Middle Scots period develops, we find Dunbar and Gawain Douglas and Sir David Lyndsay using a language of their own —Northern English in stock, with a slight French element, and a strong kinship with the spoken tongue of the Lowlands, which had developed its own idiosyncrasies. But to every Scots writer, however robust his patriotism, his speech was " English," [1] and Dunbar calls Chaucer " of our Inglisch all the lycht." [2] Gawain Douglas, indeed, claims to be a " Scottis " and not an " Inglis " poet, but he confessed himself forced to use some " Sudroun " words,[3] and his work, though it accepts more from the spoken vernacular, is in the same tradition as that of the other " makars," so that Lyndsay could speak of him as " in our Inglis rethorick the rose." A stout Scots nationalist like Hume of Godscroft, who lived at the close of the sixteenth century, might maintain that he wrote his Scottish mother-tongue, and that he had " ever accounted it a mean study to learn to read or speak English . . . esteeming it but a dialect of our own, and that (perhaps) more corrupt." [4] But his claim was a mere juggling with words.

---

[1] *Cf.* the *Wallace* (IX. 295–7) of Thomas de Longueville :—

> " Lykly he was, manlik of countenance,
> Lik to the Scottis be mekill governance,
> Saiff off his tong, for Inglis had he nane."

[2] *The Golden Targe.*
[3] Prologue to *Eneados*, Book I.
[4] Preface to the *History of the Houses of Douglas and Angus*, 1644.

Perhaps the process might be thus summarily and broadly stated. The Scots speech was in its beginnings the Northern dialect of English, which, as a spoken tongue, soon acquired minor local differences. When it came to be written it was the language of Northern England, and, though influenced to some extent by the South, it remained Northern. It was a literary speech, coloured by French and Latin, but it kept its affinities with the spoken vernacular and borrowed from it, being perhaps not much further removed from it than any book language is from that spoken in street and ale-house. As the Midland dialect became the literary language of England, Scots preserved its Northern quality and drew farther apart, developing powers and beauties of its own, though much clogged by an imperfect assimilation of its borrowings. It called itself English, but it was a substantive national speech, and its literature was a national literature, close enough to the common people to be intelligible to them, and yet capable of treating of all themes from the homeliest to the highest. Had circumstances been different Scots might have developed into a true world-speech, " perhaps," as Mr. Henderson says, " more than rivalling literary English in fertility of idioms, and in wealth, beauty, and efficacy of diction," or Southern and Northern might have united in one majestic stream.

But the sixteenth century brought a sharp fissure. The chief disruptive agent was the Reformation, which in Scotland not only involved a more violent breach with the past than elsewhere, but put secular literature under a ban and cut at the root of vernacular art and song. It led to a severance with France and a closer contact with England. It made the chief reading of

Scotland the Bible—in English ; it gave her the metrical
Psalms—in English ; and its great protagonists, like
John Knox, had so many English affiliations that they
were accused by their enemies of being " triple traitoris
quha . . . knappis suddrone." [1] The making of verse
ceased to be a pastime of people strongly troubled about
their souls, and the few who still practised the art turned,
like the poets of the *Deliciæ Poetarum Scotorum*, to
Latin, or, like Drummond of Hawthornden, Aytoun,
and Alexander, to the courtly muse of Edmund Spenser.
The tongue which was spoken at kirk and market went
out of literature for a century and more, and when it
returned it was no longer as a national speech, but as
a modish exercise. Politics, theology, a little law, and
less history held the boards in seventeenth century
Scotland, and their language was for the best part an
ungainly English.

There was a revival early in the eighteenth century
at the hands of Allan Ramsay, but its motive was antiquarian. The very men who laboured to expunge any
Scotticisms from their prose and polished their Augustan
couplets as their serious contribution to letters, turned
a curious eye back to their own sixteenth century, and
Ramsay's *Tea-Table Miscellany* and *Ever Green* were
the consequence. We owe much to this antiquarian
interest, for it preserved the old poetry when it was
in imminent danger of perishing. Thomson's *Orpheus
Caledonius* appeared in 1725 ; and following on the
publication of Bishop Percy's *Reliques* came a flood
of invaluable miscellanies, such as Herd's *Ancient and
Modern Scots Songs* (1769), Pinkerton's two volumes of

---

[1] John Hamilton's *Catholik Traictise*, 1581.

Ballads (1781 and 1783), Johnson's *Musical Museum*
(1787), culminating in Sir Walter Scott's great *Minstrelsy of the Scottish Border* (1802–3). The vernacular
had become a book tongue to be studied and annotated;
but when its students had anything to say, they said it
in that English which was now the common speech of
the literate from Devon to Aberdeen.

But Scots had one season of flowering left to it so
splendid that it is hard to believe that the blossoms were
the product of artificial tending and not the indigenous
growth of the fields. Burns is by universal admission
one of the most natural of poets, but he used a language
which was, even in his own day, largely exotic. His
Scots was not the living speech of his countrymen, like
the English of Shelley, and—in the main—the Scots of
Dunbar; it was a literary language subtly blended from
the old " makars " and the refrains of folk poetry, much
tinctured with the special dialect of Ayrshire, and with
a solid foundation of English, accented *more Boreali*.
No Scot in the later eighteenth century, whether in
Poosie Nansie's or elsewhere, spoke exactly as Burns
wrote. Perhaps the plain speech of a people can never
be the language of poetry, but a speech so limited and
specialized as the spoken vernacular of eighteenth century
Scotland could scarcely suffice for the needs of a great
poet. Burns, as he was bound to be, was retrospective and
antiquarian in his syntax and vocabulary. He created
a noble poetic diction, but it was a creation, not the
reproduction of a speech still in the ears of men.

A century and a half have passed since Burns wrote,
and the vernacular, confined to an ever-narrowing prov-
ince, has suffered a further detrition. Old words and
constructions have lapsed from use; modes of speech

which were current so late as thirty years ago among the shepherds of Ettrick and Galloway are scarcely intelligible to their successors ; in the towns the patois bids fair to become merely a broadened and dilapidated English; and though the dwellers north of Tweed will be eternally distinguishable from their neighbours by certain idiosyncrasies of speech, these idiosyncrasies will be of voice and accent, and not of language. The Scots vernacular ceased in the sixteenth century to be a language in the full sense, capable of being used on all varieties of theme, and was confined to the rustic and the parochial ; capable, indeed, in the hands of a master of sounding the depths of the human heart, but ill suited to the infinite variety of human life. Even from this narrowed orbit it has fallen, and is now little more than a robust rendering of colloquial English. The literary Scots which Burns wrote is more than ever a literary tongue, far removed from any speech in common use. It is understood by many, not because it is in their ears from hearing, but because it is in their memories from reading. To restore the Scots vernacular is beyond the power of any Act of Parliament, because the life on which it depended has gone. Thirty years ago I learned in the Tweedside glens to talk a Scots, which was then the speech of a people secluded from the modern world ; to-day if I spoke it at a Tweeddale clipping I should find only a few old men to understand me. Scots can survive only as a book-tongue, and it is to that purpose that I would bespeak the efforts of my countrymen. The knowledge of the book-tongue is still fairly common, and if, in the mill of a standardized education, it should ever be crushed out, we shall lose the power of appreciating not only the " makars," but

the best of the Ballads, Burns, and Sir Walter Scott—
that part of our literary heritage which is most inti-
mately and triumphantly our own.

It follows that the Scots poets since Burns have been
retrospective, as he was. They are all of them, from
the minor bards of *Whistle Binkie* to Stevenson and
Mrs. Jacob and Mr. Charles Murray, exponents of a
literary convention and not singers in the speech of
the common day. That is not to say that their art is
not fresh and spontaneous, for art may work through
conventions and yet be free. Poetry, composed with
infinite pains from a thousand echoes, may have the
sound of the natural voice, and to this virtue I think
some of our modern Scots verse attains. It is always
an exercise, the fruit of care and scholarship, and since
the literary tongue is so nobly pedigreed, it will preserve (so long as it has an audience to understand it)
a flavour and a grace which make it the fittest medium
for a Scot to express certain moods and longings. It
will be least successful when it is too antiquarian and
becomes a mere clot of coagulated dialect, or when it
attempts to reproduce phonetically a spoken word which
is too disintegrated for literature. It must always be
in a sense a *pastiche*, but that is not inimical to artistic
excellence. Nevertheless—let us regretfully face the fact
—the *pastiche* is not a growth of enduring vitality, and
it has the further drawback that its appeal is circum-
scribed owing to the lack of any canon of vernacular
Scots. Every shire has its variant. If we call Sir
Walter Scott's version the classic standard, what are we
to make of Burns? And if the Border speech is metro-
politan, is Mr. Charles Murray provincial?

There is a sentence in a letter of Burns to George

Thomson [1] which seems to me to point a way to the true future of Scots in our literature. " There is a *naïveté*," he wrote, " a pastoral simplicity in a slight admixture of Scots words and phraseology which is more in unison —at least to my taste, and, I would add, to any genuine Caledonian taste—with the simple pathos or rustic sprightliness of our native music, than any English verses whatever." He was speaking only of songs to be set to old airs, but the words have a wider application. It is to be noted that in some of the greatest masterpieces of our tongue, in the Ballads, in Burns's *Ae Fond Kiss*, in Scott throughout—in *Proud Maisie*, in *Wandering Willie's Tale*, in the talk of Jeanie Deans— the dialect is never emphasized ; only a word here and there provides a Northern tone. I can imagine a Scottish literature of both verse and prose based on this " slight admixture," a literature which should be, in Mr. Gregory Smith's admirable phrase, " a delicate colouring of standard English with Northern tints." In such work the drawbacks of the *pastiche* would disappear ; because of its Northern colouring it would provide the means for an expression of the racial temperament, and because it was also English, and one of the great world-speeches, no limits would be set to its range and appeal.

II

From what has been written it follows that Scots poetry after the sixteenth century has not the width and variety of a national literature, covering all the moods of life and thought. Judged by his scope, Dunbar is its greatest figure. He has been differently

[1] January 26, 1793. I owe the quotation to Mr. Gregory Smith's *Scottish Literature*.

estimated : Mr. Russell Lowell thought him a bore—
" He who is national enough to like thistles may browse
there to his heart's content " ; Mr. Andrew Lang is
tepid in his praise ; Sir Walter Scott, on the other hand,
thought him the greatest Scots poet before Burns ; and
the friends of the late W. P. Ker will remember with
what gusto he used to declare, " Dunbar is *my* poet."
To me he seems to rank with the Ballads, Burns, and
the Waverley Novels as one of the four of Scotland's
main contributions to letters. In any case it will not
be disputed that the " makars " alone essayed and suc-
ceeded in the grand manner—alone attempted (with
varying success) the full circle of poetic material. Since
their day vernacular poetry has had its wings clipped,
and though it has soared high the latitude of its flights
has shrunk.

Defects have followed from this circumscription of
area, this absorption in too narrow a world. The most
notable is a certain provincialism of theme, which is
always in danger of degenerating into a provincialism
of thought. Scots poetry is apt to be self-absorbed, to
become the scrupulous chronicle of small beer, to lack
the long perspective and the " high translunary things "
of greater art.

> " Tiny pleasures occupy the place
> Of glories and of duties : as the feet
> Of fabled fairies, when the sun goes down,
> Trip o'er the grass where wrestlers strove by day."

This in itself is no blemish, and, indeed, a confined out-
look could scarcely have been avoided in the literature
of a speech diverted from the larger uses of life and forced
back upon one class and environment. But it means

that it does not enter for the greater contests of the Muses, since a cameoist can never be a Pheidias, or a Teniers a Rembrandt.

From this inevitable provincialism spring two faults which are the prime weaknesses of Scots verse. One is a distressing facility, a preference for easy cadences and trite epithets and tedious jingles, a lack of the classic reticence and discipline. Burns is a supreme example to the contrary, and he remains a miracle in the Scots tradition. He has the sureness and the rightness of the antique, but much Scots verse is marred by a cheap glibness, an admiration for the third or fourth best, which is due to the lack of a strong artistic canon. It is a defect which is found in popular songs and popular hymns, the price which poetry must pay for popular handling. Scott said that a " vile sixpenny planet " looked in at the window when James Hogg was born, and that planet has not lost its baneful influence. The second defect is sentimentality, which is a preference for the inferior in feeling as the other is a preference for the inferior in form. A study of *Whistle Binkie* and the immense body of minor Scots verse in the last century shows us writers painfully at ease in Zion, who gloat over domestic sentiment till the charm has gone, who harp on obvious pathos till the last trace of the pathetic vanishes, who make so crude a frontal attack upon the emotions that the emotions are left inviolate. Whether it be children, or lost love, or death, or any other of the high matters of poetry, there is the same gross pawing which rubs off the delicate bloom. Heaven is as frequent and as foolish a counter in such verse as in bad hymns, and there is a perpetual saccharine sweetness which quickly cloys. Instead of Burns's " stalk of carle

hemp," there seems to be in such writers a stalk of coarse
barley sugar.

The misfortune is that these faults are found not only
in trumpery verse, but in work of real and often of high
merit. Burns is free from them, but they are rampant
in Hogg, Tannahill, Allan Cunningham, and most of
their successors. They are the result of the provincialism into which the vernacular speech fell, and the con-
sequent " in-breeding " of vernacular literature. But
the same cause has produced qualities which may well
be held to redress the balance. They are qualities, too,
which belong to the whole literature from Henryson to our
own day. Vernacular poetry is in a peculiar degree the
reflex of the Scots character, and, like that character,
combines within itself startling anomalies. It has on
one side a hardy and joyous realism, a gusto for close
detail, a shrewd, observing intimacy with the natural
world. Even in conventional work there will come
pieces of sharp concrete experience which give it a rude
life, and at the best there is a constant sense of the three
dimensions of space, of men and women moving in a
world riotously alive. The other side is within hearing of the horns of Elfland—a paradox from the point
of view of art, but complementary when seen in relation to the national character, which is founded on
these opposites. Romance is always at call, an airy,
diaphanous romance, so that Scots poetry is like some
cathedral of the Middle Ages, with peasants gossiping
in the nave and the devout at prayer in side chapels,
carved grotesques adjacent to stained-glass saints, and
beams of heavenly light stealing through the brooding
upper darkness. The Hogg of the *Shepherd's Calendar*
can claim with justice to be a " king of the mountain

and the fairy school." The combination is found in every literature, but in Scots the transition from the commonplace to the fantastic and back again is especially easy, since each mood has its source in the history and character of the race. Our Muse is like the Gifted Gilfillan in *Waverley*, who turned readily from the New Jerusalem of the Saints to the price of beasts at Mauchline fair, or like Shakespeare's Cleopatra, who can pass from banter with a peasant to a mood of sublime soliloquy. Romance in the North has always some salt of the pedestrian, and the most prosaic house of life has casements opening upon fairy seas.

J. B.

ACKNOWLEDGMENTS

THE Editor desires to offer his sincere thanks to the following authors and publishers who have permitted him to quote copyright poems: Professor Alexander Gray, Mr. Hamish Hendry, Mrs. Jacob, Mr. Joseph Lee, Mr. G. K. Menzies, Mr. W. S. Morrison, Mr. Neil Munro, and Mr. Charles Murray ; Messrs. Blackwood and Sons, Messrs. Chatto and Windus, Messrs. Constable and Co., Messrs. Alexander Gardner, Messrs. Gowans and Gray, Messrs. Longmans, Green, and Co., Mr. John Murray, and Mr. Grant Richards. He is also indebted to Mr. H. P. Brown for an extract from a poem by " J. B. Selkirk " ; to Mrs. R. A. Dyer Connon for permission to use a poem by her father, Mr. William Carnie ; to Mrs. Andrew Lang for four poems by the late Andrew Lang ; to Mrs. Logie Robertson for extracts from the work of " Hugh Haliburton " ; to Miss Margaret Warrender for the pieces by Lady John Scott ; and to the executors of George Macdonald for their assent to the inclusion of three of his poems. Finally, he has to thank Professor W. A. Craigie of Oxford, who does not share some of his views, for invaluable criticism and advice.

BOOK I
YOUTH AND SPRING

THE NORTHERN MUSE

MEDITATION IN WINTER

In to thir dirk and drublie dayis,
Whone sabill all the Hevin arrayis,
   With mystie vapouris, cluddis and skyis,
   Nature all curage me denyis
Off sangis, ballattis, and of playis.

When that the nycht dois lenthin houris,
With wind, with haill, and havy schouris,
   My dule spreit dois lurk for schoir ;
   My hairt for languor dois forloir,
For laik of symmer with his flouris.

I walk, I turne, sleip may I nocht,
I vexit am with havy thocht ;
   This warld all ouir I cast about,
   And ay the mair I am in dout,
The mair that I remeid have socht. . . .

For feir of this all day I drowp ;
No gold in kist, nor wine in cowp,
   No ladeis bewtie, nor luiffis blyss
   May lat me to remember this :
How glaid that ever I dine or soup.

dirk and drublie, dark and dripping   *dule*, sad
lurk for schoir, cower for fear   *forloir*, weary
         lat, prevent

Yit, whone the nycht begynnis to schort,
It dois my spreit sum part confort,
  Off thocht oppressit with the schouris.
  Cum, lustie symmer ! with thy flouris,
That I may leif in sum disport.

William Dunbar.

2 WHEN AINCE APRILE HAS FAIRLY COME

WHEN aince Aprile has fairly come,
An' birds may bigg in winter's lum,
An' pleisure's spreid for a' and some
    O' whatna state,
Love, wi' her auld recruitin' drum,
    Than taks the gate.

The heart plays dunt wi' main an' micht ;
The lasses' een are a' sae bricht,
Their dresses are sae braw an' ticht,
    The bonnie birdies !—
Puir winter virtue at the sicht
    Gangs heels ower hurdies.

An' aye as love frae land to land
Tirls the drum wi' eident hand,
A' men collect at her command,
    Toun-bred or land'art,
An' follow in a denty band
    Her gaucy standart.

bigg, build   *lum,* chimney   *hurdies,* thighs
land'art, country bred   *gaucy,* showy

An' I, wha sang o' rain an' snaw,
An' weary winter weel awa',
Noo busk me in a jacket braw,
    An' tak my place
I' the ram-stam, harum-scarum raw,
    Wi' smilin' face.

R. L. Stevenson.

DIFFUGERE NIVES

3

Noo swallow-birds begin to big,
    An' primrose-flooers to blaw ;
An' Jockie whistles doun the rig
    A fareweel to the snaw ;

An' glints o' sunshine, glancin' gleg,
    Licht up the buddin' shaw ;
An' wrestlin' winds are playin' tig
    Round ae bewildered craw.

Auld Tammas to the gavle-wa'
    Nails up a cherry-twig ;
An' Mar'an waters, raw by raw,
    Her bleachin' wi' a pig ;

An' yonder—he's been lang awa'—
    Comes Packie owre the brig ;
An' country lads may noo gang braw,
    An' country lasses trig.

James Logie Robertson.

gleg, quick   *gavle-wa'*, gable wall
pig, earthenware jug   *trig*, smart

4   SONG AT SUNRISE

HAY! now the day dauis,
The jolie cok crauis,
Now shroudis the shauis
    Throu Nature anone.
The thissell-cok cryis
On lovers wha lyis,
Now skaillis the skyis :
    The night is neir gone.

The feildis ouerflouis
With gouans that grouis
Where lilies like lou is,
    Als rid as the rone.
The turtill that treu is,
With notes that reneuis,
Her partie perseuis :
    The night is neir gone.

Now hartis with hyndis,
Conform to their kyndis,
Hie tursis their tyndis,
    On grund where they grone.
Now hurchonis, with hairis,
Ay passis in pairis ;
Whilk deuly declaris
    The night is neir gone.

shauis, woods   *skaillis*, clears   *lou*, flame
rone, rowan   *tursis their tyndis*, toss their antlers
                  hurchonis, hedgehogs

The sesone excellis
Thrugh sweetness that smellis ;
Now Cupid compellis
   Our heartis echone.
On Venus wha waikis,
To muse on our maikis,
Syn sing, for their saikis :
   " The night is neir gone."

All curageous knichtis
Aganis the day dichtis
The breist plate that bright is,
   To feght with their fone.
The stoned steed stampis
Through courage and crampis,
Syn on the land lampis :
   The night is neir gone.

The freikis on feildis
That wight wapins weildis
With shining bright shieldis
   As Titan in trone ;
Stiff speiris in reistis,
Ouer cursoris crestis,
Are brok on their breistis :
   The night is neir gone.

So hard are their hittis,
Some sweyis, some sittis,
And some perforce flittis
   On grund whill they grone.

echone, each one	*maikis*, mates	*syn*, then
dichtis, scour	*stoned steed*, stallion	*crampis*, rears
lampis, gallops	*freikis*, men	*trone*, throne

Syn groomis that gay is,
On blonkis that brayis,
With swordis assayis :
    The night is neir gone.

                        Alexander Montgomerie.

5   A MAY MORNING

RYGHT as the stern of day begouth to schyne,
When gone to bed war Vesper and Lucyne,
    I raise, and by a rosere did me rest ;
Up sprang the goldyn candill matutyne,
With clere depurit bemes cristallyne,
    Glading the mery foulis in thair nest ;
    Or Phebus was in purpur cape revest
Up raise the lark, the hevyns menstrale fyne
In May, in-till a morow myrthfullest.

Full angel-like thir birdis sang thair houris
Within thair courtyns grene, in-to thair bouris,
    Apparalit white and red, wyth blomes suete ;
Enamalit was the felde wyth all colouris,
The perly droppis schake in silvir schouris,
    Whill all in balme did branch and levis flete ;
    To part fra Phebus, did Aurora grete,
Hir cristall teris I saw hyng on the flouris,
    Whilk he for lufe all drank up with his hete.

blonkis, white chargers   *stern*, star   *begouth*, began
Or, ere   *flete*, float

For mirth of May, wyth skippis and wyth hoppis,
The birdis sang upon the tender croppis,
  With curiouse note, as Venus chapell-clerkis :
The rosis yong, new spreding of thair knoppis,
War powderit brycht with hevinly beriall droppis,
  Throu bemes rede, birnyng as ruby sperkis ;
  The skyes rang for schoutyng of the larkis,
The purpur hevyn our-scailit in silver sloppis
  Our-gilt the treis, branchis, lefis and barkis.

Doun throu the ryce a ryvir ran wyth stremys,
So lustily agayn thai lykand lemys,
  That all the lake as lamp did leme of licht,
Whilk schadowit all about wyth twynkling glemis ;
That bewis bathit war in secund bemys
  Throu the reflex of Phebus' visage brycht ;
  On every syde the hegies raise on hicht,
The bank was grene, the bruke was full of bremys,
  The stanneris clere as stern in frosty nycht.

The cristall air, the sapher firmament,
The ruby skyes of the orient,
  Kest beriall bemes on emerant bewis grene ;
The rosy garth depaynt and redolent,
With purpur, azure, gold and goulis gent

croppis, shoots   *knoppis*, buds   *beriall*, beryl
our-scailit in silver sloppis, scaled over with silver clouds
ryce, brushwood   *agayn thai lykand lemys*, against
    those delightful flashes—perhaps a " mackerel sky "
bewis, boughs   *hegies*, hedges   *bremys*, shallows
stanneris, stones   *rosy garth*, rose garden
                    goulis gent, lovely red

Arayed was, by dame Flora the quene,
  So nobily, that joy was for to sene ;
The roch agayn the rywir resplendent
  As low enlumynit all the leves schene.

William Dunbar.

6   O LUSTY MAY

O LUSTY May with Flora quene !
The balmy dropis from Phebus schene !
  Preluciand beams befoir the day
  Be that Diana growis grene,
    Through glaidnes of this lusty May.

Than Esperus, that is so bricht,
Till woeful hairtis castis his licht,
  With bankis that blumis on every brae ;
And schuris are shed furth of their sicht,
    Through glaidnes of this lusty May.

Birdis on bewis of every birth,
Rejoicing nottis makand their mirth
  Right plesandly upoun the spray,
With flourishing our field and firth,
    Through glaidnes of this lusty May.

All luvaris that are in cair,
To their ladeis they do repair,
  In fresh mornyngis befoir the day,
And are in mirth ay mair and mair,
    Through glaidnes of this lusty May.

low, fire   *schene,* brightness   *Be that,* by which
Till, to   *our,* over

Of everie moneth in the yeir,
To mirthful May there is no peir,
    Hir glistrine garments are so gay ;
You lovaris all mak merie cheir,
    Through glaidnes of this lusty May.

7   THE MOTHER OF FLOWERS

WHEN Merche was with variand windis past,
    And Appryll had, with hir silver shouris,
Tane leif at Nature with ane orient blast,
    And lusty May, that moder is of flouris,
    Had maid the birdis to begyn thair houris
Amang the tendir odouris reid and whyt,
Whois armony to heir it wes delyt ;

In bed at morrow, sleiping as I lay,
    Me-thocht Aurora with hir cristall ene,
In at the window lukit by the day,
    And halsit me, with visage paill and grene ;
    On whois hand a lark sang fro the splene,
" Awalk, luvaris, out of your slumbering !
See how the lusty morrow dois up-spring."

Me-thocht fresche May befoir my bed upstude,
    In weid depaint of mony diverss hew,
Sobir, benyng, and full of mansuetude,
    In brycht atteir of flouris forgit new,
    Hevinly of color, whyt, reid, broun, and blew,
Balmit in dew, and gilt with Phebus' bemys,
Whill all the houss illumynit of hir lemys.

halsit, hailed   *weid*, attire   *benyng*, benign

" Sluggird," scho said, " awalk anone for schame,
  And in my honour sum thing thow go wryt ;
The lark has done the mirry day proclame,
  To raiss up luvaris with confort and delyt ;
  Yit nocht incressis thy curage to indyt,
Whois hairt sumtyme has glaid and blisfull bene,
Sangis to mak undir the levis grene."

William Dunbar.

8   MOORLAND SPRING

THERE'S no a muir in my ain land but's fu' o' sang the day,
Wi' the whaup, and the gowden plover, and the lintie
    upon the brae.
The birk in the glen is springin', the rowan-tree in the
    shaw,
And every burn is rinnin' wild wi' the meltin' o' the snaw.

The wee white cluds in the blue lift are hurryin' light and
    free,
Their shadows fleein' on the hills, where I, too, fain wad be;
The wind frae the west is blawin', and wi' it seems to bear
The scent o' the thyme and gowan thro' a' the caller air.

The herd doon the hillside's linkin'.   O licht his heart
    may be
Whose step is on the heather, his glance ower muir and
    lea !
On the moss are the wild ducks gatherin', whar the pules
    like diamonds lie,
And far up soar the wild geese, wi' weird, unyirdly cry.

lintie, linnet   *lift*, heaven   *caller*, fresh
        linkin', striding   *unyirdly*, unearthly

In mony a neuk the primrose lies hid frae stranger een,
An' the broom on the knowes is wavin' wi' its cludin o'
    gowd and green ;
Ower the first green sprigs o' heather, the muir-fowl
    faulds his wing,
And there's nought but joy in my ain land at the comin'
    o' the Spring !

                      Lady John Scott.

9   THE COMING OF LOVE

BEWAILLING in my chamber thus allone,
   Despeired of all joye and remedye,
For-tiret of my thought and wo-begone,
   And to the wyndow gan I walk in hye,
To see the warld and folk that went forbye,
   As for the tyme though I of mirthis fude
   Mycht have no more, to luke it did me gude.

Now was there maid fast by the Touris wall
   A gardyn faire, and in the corneris set
Ane herbere greene, with wandis long and small
   Railit about, and so with treis set
Was all the place, and hawthorn hegis knet,
   That lyf was non walkyng there forbye,
   That mycht within scarce any wight aspy.

So thick the bewis and the levis grene
   Beschadit all the allyes that there were,

neuk, dell	*cludin,* clothing	*herbere,* arbour
hegis, hedges	*lyf,* living thing	*bewis,* boughs

And myddis every herbere mycht be sene
 The scharpe grene suete jenepere,
Growing so fair with branchis here and there,
 That, as it semyt to a lyf without,
 The bewis spred the herbere all about.

And on the smale grene twistis sat
 The lytil suete nyghtingale, and song
So loud and clere, the ympnis consecrat
 Of luvis use, now soft now lowd among,
That all the gardynis and the wallis rong
 Ryght of thaire song, and on the copill next
 Of thaire suete armony, and lo the text :

" Worschippe, ye that loveris bene, this May,
 For of your bliss the kalendis are begonne,
And sing with us, away winter, away,
 Come somer, come, the suete seson and sonne,
Awake, for schame ! that have your hevynis wonne,
 And amourously lift up your hedis all,
 Thank Lufe that list you to his merci call."

When thai this song had song a littil thrawe,
 Thai stent a quhile, and therewith unafraid,
As I beheld, and kest myn eyen a-lawe,
 From beugh to beugh thay hippit and thai plaid,
And freschly in thair birdis kynd araid
 Thair fatheris new, and fret thame in the sonne,
 And thankit Lufe, that had their makis wonne.

ympnis, hymns	*copill next*, next verse
thrawe, measure	*a-lawe*, below *makis*, mates

And therewith kest I doun myn eye ageyne,
  Whare as I saw walkyng under the Toure,
Full secretely, new cumyn hir to playne,
  The fairest or the freschest younge floure
That ever I sawe, methought, before that houre,
  For which sodayne abate, anon astert
  The blude of all my body to my hert.

And though I stood abaisit tho a lyte,
  No wonder was ; for why ? my wittis all
Were so ouercome with plesance and delyte,
  Only through latting of myn eyen fall,
That sudaynly my hert become hir thrall,
  For ever of free wyll, for of manace
  There was no takyn in her suete face.

And in my hede I drew rycht hastily,
  And eft sones I lent it out ageyne,
And saw hir walk that verray womanly,
  With no wight mo, bot only women tueyne,
Than gan I studye in myself and seyne :
  " Ah ! suete, are ye a warldly creature,
  Or hevinly thing in likeness of nature ?

" Or ye god Cupidis owin princess ?
  And cumyn are to louse me out of band,
Or are ye veray Nature the goddesse,
  That have depayntit with your hevinly hand
This gardyn full of flouris, as they stand ?
  What sall I think, allace ! what reverence
  Sall I minister to your excellence ?

tho a lyte, then a little   *manace*, compulsion   *takyn*, token

" Giff ye a goddess be, and that ye like
    To do me payne, I may it not astert ;
Giff ye be warldly wight, that dooth me sike,
    Why lest God mak you so, my derest hert,
To do a sely prisoner thus smert,
    That lufis you all, and wote of nought but wo ?
    And, therefore, merci, suete ! sen it is so."

When I a lytill thrawe had maid my mone,
    Bewailing myn infortune and my chance,
Unknawin how or what was best to done,
    So ferre I fallyng into lufis dance,
That sodeynly my wit, my contenance,
    My hert, my will, my nature, and my mynd,
    Was changit clene rycht in ane other kind.
                            James I. of Scotland.

astert, avoid   *dooth me sike*, makest me sigh
lest, pleased   *sely*, weak   *all*, wholly

BOOK II
PLAISIR D'AMOUR

MY HEART IS HEICH ABUFE

MY heart is heich abufe,
  My body is full of bliss,
For I am set in lufe,
  As weil as I wald wiss ;
I lufe my lady pure,
  And scho luvis me again ;
I am her serviture,
  Scho is my soverane.

Scho is my very heart,
  I am her hope and heal ;
Scho is my joy inwart,
  I am her luvar leal ;
I am her bound and thrall,
  Scho is at my command ;
I am perpetual
  Her man, both fute and hand.

The thing that may her please
  My body sall fulfil ;
Whatever her disease,
  It dois my body ill.
My bird, my bonnie ane,
  My tender babe venust,
My lufe, my life alane,
  My liking and my lust.

heich, high   *bird*, maiden   *venust*, beautiful

We interchange our hairtis
  In otheris armis soft ;
Spreitless we twa depairtis
  Usand our luvis oft ;
We murne when licht day dawis,
  We 'plain the nicht is short,
We curse the cock that crawis,
  That hinderis our disport.

I glowffin up agast,
  When I her miss on nicht,
And in my oxter fast
  I find the bowster richt ;
Then languor on me lies,
  Like Morpheus the mair,
Whilk causis me uprise
  And to my sweet repair :

And then is all the sorrow
  Furth of remembrance,
That ever I had a sorrow
  In luvis observance.
Thus never I do rest,
  So lusty a life I lead,
When that I list to test
  The well of womanheid.

Luvaris in pain I pray
  God send you sic remead
As I haif nicht and day,
  You to defend from dede ;

glowffin, wake with a start   *oxter*, bosom
                dede, death

> Therefore be ever true
>   Unto your ladies free,
> And they will on you rue,
>   As mine has done on me.

11 O, MY LUVE IS LIKE A RED, RED ROSE

> O, MY luve is like a red, red rose,
>   That's newly sprung in June :
> O, my luve is like the melodie
>   That's sweetly played in tune.
>
> As fair art thou, my bonnie lass,
>   So deep in luve am I ;
> And I will luve thee still, my dear,
>   Till a' the seas gang dry.
>
> Till a' the seas gang dry, my dear,
>   And the rocks melt wi' the sun :
> And I will luve thee still, my dear,
>   While the sands o' life shall run.
>
> And fare thee weel, my only luve,
>   And fare thee weel a while !
> And I will come again, my luve,
>   Tho' it were ten thousand mile !

Robert Burns.

12   TO A LADYE

SWEIT rose of vertew and of gentilnes,
Delytsum lyllie of everie lustynes,
    Richest in bountie, and in bewtie cleir,
    And everie vertew that is held most deir,
Except onlie that ye are mercyless.

In to your garth this day I did persew,
Thair saw I flowris that fresche wer of hew ;
    Baithe whyte and reid most lusty wer to seyne,
    And halesum herbis upone stalkis grene ;
Yit leif nor flour fynd could I nane of rue.

I doubt that Merche, with his cauld blastis keyne,
Hes slane this gentill herbe, that I of mane ;
    Whois petewous deithe dois to my hert sic pane
    That I wald mak to plant his rute agane,
So confortand his levis unto me bene.

                                    William Dunbar.

13   BAYTH GUD AND FAIR AND WOMANLIE

        BAYTH gud and fair and womanlie,
            Debonair, steidfast, wise and trew,
        Courtass, hummill and lawlie,
            And grundid weill in all vertew ;
            To whois service I sall persew
        Worship without villony,
            And evir annone I sal be trew ;
        Bayth gud and fair and womanlie.

                  of mane, moan for

Honour for evir unto that fre
   That natur formit hes so fair ;
In worship of hir fresh bewtie,
   To Luvis court I will repair,
   To serve and lufe without despair ;
For this I wit her most wirthy,
   For to be callit our all whair,
" Bayth gud and fair and womanlie."

Sen that I gif my hairt hir to,
   Why wyt I hir of my mournyng ?
Thocht I be wo, what wyt hes scho ?
   What wald I moir of my sweit thing,
   That wit nocht of my womenting ?
When I hir see confort am I :
   Hir fair effeir and fresh having
Is gud and fair and womanlie.

Thing in this warld that I best luf,
   My very hairt and conforting,
To whois service I sall persew,
   Till deid mak our depairting ;
   Faithful, constant and bening,
I sall be whill the lyfe is in me,
   And luf hir best attour all thing :
Bayth gud and fair and womanlie.

fre, maid	*all whair*, everywhere	*wyt*, blame
Thocht, though	*womenting*, lamenting	
confort, comforted	*effeir*, aspect	*having*, beauty
deid, death	*attour*, above	

14   MY AIN KIND DEARIE, O

WHEN o'er the hill the eastern star
    Tells bughtin-time is near, my jo ;
And owsen frae the furrow'd field
    Return sae dowf and weary, O ;
Down by the burn, where scented birks
    Wi' dew are hangin' clear, my jo ;
I'll meet thee on the lea-rig,
    My ain kind dearie, O !

In mirkest glen at midnight hour
    I'd rove, and ne'er be eerie, O !
If thro' that glen I gaed to thee,
    My ain kind dearie, O !
Altho' the night were ne'er sae wild,
    And I were ne'er sae wearie, O,
I'll meet thee on the lea-rig,
    My ain kind dearie, O !

The hunter lo'es the morning sun,
    To rouse the mountain deer, my jo ;
At noon the fisher takes the glen,
    Adown the burn to steer, my jo ;
Gie me the hour o' gloamin grey,
    It makes my heart sae cheery, O,
To meet thee on the lea-rig,
    My ain kind dearie, O !

                                    Robert Burns.

        jo, love

15   O' A' THE AIRTS THE WIND CAN BLAW

O' A' the airts the wind can blaw,
    I dearly like the west,
For there the bonnie lassie lives,
    The lassie I lo'e best :
There wild woods grow, and rivers row,
    And mony a hill between ;
But day and night my fancy's flight
    Is ever wi' my Jean.

I see her in the dewy flowers,
    I see her sweet and fair :
I hear her in the tunefu' birds,
    I hear her charm the air :
There's not a bonnie flower that springs
    By fountain, shaw, or green,
There's not a bonnie bird that sings,
    But minds me o' my Jean.
                   Robert Burns

16   ANNIE LAURIE

MAXWELLTON braes are bonnie,
    Where early fa's the dew,
And it's there that Annie Laurie
    Gie'd me her promise true ;
Gie'd me her promise true,
    That ne'er forgot sall be ;
But for bonnie Annie Laurie
    I'd lay doun my head and dee.

Her brow is like the snaw-drift,
  Her neck is like the swan,
Her face it is the fairest
  That e'er the sun shone on ;
That e'er the sun shone on,
  And dark blue is her e'e ;
And for bonnie Annie Laurie
  I'd lay doun my head and dee.

Like dew on the gowan lying
  Is the fa' o' her fairy feet ;
And like winds in simmer sighing,
  Her voice is low and sweet ;
Her voice is low and sweet,
  And she's a' the world to me ,
And for bonnie Annie Laurie
  I'd lay doun my head and dee.

Lady John Scott.

17   THE EWE-BUGHTS

WILL ye go to the ewe-bughts, Marion,
  And wear in the sheep wi' me ?
The sun shines sweet, my Marion ;
  But nae half sae sweet as thee.
O, Marion's a bonnie lass,
  And the blythe blink's in her e'e ;
And fain wad I marry Marion,
  Gin Marion wad marry me.

ewe-bughts, folds for the ewes   *wear*, drive

There's gowd in your garters, Marion,
　　And silk on your white hause-bane ;
Fu' fain wad I kiss my Marion,
　　At e'en when I come hame.
There's braw lads in Earnslaw, Marion,
　　Wha gape and glower with their e'e,
At kirk, when they see my Marion ;
　　But nane of them lo'es like me.

I've nine milk-ewes, my Marion ;
　　A cow and a brawny quey,
I'll gie them a' to my Marion,
　　Just on her bridal day ;
And ye's get a green sey apron,
　　And waistcoat of the London brown,
And wow but ye will be vap'ring,
　　Whene'er ye gang to the town.

I'm young and stout, my Marion ;
　　Nane dances like me on the green :
And gin ye forsake me, Marion,
　　I'll e'en gae draw up wi' Jean :
Sae put on your pearlins, Marion,
　　And kirtle o' cramasie ;
And as sune as my chin has nae hair on,
　　I shall come west, and see ye.

hause-bane, neck-bone		*quey*, heifer
sey, woollen	*pearlins*, laces	*cramasie*, crimson

18   I'LL AYE CA' IN BY YON TOUN

I'LL aye ca' in by yon toun,
    And by yon garden green again ;
I'll aye ca' in by yon toun,
    And see my bonnie Jean again.

There's nane shall ken, there's nane shall guess,
    What brings me back the gate again,
But she, my fairest faithfu' lass ;
    And stow'nlins we sall meet again.

She'll wander by the aiken tree,
    When trystin time draws near again ;
And when her lovely form I see,
    O haith ! she's doubly dear again.

I'll aye ca' in by yon toun,
    And by yon garden green again ;
I'll aye ca' in by yon toun,
    And see my bonnie Jean again.

                                    Robert Burns.

19   THE WAUKIN' O' THE FAULD

My Peggy is a young thing,
    Just enter'd in her teens,
Fair as the day, and sweet as May,
    Fair as the day, and always gay.

waukin' o' the fauld, gathering the sheep to the fold

My Peggy is a young thing,
    And I'm nae very auld,
And weel I like to meet her at
    The waukin' o' the fauld.

My Peggy speaks sae sweetly,
    Whene'er we meet alane,
I wish nae mair to lay my care,
I wish nae mair of a' that's rare.
My Peggy speaks sae sweetly,
    To a' the lave I'm cauld ;
But she gars a' my spirits glow,
    At waukin' o' the fauld.

My Peggy smiles sae kindly,
    Whene'er I whisper love,
That I look down on a' the toun,
That I look down upon a croun.
My Peggy smiles sae kindly,
    It makes me blyth and bauld ;
And naething gies me sic delight
    As waukin' o' the fauld.

My Peggy sings sae saftly,
    When on my pipe I play,
By a' the rest it is confest,—
By a' the rest, that she sings best.
My Peggy sings sae saftly,
    And in her sangs are tauld,
With innocence, the wale o' sense,
    At waukin' o' the fauld.
                Allan Ramsay.

lave, rest   *gars,* makes   *wale,* pick

20   TAM I' THE KIRK

O JEAN, my Jean, when the bell ca's the congregation
Owre valley an' hill wi' the ding frae its iron mou',
When a'body's thochts is set on his ain salvation,
            Mine's set on you.

There's a reid rose lies on the Buik o' the Word afore ye
That was growin' braw on its bush at the keek o' day,
But the lad that pu'd yon flower i' the mornin's glory,
            He canna pray.

He canna pray ; but there's nane i' the kirk will heed him
Whaur he sits sae still his lane at the side o' the wa',
For nane but the reid rose kens what my lassie gie'd him :
            It an' us twa !

He canna sing for the sang that his ain he'rt raises,
He canna see for the mist that's afore his een,
And a voice drouns the hale o' the psalms an' the para-
    phrases,
            Cryin' " Jean, Jean, Jean ! "
                                    Violet Jacob.

21   THE YELLOW-HAIR'D LADDIE

THE yellow-hair'd laddie sat down on yon brae,
Cries, " Milk the ewes, lassie, let nane of them gae.
And ay she milked, and ay she sang :
" The yellow-hair'd laddie shall be my gudeman.

        keek, break   *his lane,* alone

" The weather is cauld, and my claithing is thin ;
The ewes are new clipped, they winna bught in ;
They winna bught in tho' I should dee,
O yellow-hair'd laddie, be kind to me."

22   TO DAUNTON ME

THE blude-red rose at Yule may blaw,
The simmer lilies blume in snaw,
The frost may freeze the deepest sea,
But an auld man shall never daunton me.

    To daunton me, and me sae young,
    Wi' his fause heart and flatterin' tongue !—
    That is the thing ye ne'er shall see ;
    For an auld man shall never daunton me.

For a' his meal, for a' his maut,
For a' his fresh beef and his saut,
For a' his white and red monie,
An auld man shall never daunton me.

His gear may buy him kye and yowes,
His gear may buy him glens and knowes,
But me he shall not buy nor fee,
For an auld man shall never daunton me.

He hirples twa-fauld as he dow,
Wi' his toothless gab and his auld beld pow—
And the rain dreeps doun frae his bleared e'e,
That auld man that wad daunton me.
                       Robert Burns.

bught, fold	*maut*, malt	*saut*, salt
dow, can	*gab*, mouth	*beld pow*, bald head

23   I LO'E NAE A LADDIE BUT ANE

I lo'e nae a laddie but ane,
    He lo'es nae a lassie but me ;
He's willing to make me his ain,
    And his ain I am willing to be.
He coft me a rokelay of blue,
    A pair of mittens of green—
The price was a kiss of my mou,
    And I paid him the debt yestreen.

My mither's ay making a phrase,
    That I'm rather young to be wed ;
But lang ere she counted my days,
    O' me she was brought to bed.
Sae, mither, just settle yere tongue,
    And dinna be flyting sae bauld,
We can weel do the thing when we're young,
    That we canna do weel when we're auld.
                            John Clunie.

24   SAW YE JOHNNIE COMIN'?

" Saw ye Johnnie comin' ? " quo' she,
    " Saw ye Johnnie comin' ?
Wi' his blue bonnet on his head
    And his doggie runnin' ?
Yestreen, about the gloamin' time,
    I chanced to see him comin',

coft, bought   *rokelay*, a short cloak
            flyting, scolding

Whistlin' merrily the tune
  That I am a' day hummin'," quo' she ;
    " I am a' day hummin'.

" Fee him, faither, fee him," quo' she,
  " Fee him, faither, fee him ;
A' the wark about the house
  Gaes wi' me when I see him :
A' the wark about the house,
  I gang sae lightly through it :
And though ye pay some merks o' gear,
  Hoot ! ye winna rue it," quo' she :
    " No, ye winna rue it."

" What wad I do wi' him, hizzy ?
  What wad I do wi' him ?
He's ne'er a sark upon his back,
  And I hae nane to gie him."
" I hae twa sarks into my kist,
  And ane o' them I'll gie him ;
And for a merk o' mair fee,
  O, dinna stand wi' him," quo' she ;
    " Dinna stand wi' him.

" Weel do I lo'e him," quo' she,
  " Weel do I lo'e him ;
The brawest lads about the place
  Are a' but hav'rels to him.
O fee him, faither ; lang, I trow,
  We've dull and dowie been ;

sark, shirt   *hav'rels*, fools   *dowie*, dreary

He'll haud the plough, thrash i' the barn,
And crack wi' me at e'en," quo' she,
    " Crack wi' me at e'en."

Joanna Baillie.

25   CA' THE YOWES TO THE KNOWES

Ca' the yowes to the knowes,
Ca' them where the heather grows,
Ca' them where the burnie rowes,
    My bonnie dearie.

As I gaed down the water side,
There I met my shepherd lad,
He rowed me sweetly in his plaid,
    An' he ca'd me his dearie.

Will ye gang down the water side
And see the waves sae sweetly glide
Beneath the hazels spreading wide ?
    The moon it shines fu' clearly. . . .

Ye sall get gowns and ribbons meet,
Cauf-leather shoon upon your feet ;
And in my arms thou'lt lie and sleep,
    And ye sall be my dearie.

If ye'll but stand to what ye've said,
I'se gang wi' you, my shepherd lad,
And ye may rowe me in your plaid,
    And I sall be your dearie.

rowes, rolls   *shoon*, shoes

While waters wimple to the sea,
While day blinks in the lift sae hie,
Till clay-cauld death sall blin' my e'e,
    Ye sall be my dearie.
               Robert Burns.

26   THE SHEPHERD'S SONG

THE gowan glitters on the sward,
    The lavrock's in the sky,
And Colley on my plaid keeps ward,
    And time is passing by.
    Oh no ! sad and slow !
    I hear nae welcome sound,
The shadow of our trysting bush
    It wears sae slowly round.

My sheep-bell tinkles from the west,
    My lambs are bleating near,
But still the sound that I lo'e best,
    Alack ! I canna hear.
    Oh no ! sad and slow !
    The shadow lingers still,
And like a lanely ghaist I stand
    And croon upon the hill.

I hear below the water roar,
    The mill with clacking din ;
And Lucky scolding frae her door,
    To bring the bairnies in.

    lift, heaven   *lavrock*, lark

Oh no ! sad and slow !
  These are nae sounds for me ;
The shadow of our trysting bush
  It creeps sae drearilie.

I coft yestreen frae chapman Tam
  A snood o' bonnie blue,
And promised, when our trysting cam,
  To tye it round her brow.
  Oh no ! sad and slow !
  The time it winna pass ;
The shadow of that weary thorn
  Is tether'd on the grass.

Oh ! now I see her on the way !
  She's past the Witches' Knowe ;
She's climbing up the Brownie's Brae—
  My heart is in a lowe !
  Oh no ! 'tis not so !
  'Tis glaumrie I hae seen ;
The shadow of the hawthorn bush
  Will move nae mair till e'en.

My book of grace I'll try to read,
  Tho' conn'd wi' little skill,
When Colley barks I'll raise my head,
  And find her on the hill !
  Oh, no ! sad and slow !
  The time will ne'er be gane ;
The shadow of the trysting bush
  Is fix'd like ony stane.

Joanna Baillie.

coft, bought   *lowe*, flame   *glaumrie*, glamour

27   O, FOR ANE-AND-TWENTY, TAM

An' O, for ane-and-twenty, Tam !
    And hey, sweet ane-and-twenty, Tam !
I'll learn my kin a rattlin' sang,
    An I saw ane-and-twenty, Tam.

They snool me sair, and haud me down,
    And gar me look like bluntie, Tam ;
But three short years will soon wheel roun'—
    And then comes ane-and-twenty, Tam.

A gleib o' lan', a claut o' gear,
    Was left me by my auntie, Tam ;
At kith or kin I need na spier,
    An I saw ane-and-twenty, Tam.

They'll hae me wed a wealthy coof,
    Tho' I mysel hae plenty, Tam :
But hear'st thou, laddie—there's my loof—
    I'm thine at ane-and-twenty, Tam.

                                        Robert Burns.

28   O WHISTLE, AND I'LL COME TO YOU

O whistle, and I'll come to you, my lad,
O whistle, and I'll come to you, my lad :
Tho' father and mither and a' should gae mad,
O whistle, and I'll come to you, my lad.

snool, snub	*sair*, sore	*bluntie*, stupid
gleib, small farm	*claut o' gear*, handful of money	
spier, ask	*coof*, fool	*loof*, palm

But warily tent, when you come to court me,
And come na unless the back-yett be a-jee ;
Syne up the back-stile, and let naebody see,
And come as ye were na comin' to me,
And come as ye were na comin' to me.

At kirk, or at market, whene'er ye meet me,
Gang by me as tho' that ye car'd na a flie ;
But steal me a blink o' your bonnie black e'e,
Yet look as ye were na lookin' at me,
Yet look as ye were na lookin' at me.

Aye vow and protest that ye care na for me,
And whyles ye may lightly my beauty a wee ;
But court na anither, tho' jokin' ye be,
For fear that she wyle your fancy frae me,
For fear that she wyle your fancy frae me.

O whistle, and I'll come to you, my lad,
O whistle, and I'll come to you, my lad :
Tho' father and mither and a' should gae mad,
O whistle, and I'll come to you, my lad.

                                    Robert Burns.

29   LAST MAY A BRAW WOOER

LAST May a braw wooer cam down the lang glen,
    And sair wi' his love he did deave me ;
I said there was naething I hated like men.
    The deuce gae wi 'm, to believe, believe me,
    The deuce gae wi 'm, to believe me.

tent, take care   *yett*, gate   *a-jee*, ajar   *Syne*, then
    whyles, sometimes   *lightly*, disparage   *deave*, deafen

He spak o' the darts in my bonnie black een,
 And vow'd for my love he was dyin';
I said he might die when he liket for Jean,
 The Lord forgie me for lyin', for lyin',
 The Lord forgie me for lyin'.

A weel-stocked mailen—himsel for the laird—
 And marriage aff-hand were his proffers:
I never loot on that I kenn'd it, or car'd,
 But thought I might hae waur offers, waur offers,
 But thought I might hae waur offers.

But what wad ye think? in a fortnight or less—
 The deil tak his taste to gae near her!
He up the gate-slack to my black cousin Bess,
 Guess ye how, the jad! I could bear her, could bear
  her,
 Guess ye how, the jad! I could bear her.

But a' the niest week as I petted wi' care,
 I gaed to the tryste o' Dalgarnock,
And wha but my fine fickle lover was there!
 I glowr'd as I'd seen a warlock, a warlock,
 I glowr'd as I'd seen a warlock.

But owre my left shouther I gae him a blink,
 Lest neebors might say I was saucy;
My wooer he caper'd as he'd been in drink,
 And vow'd I was his dear lassie, dear lassie,
 And vow'd I was his dear lassie.

mailen, farm *loot,* let *niest,* next
tryste, fair *glowr'd,* stared

I spier'd for my cousin fu' couthy and sweet,
   Gin she had recover'd her hearin',
And how her new shoon fit her auld shachl't feet,
    But, heavens ! how he fell a-swearin', a-swearin',
    But, heavens ! how he fell a-swearin' !

He begged, for gudesake, I wad be his wife,
   Or else I wad kill him wi' sorrow ;
Sae e'en to preserve the poor body his life,
    I think I maun wed him to-morrow, to-morrow,
    I think I maun wed him to-morrow.

Robert Burns.

30   THE GOWK

> I see the Gowk an' the Gowk sees me
> Beside a berry-bush by the aipple tree.
> *Old Scots Rhyme.*

Tib, my auntie's a deil to wark,
   Has me risin' afore the sun ;
Aince her heid is abune her sark
   Then the clash o' her tongue's begun !
Warslin', steerin' wi' hens an' swine,
Naucht kens she o' a freend o' mine—
But the Gowk that bides i' the woods o' Dun
    He kens him fine !

Past the yaird an' ahint the stye,
   O the aipples grow bonnilie !
Tib, my auntie, she canna spy
   Wha comes creepin' to kep wi' me.

spier'd, asked	*couthy*, gracious	*shachl't*, shapeless
Warslin', wrestling	*Gowk*, cuckoo	*kep*, keep company

Aye ! she'd sort him, for, dod, she's fell !
Whisht now, Jimmie, an' hide yersel',
An' the wise-like bird i' the aipple tree
    He winna' tell !

Aprile-month, or the aipples flower,
  Tib, my auntie, will rage an' ca' ;
Jimmie, lad, she may rin an' glower—
  What care I ? We'll be far awa' !
Let her seek me the leelang day,
Wha's to tell her the road we'll gae ?
For the cannie Gowk, tho' he kens it a',
    He winna' say !

                Violet Jacob.

31   ROBENE AND MAKYNE

ROBENE sat on gud grene hill
  Kepand a flock of fe,
Mirry Makyne said him till :
  " Robene, thou rew on me ;
I haif thee luvit loud and still
  Thir yeiris two or three ;
My dule in dern bot gif thou dill,
  Doubtless but dreid I de."

Robene answerit : " Be the Rude
  Na thing of lufe I knaw,

or, ere   *glower,* gloom   *leelang,* livelong
fe, sheep   *him till,* to him   *rew on,* have pity
             thir, these
my dule in dern, etc., my secret grief unless thou share
dreid, for sorrow   *Be the Rude,* By the Cross

Bot keipis my scheip under yone wude,
  Lo ! whair they raik on raw :
What hes marrit thee in thy mude,
  Makyne, to me thou shaw ?
Or what is lufe, or to be lude,
  Fane wald I leir that law."

" At luvis lair gif thou will leir,
  Tak thair ane A, B, C ;
Be heynd, courtass, and fair of feir,
  Wyse, hardy, and free :
So that no danger do thee deir,
  What dule in dern thou dree ;
Press thee with pain at all poweir,
  Be pacient, and privie."

Robene answerit her agane :
  " I wait nocht what is lufe,
But I haif mervell intertane
  What makis thee this wanrufe.
The weddir is fair, and I am fain,
  My scheip gois haill aboif,
And we wald play us in this plane
  They wald us baith reproif."

" Robene, tak tent unto my tale
  And wirk all as I reid,
And thou sall haif my hairt all haill,
  Eik and my maidenheid.

raik on raw, range in row *lude*, loved   *leir*, learn
lair, lore   *heynd*, gentle *feir*, complexion
deir, daunt   *dree*, suffer   *wait*, wot
this wanrufe, thus uneasy   *reid*, advise *haill*, whole

Sen God sendis bute for baill,
    And for murnyng remeid ;
In dern with thee bot giff I daill,
    Doubtless I am bot deid."

" Makyne, to-morne this ilka tyde
    And ye will meet me heir,
Peraventure my scheip may gang besyd
    While we haif liggit full neir ;
Bot mawgre haif I and I byd
    Fra they begin to steir,
What lyis on hairt I will nocht hyd ;
    Makyne, than mak gud cheir."

" Robene, thou reivis me rois and rest !
    I luve bot thee alane."
" Makyne, adew ! the sone gois west,
    The day is neir-hand gane."
" Robene, in dule I am so drest,
    That lufe will be my bane."
" Ga lufe, Makyne, wherever thou list,
    For leman I luve nane."

" Robene, I stand in sic a style,
    I sich and that full sair."
" Makyne, I haif bene heir this while,
    At hame God gif I wair."

bute for baill, succour for sorrow
ilka tyde, same hour   *liggit*, lain
Bot mawgre, etc., but ill-will may I have if I stay
steir, move   *reivis me rois*, robbest me of quiet
sich, sigh   *gif*, grant

" My huny, Robene, talk ane while,
  Gif thou will do na mair."
" Makyne, sum other man begile,
  For hamewart I will fair."

Robene on his wayis went
  Als licht as leif of tree ;
Makyne murnit in hir intent,
  And trowd him never to see.
Robene brayd attour the bent ;
  Than Makyne cryit on hie :
" Now ma thou sing, for I am schent ;
  What alis lufe at me ? "

Makyne went hame withouttin faill
  Full wery eftir couth weep,
Than Robene in a full fair daill
  Assemblit all his scheip.
Be that some part of Makyne's aill
  Outthrow his hairt cowd creip ;
He fallowit her fast thair till assail
  And till her took gude keep.

" Abyd, abyd, thou fair Makyne !
  A word for ony-thing !
For all my luve it sal be thyne,
  Withouttin departing.
All haill thy heart for till haif myne
  Is all my coveting.

brayd attour, strode over   *schent*, undone
Be that, by that time   *gude keep*, good heed
         departing, sharing
     All haill, etc., to have thy whole heart mine

My scheip to-morn quhill houris nyne,
    Will neid of no keping."

"Robene, thou hes heard soung and say,
    In gestis and storeis auld :
' The man that will nocht when he may
    Sall haif nocht when he wald.'
I pray to Jesu, every day,
    Mot eik thair cairis cauld,
That first preissis with thee to play
    Be firth, forrest, or fauld."

"Makyne, the nicht is soft and dry,
    The weddir is warm and fair,
And the grene wood rycht neir us by
    To walk attour all quhair :
Thair ma na janglour us espy
    That is to lufe contrair ;
Thairin, Makyne, bath ye and I
    Unseen we ma repair."

"Robene, that warld is all away,
    And quite brocht till ane end ;
And nevir agane thairto, perfay,
    Sall it be as thou wend.
For of my pain thou made it play,
    And all in vain I spend ;
As thou hes done, sa sall I say,
    Murne on, I think to mend."

quhill houris nyne, till nine o'clock   *mot eik*, may add to
janglour, tale-bearer   *perfay*, by my troth
         wend, thought

" Makyne, the howp of all my heill,
    My hairt on thee is set,
And ever-mair to thee be leill
    While I may leif, but let ;
Nevir to fail, as utheris feill,
    What grace that ever I get."
" Robene, with thee I will nocht deill ;
    Adew, for thus we met."

Makyne went hame, blyth anewche
    Attour the holtis hair.
Robene murnit, and Makyne lewche,
    Scho sang, he sichit sair :
And so left him bayth wo and wreuch,
    In dolour and in cair,
Kepand his hird under a huche
    Amang the holtis hair.

Robert Henryson.

32   DUNCAN GRAY

DUNCAN GRAY cam here to woo,
    Ha, ha, the wooing o't,
On blythe Yule night when we were fou,
    Ha, ha, the wooing o't.

heill, well-being	*leill,* true
but let, without ceasing	*anewche,* enough
Attour the holtis hair, over the grey moorlands	
lewche, laughed	*sichit sair,* sighed sore
wo and wreuch, sad and wretched	*huche,* height

Maggie coost her head fu' high,
Look'd asklent and unco skeigh,
Gart poor Duncan stand abeigh ;
    Ha, ha, the wooing o't.

Duncan fleech'd, and Duncan pray'd,
    Ha, ha, the wooing o't ;
Meg was deaf as Ailsa Craig,
    Ha, ha, the wooing o't.
Duncan sigh'd baith out and in,
Grat his een baith bleer't and blin',
Spak o' lowpin' o'er a linn ;
    Ha, ha, the wooing o't.

Time and chance are but a tide ;
    Ha, ha, the wooing o't ;
Slighted love is sair to bide ;
    Ha, ha, the wooing o't.
Shall I, like a fool, quoth he,
For a haughty hizzie die ?
She may gae to—France for me !
    Ha, ha, the wooing o't.

How it comes let doctors tell ;
    Ha, ha, the wooing o't ;
Meg grew sick—as he grew hale ;
    Ha, ha, the wooing o't.
Something in her bosom wrings,
For relief a sigh she brings ;
And O, her een, they spak sic things !
    Ha, ha, the wooing o't.

asklent, askew   *unco skeigh*, very skittish
abeigh, off   *fleech'd*, wheedled   *grat*, wept

Duncan was a lad o' grace ;
    Ha, ha, the wooing o't ;
Maggie's was a piteous case ;
    Ha, ha, the wooing o't.
Duncan could na be her death,
Swelling pity smoor'd his wrath ;
Now they're crouse and canty baith ;
    Ha, ha, the wooing o't.

                                    Robert Burns.

33   A CHANGE O' DEILS

    " A change o' deils is lichtsome."
                                    Scots Proverb.

My Grannie spent a merry youth,
    She niver wantit for a joe,
And gin she tell't me aye the truth,
    Richt little was't she kent na o'.

An' while afore she gae'd awa'
    To bed her doon below the grass,
Says she, " Guidmen I've kistit twa,
    But a change o' deils is lichtsome, lass ! "

Sae dinna think to maister me,
    For Scotland's fu' o' brawlike chiels,
And ablins ither folk ye'll see
    Are fine an' pleased to change their deils.

smoor'd, smothered   *crouse and canty*, proud and cheerful
joe, sweetheart   *kistit*, coffined   *ablins*, perhaps

Aye, set yer bonnet on yer heid,
　　An' cock it up upon yer bree,
O' a' yer tricks ye'll hae some need
　　Afore ye get the best o' me !

Sma' wark to fill yer place I'd hae,
　　I'll seek a sweethe'rt i' the toon,
Or cast my he'rt across the Spey
　　An' tak' some pridefu' Hieland loon.

I ken a man has hoose an' land,
　　His arm is stoot, his een are blue,
A ring o' gowd is on his hand,
　　An' he's a bonnier man nor you !

But hoose an' gear an' land an' mair,
　　He'd gie them a' to get the preen
That preened the flowers in till my hair
　　Beside the may-bush yestere'en.

Jist tak' you tent, an' mind forbye,
　　The braw guid sense my Grannie had,
My Grannie's dochter's bairn am I,
　　And a change o' deils is lichtsome, lad !
　　　　　　　　　　　　Violet Jacob.

34　　　LOW DOUN IN THE BROOM

　　My daddy is a cankert carle,
　　　　He'll no twine wi' his gear ;
　　My minnie is a scauldin' wife
　　　　Hauds a' the house asteer.

preen, pin　　　　*tent,* care　　　　*twine,* part

But let them say, or let them dae,
  It's a' ane to me ;
For he's low doun, he's in the broom
  That's waitin' for me ;

A-waitin' for me, my love,
  That's waitin' for me,
For he's low doun, he's in the broom
  That's waitin' for me.

My Auntie Kate sits at her wheel,
  And sair she lightlies me ;
But weel I ken it's a' for spite,
  For ne'er a jo has she.

But let them say, or let them dae,
  It's a' ane to me ;
For he's low doun, he's in the broom
  That's waitin' for me.

35   KISS'D YESTREEN

Kiss'd yestreen, and kiss'd yestreen,
Up the Gallowgate, down the Green :
I've woo'd wi' lords, and woo'd wi' lairds,
I've mool'd wi' carles and mell'd wi' cairds,
I've kiss'd wi' priests—'twas done i' the dark,
Twice in my gown and thrice in my sark ;
But priest, nor lord, nor loon can gie
Sic kindly kisses as he gae me.

   mool'd, played   *mell'd*, meddled

36

TAM GLEN

My heart is a-breaking, dear tittie ;
  Some counsel unto me come len' ;
To anger them a' is a pity ;
  But what will I do wi' Tam Glen ?

I'm thinking, wi' sic a braw fallow,
  In poortith I might make a fen' ;
What care I in riches to wallow,
  If I mauna marry Tam Glen ?

There's Lowrie the laird o' Dumeller,
  " Gude-day to you, brute ! " he comes ben :
He brags and he blaws o' his siller,
  But when will he dance like Tam Glen ?

My minnie does constantly deave me,
  And bids me beware o' young men ;
They flatter, she says, to deceive me ;
  But wha can think sae o' Tam Glen ?

My daddie says, gin I'll forsake him,
  He'll gie me gude hunder marks ten ;
But, if it's ordain'd I maun take him,
  O wha will I get but Tam Glen ?

Yestreen at the valentines' dealing,
  My heart to my mou gied a sten ;
For thrice I drew ane without failing,
  And thrice it was written, Tam Glen.

tittie, sister	*poortith*, poverty	*fen'*, shift
siller, money	*minnie*, mother	*deave*, deafen
mou, mouth	*sten*, spring	

The last Hallowe'en I was waukin
   My droukit sark-sleeve, as ye ken ;
His likeness came up the house staukin—
   The very grey breeks o' Tam Glen !

Come counsel, dear tittie, don't tarry ;
   I'll gie you my bonnie black hen,
Gif ye will advise me to marry
   The lad I lo'e dearly, Tam Glen.

Robert Burns.

37 LET ME IN THIS AE NIGHT

" O LASSIE, art thou sleeping yet,
   Or are ye waking, I wad wit ?
Thy love has bound me hand and foot,
   And here I maun remain-o.
O let me in this ae night,
   This ae, ae, ae night ;
O let me in this ae night,
   Or I'll ne'er come back again-o.

" Deep is the way wi' snaw and sleet,
And wild the night wi' wind and weet ;
My shoon are frozen on my feet,
   Sae lang I maun remain-o.
O let me in this ae night,
   This ae, ae, ae night ;
The wildness o' this winter night
   Might conquer thy disdain-o."

droukit sark, soaked shift   *breeks*, breeches

"Now, where dwell ye when ye're at hame—
What are ye like—have ye a name—
Are ye heav'n's wark, and think ye shame
   In sunshine to be seen-o?
Away thy ways, this ae night,
   This ae, ae, ae night,
And come this way in daylight—
   It's honester than e'en-o."

"Some ca' me fair, some ca' me fause,
Of mickle mirth I am the cause,
For I'm the laird o' Windie-waas,
   A house of ancient fame-o.
Sae let me in this ae night,
   This ae, ae, ae night;
Show me the way this ae night,
   And I'll ken the way again-o."

"My daddie's wondrous light o' sleep;
My aunt my chamber keys maun keep;
I wot my casements chirp and cheep,
   Else I wad let ye in-o.
I'd let ye in this ae night,
   This ae, ae, ae night,
I'll let ye in this ae night,
   If ye'll ne'er do it again-o."

"O, I'll steal in like sweet moonlight
And ere the laverock takes his flight
I'll glide awa like glamour slight,
   Ye'll hardly think I've been-o.

Windie-waas, windy walls—that is, nowhere
     laverock, lark

Sae let me in this ae night,
    This ae, ae, ae night ;
A wa'er heart, a wearier wight,
    Never woo'd at e'en-o."

                    Allan Cunningham.

38   O ! ARE YE SLEEPIN', MAGGIE ?

" O ! ARE ye sleepin', Maggie ?
    O ! are ye sleepin', Maggie ?
Let me in, for loud the linn
    Is roarin' o'er the warlock craigie !

" Mirk an' rainy is the nicht,
    No a starn in a' the carry ;
Lightnin's gleam athwart the lift,
    An' win's drive on wi' winter's fury.

" Fearfu' soughs the bour-tree bank,
    The rifted wood roars wild an' dreary,
Loud the iron yett does clank,
    The cry o' howlets mak's me eerie.

" Aboon my breath I daurna speak,
    For fear I rouse your waukrife daddie.
Cauld's the blast upon my cheek,—
    O rise, rise, my bonnie lady ! "

warlock craigie, wizard's crag		*starn*, star
carry, sky	*lift*, heavens	*soughs*, wails
bour-tree, elderberry	*yett*, gate	*howlets*, owls
	waukrife, wakeful	

She oped the door, she loot him in :
   He cuist aside his dreepin' plaidie :
" Blaw your warst, ye rain an' win',
   Since, Maggie, now I'm in aside ye.

   " Now, since ye're waukin', Maggie,
   Now, since ye're waukin', Maggie,
   What care I for howlet's cry,
   For bour-tree bank, or warlock craigie ? "
                    Robert Tannahill.

39   MARY MORISON

O MARY, at thy window be,
   It is the wish'd, the trysted hour !
Those smiles and glances let me see
   That make the miser's treasure poor :

How blithely wad I bide the stoure,
   A weary slave frae sun to sun.
Could I the rich reward secure—
   The lovely Mary Morison !

Yestreen, when to the trembling string,
   The dance gaed thro' the lighted ha',
To thee my fancy took its wing,
   I sat, but neither heard nor saw :
Tho' this was fair, and that was braw,
   And yon the toast of a' the town,
I sigh'd, and said, amang them a',
   " Ye are na Mary Morison."

            stoure, dust

O Mary, canst thou wreck his peace
  Wha for thy sake wad gladly die ?
Or canst thou break that heart of his
  Whase only faut is loving thee ?

If love for love thou wilt na gie,
  At least be pity to me shown ;
A thought ungentle canna be
  The thought o' Mary Morison.

Robert Burns.

40   WHEN FLORA HAD OURFRET THE
              FIRTH

When Flora had ourfret the firth,
  In May of every moneth quene ;
When merle and mavis singis with mirth,
  Sueit melling in the schawis schene ;
  When all luvaris rejoicit bene,
And most desirous of their prey ;
  I heard a lusty luvar mene :
" I luve but I dar nocht assay.

" Strang are the panis I dayly prufe
  Bot yit with patience I sustene,
I am so fetterit with the lufe
  Onlie of my lady schene,
  Whilk for hir beauty mycht be quene ;
Natour sa craftily alway
  Hes done depaint that sweit serene ;
Whom I luf I dar nocht assay.

firth, enclosed place   *melling*, playing
schawis schene, bright woods   *mene*, moan

" Scho is so brycht of hide and hew,
   I lufe bot hir alone, I wene ;
Is non hir luf that may eschew,
   That blenkis of that dulce amene.
   So comely cleir are hir twa ene,
That scho ma luvaris dois effrey,
   Than evir of Greece did fair Helene ;
Whom I luve I dar nocht assay."

41 O WERT THOU IN THE CAULD BLAST

O WERT thou in the cauld blast
   On yonder lea, on yonder lea,
My plaidie to the angry airt,
   I'd shelter thee, I'd shelter thee :
Or did Misfortune's bitter storms
   Around thee blaw, around thee blaw,
Thy bield should be my bosom,
   To share it a', to share it a'.

Or were I in the wildest waste,
   Sae black and bare, sae black and bare,
The desert were a paradise,
   If thou wert there, if thou wert there :
Or were I monarch o' the globe,
   Wi' thee to reign, wi' thee to reign,
The brightest jewel in my crown
   Wad be my queen, wad be my queen.
Robert Burns.

hide and hew, skin and colouring
blenkis, catches a glimpse
dulce amene, sweet darling   *ma*, more
airt, quarter   *bield*, shelter

42   FOR THE SAKE O' SOMEBODY

My heart is sair—I darena tell—
    My heart is sair for Somebody ;
I could wake a winter night
    For the sake o' Somebody.
        Ohon ! for Somebody !
        O-hey ! for Somebody !
I could range the world around,
    For the sake o' Somebody !

Ye Powers that smile on virtuous love,
    O, sweetly smile on Somebody !
Frae ilka danger keep him free,
    And send me safe my Somebody.
        Ohon ! for Somebody !
        O-hey ! for Somebody !
I wad do—what wad I not ?
    For the sake o' Somebody !

                            Robert Burns.

43   JOCKIE'S TA'EN THE PARTING KISS

Jockie's ta'en the parting kiss,
    Ower the mountains he is gane ;
And with him is a' my bliss ;
    Nought but griefs wi' me remain.

Spare my love, ye winds that blaw,
    Plashy sleets and beating rain !
Spare my love, thou feathery snaw,
    Drifting o'er the frozen plain !

When the shades of evening creep
  Ower the day's fair gladsome e'e,
Sound and safely may he sleep,
  Sweetly blythe his waukening be !

He will think on her he loves,
  Fondly he'll repeat her name ;
For, where'er he distant roves,
  Jockie's heart is still at hame.

Robert Burns.

44   WANDERING WILLIE

HERE awa, there awa, wandering Willie !
  Here awa, there awa, haud awa hame !
Lang have I sought thee, dear have I bought thee ;
  Now I have gotten my Willie again.

Through the lang muir I have followed my Willie ;
  Through the lang muir I have followed him hame.
Whatever betide us, nought shall divide us ;
  Love now rewards all my sorrow and pain.

Here awa, there awa, here awa, Willie !
  Here awa, there awa, here awa, hame !
Come, love, believe me, nothing can grieve me,
  Ilka thing pleases, when Willie's at hame.

45   LOGIE O' BUCHAN

O LOGIE o' Buchan, O Logie the laird,
They hae ta'en awa' Jamie that delved in the yaird ;
He play'd on the pipe and the viol sae sma' ;
They hae ta'en awa' Jamie, the flower o' them a'.

He said : " Think na lang, lassie, tho' I gang awa' ; "
He said : " Think na lang, lassie, tho' I gang awa' ;
For the simmer is coming, cauld winter's awa',
And I'll come and see thee in spite o' them a'."

O, Sandie has owsen, and siller, and kye,
A house and a haddin, and a' things forbye,
But I wad hae Jamie, wi's bonnet in's hand,
Before I'd hae Sandie wi' houses and land.

My daddie looks sulky, my minnie looks sour,
They frown upon Jamie, because he is poor ;
But daddie and minnie altho' that they be,
There's nane o' them a' like my Jamie to me.

I sit on my creepie, and spin at my wheel,
And think on the laddie that lo'ed me sae weel ;
He had but ae saxpence—he brak it in twa,
And he gied me the hauf o't when he gaed awa'.
        Then haste ye back, Jamie, and bide na awa' ;
        Then haste ye back, Jamie, and bide na awa' ;
        Simmer is comin', cauld winter's awa',
        And ye'll come and see me in spite o' them a'.

46   ADIEU TO HIS MISTRESS

        ADIEU, O daisy of delyt ;
        Adieu, most plesand and perfyte ;
            Adieu, and haif gude nicht :
        Adieu, thou lustiest on lyve ;

owsen, oxen   *kye*, cows   *haddin*, holding
        creepie, stool

Adieu, sweet thing superlatyve ;
   Adieu, my lamp of licht !
Like as the lissard does indeid
   Leiv by the manis face,
Thy beautie likewise suld me feed,
   If we had time and space.
     Adieu now ; be true now,
      Sen that we must depart.
     Forget not, and set not
      At licht my constant heart.

Albeit my body be absent,
My faithful heart is vigilent
   To do you service true ;
Bot when I hant into the place
Where I wes wont to sie that face,
   My dolour does renew.
Then all my plesur is bot pain,
   My cairis they do incres ;
Until I sie your face again
   I live in heavynes.
     Sair weeping, but sleeping
      The nichtis I ouerdryve ;
     Whylis murning, whylis turning,
      With thoghtis pensityve.

Sometime Good Hope did me comfort,
Saying, the time suld be bot short
   Of absence to endure.

     hant into, frequent
  but, without   *ouerdryve*, spend

Then curage quickins so my spreit,
When I think on my lady sweet,
   I hald my service sure.
I can not plaint of my estait,
   I thank the gods above ;
For I am first in her consait,
    Whom both I serve and love.
      Her freindis ay weindis
        To cause her to revoke ;
      Scho bydis, and slydis
        No more than does a rok.

O lady, for thy constancie,
A faithful servand sall I be,
   Thine honour to defend ;
And I sall surelie, for thy sake,
As doth the turtle for her maik,
   Love to my lyfis end.
No pene nor travell, feir nor dreid,
   Sall cause me to desist.
Then ay when ye this letter reid,
   Remember how we kist ;
      Embracing with lacing,
        With others teiris sweet,
      Sic blissing in kissing
        I quyt till we twa meit.
                Alexander Montgomerie.

plaint, complain   *weindis*, scheme
maik, mate   *quyt*, leave

BOOK III
CHAGRIN D'AMOUR

HENCE HAIRT

Hence hairt, with her that must depairt,
  And hald thee with thy soverane,
For I had lever want ane hairt
  Nor haif the hairt that dois me pane ;
  Thairfoir go, with thy lufe remane,
And lat me lif thus unmolest ;
  And see that thou come not agane,
But bide with hir thou luvis best.

Sen scho that I haif schervit lang
  Is to depart so suddanly,
Address thee now, for thou sall gang
  And beir thy lady company.
  Fra scho begone, hairtless am I,
For why thou art with hir possesst ;
  Thairfoir, my hairt, go hence in hy,
And bide with hir thou luvis best.

Thoch this belappit body heir
  Be bound to schervitude and thrall,
My faithful hairt is free inteir
  And mind to serve my lady at all.

lever, rather *Address*, prepare
Fra scho begone, from the time when she is gone
hy, haste *belappit*, burdened *at all*, wholly

Wald God that I wer perigall,
Under that redolent rose to rest !
  Yit at the leist, my hairt, thou sall
Abide with hir thou luvis best.

Sen in your garth the lilly white
  May not remain amang the laif,
Adew, the flour of haill delyte !
  Adew the succour that may me saif !
  Adew the fragrant balme suaif,
And lamp of ladeis lustiest !
  My faithful hairt scho sall it haif
To bide with hir it luvis best.

Deploir, ye ladeis cleir of hew,
  Hir absence, sen scho must depart,
And specially ye luvaris trew,
  That woundit bene with luvis dart :
  For some of yow sall want ane hairt
As weill as I : thairfoir at last
  Do go with mine, with mind inwart,
And bide with hir thou luvis best.

Alexander Scott.

48   A ROUNDEL OF LUVE

Lo ! what it is to lufe
  Learn ye, that list to prufe
Be me, I say, that nae wayis may
  The grund of greif remufe,
Bot still decay, both nicht and day :
  Lo ! what it is to lufe.

perigall, worthy   *laif*, rest
  suaif, suave, sweet   *Be*, by

Lufe is ane fervent fire
Kendillit without desire :
Short plesour, lang displesour ;
Repentance is the hire ;
Ane pure tressour without mesour :
Lufe is ane fervent fire.

To lufe and to be wyse,
To rege with gud advyce,
Now thus, now than, so gois the game.
Incertane is the dice :
Thair is no man, I say, that can
Both lufe and to be wyse.

Flee alwayis from the snare ;
Learn at me to be ware ;
It is ane pain and double trane
Of endless woe and care ;
For to refrain that denger plain,
Flee alwayis from the snare.

Alexander Scott.

49   AY WAUKIN', O

O I'm wat, wat,
O' I'm wat and wearie !
Yet fain wad I rise and rin,
If I thought I would meet my dearie.

Ay waukin', O !
Waukin' ay, and wearie,
Sleep I can get nane
For thinkin' on my dearie.

pure, poor   *rege with*, rage at   *wat*, wet

Simmer's a pleasant time,
   Flowers of every colour,
The water rins ower the heugh—
   And I lang for my true lover.

When I sleep I dream,
   When I wauk I'm eerie ;
Sleep I can get nane
   For thinkin' on my dearie.

Lanely night comes on ;
   A' the lave are sleepin' ;
I think on my love,
   And bleer my een wi' greetin'.

Feather-beds are saft,
   Pentit rooms are bonnie ;
But a kiss o' my dear love
   Is better far than ony.

                              Robert Burns.

50 WERE NA MY HEART LIGHT, I WAD DIE

THERE was ance a may, and she lo'ed na men,
She biggit her bonny bow'r down in yon glen ;
But now she cries dool ! and a well-a-day !
Come down the green gate, and come here away.
      But now she cries dool ! etc.

heugh, bank   *lave*, rest   *Pentit*, painted
may, maid   *biggit*, built   *dool*, woe

When bonny young Johnny came o'er the sea,
He said he saw naething sae lovely as me ;
He hecht me baith rings and mony braw things ;
And were na my heart light, I wad dee.
      He hecht, etc.

He had a wee titty that lo'ed na me,
Because I was twice as bonny as she ;
She rais'd sic a pother 'twixt him and his mother,
That were na my heart light, I wad dee.
      She raised, etc.

The day it was set, and the bridal to be,
The wife took a dwam, and lay down to dee ;
She main'd and she grain'd out of dolour and pain,
Till he vow'd he never wad see me again.
      She main'd, etc.

His kin was for ane of a higher degree,
Said, " What had he to do with the like of me ? "
Albeit I was bonny, I was na for Johnny ;
And were na my heart light, I wad dee.
      Albeit I was, etc.

They said I had neither cow nor calf,
Nor dribbles of drink rins thro' the draff,
Nor pickles of meal rins thro' the mill-e'e ;
And were na my heart light, I wad dee.
      Nor pickles of, etc.

hecht, promised	*titty*, sister
dwam, swoon	*grain'd*, groaned
draff, malt refuse	*pickles*, small quantities

His titty she was baith wylie and slee ;
She spy'd me as I came o'er the lea ;
And then she ran in and made a loud din ;
Believe your ain een, an ye trow na me.
     And then she, etc.

His bonnet stood ay fu' round on his broo ;
His auld ane looks ay as well as some's new :
But now he lets 't wear ony gate it will hing,
And casts himsel dowie upon the corn-bing.
     But now he, etc.

And now he gaes drooping about the dykes,
And a' he dow do is to hund the tykes ;
The live-lang night he ne'er steeks his e'e ;
And were na my heart light, I wad dee.
     The live-lang, etc.

Were I young for thee, as I hae been,
We shou'd hae been galloping doun on yon green,
And linking out o'er yon lily-white lea ;
And wow gin I were but young for thee.
     And linking, etc.

Lady Grizel Baillie.

gate, way	*hing*, hang	*dowie*, sad
dow, can	*hund the tykes*, hound the dogs	
	steeks, closes	

51 LAMENT OF THE MASTER OF ERSKINE

DEPART, depart, depart !
Allace ! I must depart
From her that hes my hart,
With hart full soir,
Aganis my will indeid,
And can find no remeid,
I wait the pains of deid
Can do no moir.

Now must I go, allace !
Frome sicht of her sweit face,
The grund of all my grace
And soverane :
What chance that may fall me,
Sall I nevir mirry be,
Unto the tyme I see
My sweit agane.

I go, and wait nocht whair,
I wandir heir and thair,
I weip and sichis rycht sair,
With panis smart ;
Now must I pass away, away,
In wildirness and willfull way ;
Allace ! this wofull day
We suld depart.

My spreit dois quaik for dreid,
My thirlit hairt dois bleid,
My painis dois exceid—

wait, wot   *sichis*, sigh   *thirlit*, transfixed

What suld I say ?
I wofull wycht allone,
Makand ane petous mone,
Allace ! my hairt is gone,
For evir and ay.

Throw langour of my sweit,
So thirlit is my spreit,
My dayis ar most compleit,
Throw hir absence :
Chryst, sen scho knew my smert,
Ingraivit in my hairt,
Becaus I must depart
Frome hir presens.

Adew, my awin sweit thing,
My joy and conforting,
My mirth and sollesing,
Of erdly gloir :
Fairweill, my lady bricht,
And my remembrance rycht ;
Fair weill, and haif gud nycht ;
I say no moir.

Alexander Scott.

52 O WALY, WALY

O WALY, waly up the bank,
  And waly, waly down the brae,
And waly, waly by yon burnside
  Where I and my Love wont to gae.

I lent my back against an aik,
  I thought it was a trusty tree ;
But first it bow'd and syne it brak :
  Sae my true Love did lichtly me.

O waly, waly, but love is bonny
  A little time while it is new ;
But when 'tis auld, it waxeth cauld
  And fades awa' like morning dew.
O wherefore should I busk my head ?
  O wherefore should I kame my hair ?
For my true Love has me forsook,
  And says he'll never lo'e me mair.

Now Arthur's Seat sall be my bed,
  The sheets sall ne'er be prest by me ;
Saint Anton's Well sall be my drink,
  Since my true Love's forsaken me.
Mart'mas wind, when wilt thou blaw
  And shake the green leaves aff the tree ?
O gentle Death, when wilt thou come ?
  For of my life I am wearie.

'Tis not the frost, that freezes fell,
  Nor blawing snaw's inclemencie,
'Tis not sic cauld that makes me cry,
  But my Love's heart grown cauld to me.
When we came in by Glasgow town
  We were a comely sight to see :
My Love was clad in the black velvet,
  And I myself in cramasie.

aik, oak   *syne*, then

But had I wist, before I kist,
  That love had been sae ill to win,
I had lockt my heart in a case of gowd
  And pinn'd it with a siller pin.
And O ! if my young babe were born,
  And set upon the nurse's knee,
And I mysell were dead and gane,
  And the green grass growing over me

53   AULD ROBIN GRAY

WHEN the sheep are in the fauld, and the kye's a' at
    hame,
And a' the world to rest are gane ;
The waes o' my heart fa' in showers frae my e'e,
Unkent by my gudeman, wha sleeps sound by me.

Young Jamie lo'ed me weel, and he sought me for his
    bride,
But saving a crown, he had naething else beside ;
To mak' the crown a pound, my Jamie gaed to sea,
And the crown and the pound, they were baith for me.

He hadna been gane a twelvemonth and a day,
When my faither brak' his arm, and the cow was stown
    away ;
My mither she fell sick—my Jamie at the sea ;
And Auld Robin Gray came a-courting me.

My faither couldna work, and my mither couldna spin ;
I toil'd day and nicht, but their bread I couldna win :

    fauld, fold   *kye*, cows   *stown*, stolen

Auld Rob maintain'd them baith, and wi' tears in his e'e,
Said " Jeanie, for their sakes, will ye no marry me ? "

My heart it said Na, and I looked for Jamie back ;
But hard blew the winds, and his ship it was a wrack ;
The ship was a wrack : why didna Jamie dee ?
Or why am I spared to cry, " Wae is me " ?

My faither urged me sair, my mither didna speak,
But she lookit in my face till my heart was like to break ;
They gied him my hand—my heart was in the sea ;
And so Robin Gray he was gudeman to me.

I hadna been his wife a week but only four,
When, mournfu' as I sat on the stane at my door,
I saw my Jamie's ghaist, for I couldna think it he,
Till he said : " I'm come hame, love, to marry thee."

Oh ! sair, sair did we greet, and mickle say of a' ;
I gied him a kiss, and bade him gang awa' ;
I wished that I were dead, but I'm nae like to dee :
For tho' my heart is broken, I'm young, wae's me !

I gang like a ghaist, and carena to spin ;
I darena think on Jamie, for that wad be a sin ;
But I'll do my best a gude wife to be,
For oh ! Robin Gray he is kind to me.

Lady Anne Barnard.

greet, weep   *mickle,* much

54 YE BANKS AND BRAES

YE banks and braes o' bonnie Doon,
　　How can ye bloom sae fresh and fair ;
How can ye chant, ye little birds,
　　And I sae weary, fu' o' care ?

Thou'll break my heart, thou warbling bird,
　　That wantons thro' the flowering thorn :
Thou minds me o' departed joys,
　　Departed—never to return !

Aft hae I rov'd by bonnie Doon,
　　To see the rose and woodbine twine ;
And ilka bird sang o' its luve,
　　And fondly sae did I o' mine.

Wi' lightsome heart I pu'd a rose,
　　Fu' sweet upon its thorny tree ;
And my fause luver staw my rose,
　　But, ah ! he left the thorn wi' me.
　　　　　　　　　　　　　　Robert Burns.

55 AE FOND KISS

AE fond kiss, and then we sever !
Ae farewell, and then, for ever !
Deep in heart-wrung tears I'll pledge thee,
Warring sighs and groans I'll wage thee. . . .

　　　　　　staw, stole

Had we never lov'd sae kindly,
Had we never lov'd sae blindly,
Never met—or never parted,
We had ne'er been broken-hearted.

Fare thee weel, thou first and fairest !
Fare thee weel, thou best and dearest !
Thine be ilka joy and treasure,
Peace, enjoyment, love, and pleasure !

Ae fond kiss, and then we sever !
Ae fareweel, alas ! for ever !
Deep in heart-wrung tears I'll pledge thee,
Warring sighs and groans I'll wage thee !
Robert Burns.

56   CUPID AND VENUS

FRA bank to bank, fra wood to wood I rin,
   Ourhailit with my feeble fantasie ;
   Like til a leaf that fallis from a tree,
Or til a reed ourblawin with the win'.
Twa gods guides me ; the ane of them is blin',
   Yea and a bairn brocht up in vanitie ;
   The next a wife ingenrit of the sea,
And lichter nor a dauphin with her fin.

Unhappy is the man for evermair
   That tills the sand and sawis in the air ;

      Ourhailit, overcome

But twice unhappier is he, I lairn,
That feedis in his hairt a mad desire,
And follows on a woman throw the fire,
Led by a blind and teachit by a bairn.

Mark Alexander Boyd.

BOOK IV
THE HEARTH

82   The Northern Muse

THE WAITING BRIDE

57   THE RANTIN' DOG THE DADDIE O'T

O WHA my babie-clouts will buy ?
O wha will tent me when I cry ?
Wha will kiss me where I lie ?—
    The rantin' dog the daddie o't.

O wha will own he did the fau't ?
O wha will buy the groanin' maut ?
O wha will tell me how to ca't ?—
    The rantin' dog the daddie o't.

When I mount the creepie chair,
Wha will sit beside me there ?
Gie me Rob, I'll seek nae mair,
    The rantin' dog the daddie o't.

Wha will crack to me my lane ?
Wha will mak me fidgin' fain ?
Wha will kiss me o'er again ?—
    The rantin' dog the daddie o't.

                                Robert Burns.

babie-clouts, baby-clothes   *tent*, tend
groanin' maut, ale for the midwife
creepie chair, stool of repentance
crack, talk   *fidgin' fain*, tingling with love

58   THE WAITING BRIDE

" O WHA will shoe my bonny foot ?
    And wha will glove my hand ?
And wha will lace my middle jimp,
    Wi' a lang, lang linen band ?

" O wha will kame my yellow hair,
    Wi' a haw bayberry kame ?
And wha will be my babe's father
    Till Gregory come hame ? ''

" Thy father he will shoe thy foot,
    Thy brother will glove thy hand,
Thy mither will bind thy middle jimp
    Wi' a lang, lang linen band.

" Thy sister will kame thy yellow hair,
    Wi' a haw bayberry kame ;
The Almighty will be thy babe's father,
    Till Gregory come hame.''

59   THE GARMONT OF GUDE LADIES

WALD my gude lady lufe me best,
    And work eftir my will,
I suld ane garmont gudliest
    Gar mak her body till.

jimp, trim   *kame*, comb
haw bayberry.   See note, page 473
gar mak, cause to be made

Of hie honour suld be her hude,
    Upon her heid to wear,
Garneist with governance so gude,
    Na deeming suld her deir.

Her serk suld be her body nixt,
    Of chastitie so white,
With shame and dreid togidder mixt,
    The same suld be perfite.

Her kirtle suld be of clean constance,
    Laced with leesome lufe,
The mailyeis of continuance
    For never to remufe.

Her gown suld be of gudliness,
    Weil ribbon'd with renoun,
Purfillit with pleasure in ilk place,
    Furrit with fine fassoun.

Her belt suld be of benignitie,
    About her middle meet ;
Her mantle of humilitie,
    To thole baith wind and weet.

Her hat suld be of fair-having,
    And her tepat of truth ;
Her patelet of gude-pansing ;
    Her hals-ribbon of ruth.

garneist, garnished   *deeming*, contempt
deir, daunt   *leesome*, delightful
mailyeis, lacing-holes   *Purfillit*, purfled, embroidered
fassoun, fashion   *thole*, bear   *tepat*, tippet
patelet, ruff   *gude-pansing*, good thinking
hals-, hause, neck

Her sleevis suld be of esperance,
   To keep her fra despair ;
Her glovis of gude governance,
   To guide her fingeris fair.

Her shoon suld be of siccarness,
   In sign that scho nocht slide ;
Her hose of honestie, I guess,
   I suld for her provide.

Wald scho put on this garmont gay,
   I durst swear by my seill,
That scho wore never green nor grey
   That set her half so weil.

Robert Henryson.

60   A HAPPY FIRESIDE CLIME

I HAE a wife and twa wee laddies,
They maun hae brose and brats o' duddies ;
Ye ken yoursel my heart right proud is—
          I need na vaunt,
But I'll sned besoms, thraw saugh woodies,
          Before they want. . . .

But to conclude my silly rhyme,
(I'm scant o' verse, and scant o' time),
To make a happy fireside clime
          To weans and wife ;
That's the true pathos and sublime
          Of human life.

Robert Burns.

siccarness, sureness   *seill*, felicity
   brats o' duddies, scraps of clothes   *sned*, trim
   thraw saugh woodies, weave willow twigs

61   JOHN ANDERSON, MY JO

JOHN ANDERSON, my jo, John,
    When we were first acquent ;
Your locks were like the raven,
    Your bonnie brow was brent ;

But now your brow is beld, John,
    Your locks are like the snaw ;
But blessings on your frosty pow,
    John Anderson, my jo.

John Anderson, my jo, John,
    We clamb the hill thegither ;
And mony a cantie day, John,
    We've had wi' ane anither :

Now we maun totter down, John,
    And hand in hand we'll go ;
And sleep thegither at the foot,
    John Anderson, my jo.

                            Robert Burns

62   A HIGHLAND CRADLE SONG

HEE balou, my sweet wee Donald,
Image of the great Clanronald !
Brawlie kens our wanton chief
Wha gat my young Highland thief.

jo, love   brent, straight   beld, bald
          pow, head   cantie, jolly

Leeze me on thy bonnie craigie !
An thou live thou'll steal a naigie,
Travel the country thro' and thro',
And bring me hame a Carlisle cow.

Thro' the Lawlands, o'er the Border,
Weel, my babie, may thou furder,
Herry the louns o' the laigh countrie,
Syne to the Highlands hame to me.

Robert Burns.

63   CAN YE SEW CUSHIONS ?

O CAN ye sew cushions ?
  Or can ye sew sheets ?
An' can ye sing ba-la-loo
  When the bairnie greets ?
An' hee an' ba, birdie,
  An' hee an' ba, lamb,
An' hee an' ba, birdie,
  My bonnie wee man.

  Hee O, wee O, what'll I dae wi' ye ?
  Black is the life that I lead wi' ye,
  Mony o' ye, little to gie ye,
  Hee O, wee O, what'll I dae wi' ye ?

Now hush-a-ba, lammie,
  An' hush-a-ba, dear,
Now hush-a-ba, lammie,
  Thy minnie is here.

leeze me on, blessings on	*craigie*, throat	*naigie*, horse
furder, advance	*louns*, rascals	*laigh*, low

The wild wind is ravin',
   Thy minnie's heart's sair;
The wild wind is ravin',
   An' ye dinna care.

Sing ba-la-loo, lammie,
   Sing ba-la-loo, dear,
Does wee lammie ken
   That his daddie's no here?
Ye're rockin' fu' sweetly
   Upon my warm knee,
But your daddie's a-rockin'
   Upon the saut sea.

64   MY WIFE'S A WINSOME WEE THING

My wife's a winsome wee thing,
A bonnie, blythesome wee thing,
My dear, my constant wee thing,
   And evermair sall be;
It warms my heart to view her;
I canna choose but lo'e her;
And oh, weel may I trow her,
   How dearly she lo'es me!

For tho' her face sae fair be
As nane could ever mair be;
And tho' her wit sae rare be
   As seenil do we see;
Her beauty ne'er had gain'd me,
Her wit had ne'er enchain'd me,
Nor baith sae lang retain'd me,
   But for her love to me.

      seenil, seldom

When wealth and pride disown'd me,
　A' views were dark around me ;
And sad and laigh she found me
　As friendless worth could be :
Whan ither hope gaed frae me,
Her pity kind did stay me,
And love for love she gae me ;—
　And that's the love for me !

And, till this heart is cauld, I
　That charm o' life will hald by ;
And, tho' my wife grow auld, my
　Leal love ay young will be ;
For she's my winsome wee thing,
My canty, blythesome wee thing,
My tender, constant wee thing,
　And evermair sall be.

Robert Jamieson.

65 .　　　THE FARMER'S INGLE

Et multo in primis hilarans convivia Baccho,
Ante focum, si frigus erit.—VIRG., *Buc.*

WHEN gloamin' grey out-owre the welkin keeks ; ·
　When Batie ca's his owsen to the byre ;
When Thrasher John, sair dung, his barn-door steeks,
　And lusty lasses at the dightin' tire ;
What bangs fu' leal the e'enin's coming cauld,
　And gars snaw-tappit winter freeze in vain ?
Gars dowie mortal look baith blythe and bauld,

laigh, low	*welkin*, sky	*owsen*, oxen	*sair dung*, sore tired
steeks, shuts	*dightin'*, winnowing		*bangs*, defeats

Nor fley'd wi' a' the poortith o' the plain ?
Begin, my Muse ! and chaunt in hamely strain.

Frae the big stack, weel winnow't on the hill,
  Wi' divots theekit frae the weet and drift,
Sods, peats and heathery truffs the chimley fill,
  And gar their thickening smeek salute the lift.
The gudeman, new come hame, is blythe to find,
  When he out-owre the hallan flings his een,
That ilka turn is handled to his mind ;
  That a' his housie looks sae cosh and clean ;
For cleanly house lo'es he, though e'er so mean.

Weel kens the gudewife that the pleughs require
  A heartsome meltith, and refreshing synd
O' nappy liquor, owre a bleezin' fire ;
  Sair wark and poortith downa weel be join'd.
Wi' butter'd bannocks now the girdle reeks ;
  I' the far nook the bowie briskly reams ;
The readied kail stand by the chimley cheeks,
  And haud the riggin het wi' welcome streams,
Whilk than the daintiest kitchen nicer seems. . . .

The couthy cracks begin when supper's owre ;
  The cheering bicker gars them glibly gash
O' simmer's showery blinks, and winter sour,
  Whase floods did erst their mailin's produce hash.

fley'd, scared	*poortith*, poverty	*divots*, sods
theekit, thatched	*truffs*, turfs	*smeek*, smoke
lift, sky *hallan*, partition wall in a cottage		*cosh*, neat
meltith, meal	*synd*, draught	*downa*, cannot
bowie, dish	*reams*, creams	*readied*, made ready
kail, broth	*kitchen*, flavouring	*couthy*, intimate
bicker, bowl	*gash*, chatter	*mailin*, farm

'Bout kirk and market eke their tales gae on ;
　　How Jock woo'd Jenny here to be his bride ;
And there how Marion, for a bastard son,
　　Upon the cutty stool was forced to ride,
　　The waefu' scauld o' our Mess John to bide.

The fient a cheep's amang the bairnies now,
　　For a' their anger's wi' their hunger gane :
Aye maun the childer, wi' a fastin' mou',
　　Grumble and greet, and mak an unco mane.
In rangles round, before the ingle's lowe,
　　Frae gudame's mouth auld warld tales they hear,
O' warlocks loupin' round the wirrikow ;
　　O' ghaists, that win in glen and kirk-yard drear ;
　　Whilk touzles a' their tap, and gars them shak wi'
　　　　fear ! . . .

In its auld lerroch yet the deas remains,
　　Where the gudeman aft streeks him at his ease ;
A warm and canny lean for weary banes
　　O' labourers dyolt upon the weary leas.
Round him will baudrons and the collie come,
　　To wag their tail, and cast a thankfu' e'e
To him wha kindly throws them mony a crum
　　O' kebbuck whang'd, and dainty fadge, to pree ;
　　This a' the boon they crave, and a' the fee.

cutty stool, stool of repentance		*scauld*, scolding
The fient, never	*greet*, weep	*rangles*, rows
wirrikow, bugbear	*win*, dwell	*touzles*, ruffles
lerroch, place	*deas*, dais, long seat	*streeks*, stretches
dyolt, tired	*baudrons*, the cat	*kebbuck*, cheese
	fadge, bread	

Frae him the lads their mornin' counsel tak—
   What stacks he wants to thrash, what rigs to till ;
How big a birn maun lie on Bassie's back,
   For meal and mu'ter to the thirlin' mill.
Neist, the gudewife her hirelin' damsels bids
   Glow'r through the byre, and see the hawkies bound ;
Tak tent, case Crummy tak her wonted tids,
   And ca' the laiglen's treasure on the ground ;
   Whilk spills a kebbuck nice, or yellow pound.

Then a' the house for sleep begin to grien,
   Their joints to slack frae industry a while ;
The leaden god fa's heavy on their een,
   And hafflins steeks them frae their daily toil ;
The cruizy, too, can only blink and bleer,
   The reistit ingle's done the maist it dow ;
Tacksman and cottar eke to bed maun steer,
   Upon the cod to clear their drumly pow,
   Till waken'd by the dawnin's ruddy glow. . . .

               Robert Fergusson.

66 THERE'S NAE LUCK ABOUT THE HOUSE

    FOR there's nae luck about the house,
      There's nae luck at a' ;
    There's little pleasure in the house,
      When our gudeman's awa'.

birn, burden   *mu'ter*, the miller's toll
thirlin' mill, the mill which they were bound to employ
hawkies, cows   *tids*, humours   *laiglen*, milking pail
grien, long   *hafflins*, half   *cruizy*, lamp
steer, move   *cod*, pillow   *drumly*, muddy

And are ye sure the news is true ?
    And are ye sure he's weel ?
Is this a time to think o' wark ?
    Ye jauds, fling bye your wheel.
Is this a time to think o' wark,
    When Colin's at the door ?
Rax me my cloak, I'll to the quay,
    And see him come ashore.

And gie to me my bigonnet,
    My bishop-satin gown,
For I maun tell the bailie's wife
    That Colin's come to town.
My Turkey slippers maun gae on,
    My hose o' pearl blue ;
'Tis a' to please my ain gudeman,
    For he's baith leal and true.

Rise up and mak' a clean fireside,
    Put on the muckle pat ;
Gie little Kate her cotton gown,
    And Jock his Sunday coat ;
And mak' their shoon as black as slaes,
    Their hose as white as snaw ;
It's a' to please my ain gudeman :
    He likes to see them braw.

There's twa fat hens upon the bauk,
    Been fed this month and mair ;
Mak' haste and thraw their necks about,
    That Colin weel may fare.

Rax, reach   *bigonnet*, linen cap   *bauk*, roost

And spread the table neat and clean,
    Gar ilka thing look braw,
For wha can tell how Colin fared
    When he was far awa' ?

Sae true his heart, sae smooth his speech,
    His breath like caller air ;
His very fit has music in't
    As he comes up the stair.
And will I see his face again ?
    And will I hear him speak ?
I'm downright dizzy with the thought :
    In troth, I'm like to greet.

    For there's nae luck about the house,
        There's nae luck at a' ;
    There's little pleasure in the house
        When our gudeman's awa'.

67   BESSIE AND HER SPINNING-WHEEL

O LEEZE me on my spinnin-wheel,
And leeze me on my rock and reel ;
Frae tap to tae that cleeds me bien,
And haps me fiel and warm at e'en !
I'll set me down and sing and spin,
While laigh descends the simmer sun,
Blest wi' content, and milk and meal—
O leeze me on my spinnin-wheel !

caller, fresh	*fit*, foot	*leeze me*, blessings on
cleeds, clothes		*bien*, comfortably
haps, wraps	*fiel*, well	*laigh*, low

On ilka hand the burnies trot,
And meet below my theekit cot ;
The scented birk and hawthorn white,
Across the pool their arms unite,
Alike to screen the birdies' nest,
And little fishes' caller rest :
The sun blinks kindly in the biel',
Where blithe I turn my spinnin-wheel.

On lofty aiks the cushats wail,
And echo cons the doolfu' tale ;
The lintwhites in the hazel braes,
Delighted, rival ither's lays :
The craik amang the clover hay,
The paitrick whirrin' o'er the ley,
The swallow jinkin' round my shiel,
Amuse me at my spinnin-wheel.

Wi' sma' to sell, and less to buy,
Aboon distress, below envy,
O wha would leave this humble state,
For a' the pride of a' the great ?
Amid their flaring, idle toys,
Amid their cumbrous, dinsome joys,
Can they the peace and pleasure feel
Of Bessie at her spinnin-wheel ?

Robert Burns.

theekit, thatched   *caller*, cool   *biel'*, shelter
lintwhites, linnets   *craik*, corncrake
paitrick, partridge   *shiel*, cottage   *dinsome*, noisy

68   O WEEL MAY THE BOATIE ROW

O WEEL may the boatie row,
  And better may she speed !
And weel may the boatie row,
  That wins the bairns' bread !
The boatie rows, the boatie rows,
  The boatie rows indeed ;
And happy be the lot of a'
  That wishes her to speed !

I cuist my line in Largo Bay,
  And fishes I caught nine ;
There's three to boil, and three to fry,
  And three to bait the line.
The boatie rows, the boatie rows,
  The boatie rows indeed ;
And happy be the lot of a'
  That wishes her to speed !

O weel may the boatie row,
  That fills a heavy creel,
And cleads us a' frae head to feet,
  And buys our parritch meal.
The boatie rows, the boatie rows,
  The boatie rows indeed ;
And happy be the lot of a'
  That wish the boatie speed.

cuist, cast   *cleads*, clothes   *parritch*, porridge

When Jamie vow'd he would be mine,
   And wan frae me my heart,
O muckle lighter grew my creel !
   He swore we'd never part.
The boatie rows, the boatie rows,
   The boatie rows fu' weel ;
And muckle lighter is the lade,
   When love bears up the creel.

My kurtch I put upon my head,
   An' dressed mysel' fu' braw ;
I trow my heart was dowf and wae
   When Jamie gaed awa'.
But weel may the boatie row,
   And lucky be her part ;
And lightsome be the lassie's care
   That yields an honest heart !

When Sawnie, Jock, and Janetie
   Are up and gotten lear,
They'll help to gar the boatie row,
   And lighten a' our care.
The boatie rows, the boatie rows,
   The boatie rows fu' weel ;
And lightsome be her heart that bears
   The murlain and the creel !

And when wi' age we're worn down,
   And hirpling round the door,
They'll row to keep us hale and warm,
   As we did them before.

| *lade*, load | *kurtch*, head-dress | *dowf*, dreary |
| *lear*, learning | *murlain*, fish basket | *hirpling*, hobbling |

Then weel may the boatie row,
   That wins the bairns' bread ;
And happy be the lot of a'
   That wish the boatie speed !

69   I'LL GAR OUR GUDEMAN TROW

I'LL gar our gudeman trow
   I'll sell the ladle,
If he winna buy to me
   A bonnie side-saddle,
To ride to kirk and bridal,
   And round about the town ;
Sae stand about, ye fisher jauds,
   And gie my gown room !

I'll gar our gudeman trow,
   I'll tak' the fling-strings,
If he winna buy to me
   Twal bonnie gowd rings ;
Ane for ilka finger,
   And twa for ilka thoom ;
Sae stand about, ye fisher jauds,
   And gie my gown room !

I'll gar our gudeman trow
   That I'm gaun to die,
If he winna fee to me
   Valets twa or three,

trow, understand   *jauds*, wenches
twal, twelve   *thoom*, thumb
(2,470)   4

To bear my train up frae the dirt,
    And ush me through the town;
Sae stand about, ye fisher jauds,
    And gie my gown room!

70   AN ILL WIFE

WHEN ilka herd for cauld his fingers rubs,
And cakes o' ice are seen upo' the dubs;
At mornin', when frae pleugh or fauld I come,
I'll see a braw reek rising frae my lum,
And aiblins think to get a rantin' blaze,
To fley the frost awa', and toast my taes;
But when I shoot my nose in, ten to ane,
If I weelfar'dly see my ain hearthstane.
She round the ingle wi' her gimmers sits,
Crammin' their gebbies wi' her nicest bits;
While the gudeman out-by maun fill his crap
Frae the milk coggie or the parritch cap.
                                Robert Fergusson.

71   WILLIE WASTLE

WILLIE WASTLE dwalt on Tweed,
    The spot they ca'd it Linkumdoddie,
Willie was a wabster guid,
    Cou'd stown a clue wi' ony bodie:

dubs, pools   *reek*, smoke   *lum*, chimney
aiblins, perhaps   *fley*, scare   *weelfar'dly*, comfortably
gimmers, ewes, gossips   *gebbies*, mouths   *coggie*, bowl
wabster, weaver   *stown*, have stolen.   See note, page 475

He had a wife was dour and din,
  O Tinkler Maidgie was her mither !
Sic a wife as Willie had,
  I wad na gie a button for her.

She has an e'e—she has but ane—
  The cat has twa the very colour ;
Five rusty teeth, forbye a stump,
  A clapper-tongue wad deave a miller ;
A whiskin' beard about her mou',
  Her nose and chin they threaten ither—·
Sic a wife as Willie had,
  I wad na gie a button for her.

She's bow-hough'd, she's hem-shinn'd,
  Ae limpin' leg, a hand-breed shorter ;
She's twisted right, she's twisted left,
  To balance fair in ilka quarter :
She has a hump upon her breast,
  The twin o' that upon her shouther·—
Sic a wife as Willie had,
  I wad na gie a button for her.

Auld baudrons by the ingle sits,
  An' wi' her loof her face a-washin' ;
But Willie's wife is nae sae trig,
  She dights her grunzie wi' a hushion ;

dour and din, stubborn and drab   *deave*, deafen
bow-hough'd, hem-shinn'd, bandy *hand-breed*, hand's-breadth
baudrons, pussy   *loof*, paw   *trig*, trim
dights, etc., wipes her snout with a footless stocking

Her walie nieves like midden-creels,
　　Her face wad fyle the Logan-Water—
Sic a wife as Willie had,
　　I wad na gie a button for her.

Robert Burns.

72　　　GET UP AND BAR THE DOOR

AND the barrin' o' our door weil, weil, weil,
And the barrin' o' our door weil.

It fell about the Martinmas time,
　　And a gay time it was than,
When our gudewife had puddin's to mak',
　　And she boil'd them in the pan.

The wind blew cauld frae south to north,
　　It blew into the floor ;
Says our gudeman to our gudewife :
　　" Get up and bar the door."

" My hand is in my hussyfe-skep,
　　Gudeman, as ye may see ;
An' it shouldna be barr'd this hunner year,
　　It's no' be barr'd for me."

They made a paction 'tween them twa,
　　They made it firm and sure,
The first that spak' the foremost word
　　Should rise and bar the door.

walie nieves, massive fists　　*midden-creels,* manure baskets
fyle, defile　　　　　　　　　*hussyfe-skep,* housewifery

Then by there came twa gentlemen
    At twelve o'clock at nicht ;
And they could neither see house nor ha',
    Nor coal nor candle-licht.

" Now whether is this a rich man's house
    Or whether is this a puir ? "
But never a word wad ane o' them speak,
    For the barrin' o' the door.

And first they ate the white puddin's,
    And syne they ate the black ;
And muckle thocht our gudewife to hersell,
    But never a word she spak'.

" Then said the tane unto the tother :
    " Hae, man, take ye my knife ;
Do ye tak' aff the auld man's beard,
    And I'll kiss the gudewife."

" But there's nae water in the house,
    And what shall we do than ? "
" What ails ye at the puddin' broo
    That boils into the pan ? "

O up then startit our gudeman,
    And an angry man was he :
" Wad ye kiss my wife before my face,
    And scaud me wi' puddin' bree ? "

Then up and startit our gudewife,
    Gied three skips on the floor :
" Gudeman, ye've spoken the foremost word,
    Get up and bar the door."

      broo, broth   *scaud,* scald

73   BENTY BOWS, ROBIN

ROBIN's gane to the south countree,
  Holland, green Holland !
And there he's courted a gay ladye,
  Benty bows, Robin !

He's wed her, and he's brought her hame,
  Holland, green Holland !
Weel I wat, she's a denty dame,
  Benty bows, Robin !

She winna wash, she winna wring,
  Holland, green Holland !
For wearing o' her gay gold ring,
  Benty bows, Robin !

She winna bake, she winna brew,
  Holland, green Holland !
For spoiling o' her comely hue,
  Benty bows, Robin !

She winna spin, she winna card,
  Holland, green Holland !
But she will gallant wi' the laird,
  Benty bows, Robin !

Robin's came hame frae the plough,
  Holland, green Holland !
Cries, " Is my dinner ready now ? "
  Benty bows, Robin !

" You're a' mista'en, gudeman," says she,
  Holland, green Holland !
" To think I'll servant be to thee,"
  Benty bows, Robin !

Robin's gane unto the faul',
  Holland, green Holland !
He's catch'd a wedder by the spaul,
  Benty bows, Robin !

He's carried it, and brought it hame,
  Holland, green Holland !
To gi'e it to his denty dame,
  Benty bows, Robin !

Robin's killed his wedder black,
  Holland, green Holland !
He's laid the skin upon her back,
  Benty bows, Robin !

He's laid the skin upon her back,
  Holland, green Holland !
And on the skin he's laid a whack,
  Benty bows, Robin !

" I daurna pay thee for thy kin,"
  Holland, green Holland !
" But I may pay my wedder's skin,"
  Benty bows, Robin !

" I daurna pay my lady's back,"
  Holland, green Holland !
" But I may pay my wedder black,"
  Benty bows, Robin !

  wedder, wether   *spaul*, shoulder

"O Robin, Robin, let me be,"
   Holland, green Holland !
"And I'll a gude wife be to thee,"
   Benty bows, Robin !

74 TAK' YOUR AULD CLOAK ABOUT YE

In winter when the rain rain'd cauld
   And frost and snaw on ilka hill ;
And Boreas, wi' his blasts sae bauld,
   Was threat'ning a' our kye to kill.
Then Bell, my wife, wha lo'es nae strife,
   She said to me right hastily,
"Get up, gudeman, save Crummie's life,
   And tak' your auld cloak about ye.

"My Crummie is a usefu' cow,
   An' she has come o' a gude kin',
Aft has she wet the bairns' mou',
   And I am laith that she should tine.
Get up, gudeman, it is fu' time,
   The sun shines in the lift sae hie ;
Sloth never made a gracious end,
   Gae tak' your auld cloak about ye."

"My cloak was ance a gude grey cloak,
   When it was fitting for my wear ;
But now it's scantly worth a groat,
   For I hae worn't this thretty year,

tine, perish   *lift*, sky   *thretty*, thirty

Let's spend the gear that we hae won,
  We little ken the day we'll dee ;
Then I'll be proud, sin' I hae sworn
  To hae a new cloak about me."

" In days when gude King Robert rang,
  He's trews they cost but half-a-croun ;
He said they were a groat ower dear,
  And ca'd the tailor thief and loon.
He was the king that wore the croun,
  And thou'rt a man of laich degree ;
It's pride puts a' the country doun,
  Sae tak' your auld cloak about ye."

" Ilka land has its ain lauch,
  Ilk' kind o' corn has its ain hool ;
I think the warld is a' gane wrang,
  When ilka wife her man maun rule.
Do you see Rob, Jock, and Hab,
  How they are girded gallantlie ;
While I sit hirklin' i' the ase ?
  I'll hae a new cloak about me ! "

" Gudeman, I wat it's thretty year
  Sin' we did ane anither ken ;
An' we ha'e had atween us twa
  Of lads and bonnie lasses ten ;

rang, reigned   *laich*, low
lauch, laugh   *hool*, husk
  hirklin' i' the ase, crouching among the ashes

Now they are women grown and men,
  I wish and pray weel may they be ;
And if you prove a good husband,
  E'en tak' your auld cloak about ye."

Bell, my wife, she lo'es nae strife,
  But she would guide me if she can ;
And to maintain an easy life,
  I aft maun yield, though I'm gudeman.
Nocht's to be won at woman's han',
  Unless you gi'e her a' the plea ;
Then I'll leave aff where I began,
  And tak' my auld cloak about me.

BOOK V
THE OPEN ROAD

75   THE GREENWOOD

THE king's young dochter was sitting in her window,
　　Sewing at her silken seam ;
She lookt out o' a bow-window,
　　And she saw the leaves growing green,
　　　　　My luve ;
　　And she saw the leaves growing green.

She stuck her needle into her sleeve,
　　Her seam down by her tae,
And she is awa' to the merrie greenwood,
　　To pu' the nit and the slae,
　　　　　My luve ;
　　To pu' the nit and the slae.

76   THE STIRRUP CUP

Go fetch to me a pint o' wine,
　　An' fill it in a silver tassie,
That I may drink, before I go,
　　A service to my bonnie lassie ;

The boat rocks at the pier o' Leith ;
　　Fu' loud the wind blaws frae the ferry ;
The ship rides by the Berwick-Law,
　　And I maun leave my bonnie Mary.

dochter, daughter 　　　*tae*, toe 　　　*slae*, sloe
109

The trumpets sound, the banners fly,
   The glittering spears are rankèd ready :
The shouts o' war are heard afar,
   The battle closes thick and bloody.

It's not the roar o' sea or shore
   Wad make me langer wish to tarry ;
Nor shout o' war that's heard afar—
   It's leaving thee, my bonnie Mary.
                      Robert Burns.

77   LEEZIE LINDSAY

" WILL you gang wi' me, Leezie Lindsay,
   Will ye gang to the Highlands wi' me ?
Will ye gang wi' me, Leezie Lindsay,
   My bride and my darling to be ? "

" To gang to the Highlands wi' you, sir,
   I dinna ken how that may be ;
For I ken nae the land that ye live in,
   Nor ken I the lad I'm gaun wi'."

" O Leezie, lass, ye maun ken little,
   If sae be ye dinna ken me ;
For my name is Lord Ronald Macdonald,
   A chieftain o' high degree."

She has kilted her coats o' green satin,
   She has kilted them up to the knee,
And she's aff wi' Lord Ronald Macdonald,
   His bride and his darling to be.

78   JOCK O' HAZELDEAN

" Why weep ye by the tide, ladye ?
    Why weep ye by the tide ?
I'll wed ye to my youngest son,
    And ye sall be his bride ;
And ye sall be his bride, ladye,
    Sae comely to be seen : "
But aye she loot the tears down fa'
    For Jock o' Hazeldean.

" Now let this wilfu' grief be done,
    And dry that cheek sae pale ;
Young Frank is chief of Errington
    And lord of Langley-dale ;
His step is first in peaceful ha',
    His sword in battle keen : "
But aye she loot the tears down fa'
    For Jock o' Hazeldean.

" A chain of gold ye sall not lack,
    Nor braid to bind your hair ;
Nor mettled hound, nor managed hawk,
    Nor palfrey fresh and fair ;
And you the foremost o' them a'
    Shall ride—our forest queen : "
But aye she loot the tears down fa'
    For Jock o' Hazeldean.

loot, let

The kirk was deck'd at morning-tide,
    The tapers glimmer'd fair ;
The priest and bridegroom wait the bride,
    And dame and knight are there.
They sought her baith by bower and ha' ;
    The ladye was not seen :
She's o'er the border, and awa'
    Wi' Jock o' Hazeldean.

                    Sir Walter Scott.

79   JOHNIE FAA

THE gypsies cam to our gude lord's yett,
    And wow but they sang sweetly ;
They sang sae sweet and sae very complete,
    That doun cam our fair lady.

And she cam tripping down the stair,
    And all her maids before her ;
As sune as they saw her weel-faured face
    They cuist the glamourye ower her.

" O come with me," says Johnie Faa ;
    " O come with me, my dearie :
For I vow and I swear by the hilt of my sword,
    That your lord shall nae mair come near ye ! "

Then she gied them the gude wheit breid,
    And they ga'e her the ginger ;
But she gied them a far better thing,
    The gowd ring aff her finger.

            weel-faured, well-favoured

" Gae tak' frae me this gay mantill,
  And bring to me a plaidie ;
For if kith and kin and a' had sworn,
  I'll follow the gipsy laddie.

" Yestreen I lay in a weel-made bed,
  Wi' my gude lord beside me ;
This night I'll lie in a tenant's barn,
  Whatever shall betide me."

" Come to your bed," says Johnie Faa ;
  " Come to your bed, my dearie :
For I vow and I swear by the hilt o' my sword,
  That your lord shall nae mair come near ye."

" I'll go to bed to my Johnie Faa ;
  I'll go to bed to my dearie :
For I vow and I swear by the fan in my hand,
  That my lord shall nae mair come near me.

" I'll mak' a hap to my Johnie Faa ;
  I'll mak' a hap to my dearie :
And he's get a' the sash gaes round ;
  And my lord shall nae mair come near me."

And when our lord cam hame at e'en,
  And speired for his fair lady,
The tane she cried, and the other replied,
  " She's awa' wi' the gipsy laddie."

" Gae saddle to me the black black steed ;
  Gae saddle and mak him ready :
Before that I either eat or sleep,
  I'll gae seek my fair lady."

  hap, warm covering   *speired*, inquired

And we were fifteen weel-made men,
  Although we were na bonnie ;
And we were a' put down for ane,
  A fair young wanton lady.

80   BONNIE DUNDEE

" COME fill up my cup, come fill up my can,
  Come saddle your horses, and call up your men ;
  Come open the West Port, and let me gang free,
  And it's room for the bonnets o' Bonnie Dundee ! "

To the Lords of Convention 'twas Claver'se who spoke :
" Ere the king's crown shall fall there are crowns to be
      broke ;
So let each cavalier who loves honour and me,
Come follow the bonnet o' Bonnie Dundee."

Dundee he is mounted, he rides up the street,
The bells are rung backward, the drums they are beat ;
But the Provost, douce man, said : " Just e'en let him be,
The guid toun is weel quit of that deil of Dundee."

As he rode down the sanctified bends of the Bow,
Ilk carline was flyting, and shaking her pow ;
But the young plants of grace they look'd couthie and
      slee,
Thinking, " Luck to thy bonnet, thou Bonnie Dundee ! "

> *douce*, decent   *carline*, old woman
> *flyting*, scolding   *pow*, head

With sour-featur'd Whigs the Grassmarket was cramm'd,
As if half the West had set tryst to be hang'd ;
There was spite in each look, there was fear in each e'e,
As they watch'd for the bonnets o' Bonnie Dundee !

These cowls of Kilmarnock had spits and had spears,
And lang-hafted gullies to kill cavaliers ;
But they shrunk to close-heads, and the causeway was
    free,
At the toss of the bonnet o' Bonnie Dundee.

He spurr'd to the foot of the proud Castle rock,
And with the gay Gordon he gallantly spoke :
" Let Mons Meg and her marrows speak twa words or
    three,
For the love of the bonnet o' Bonnie Dundee."

The Gordon demands of him which way he goes—
" Where'er shall direct me the shade of Montrose !
Your Grace in short space shall hear tidings of me,
Or that low lies the bonnet o' Bonnie Dundee.

" There are hills beyond Pentlands, and lands beyond
    Forth ;
If there's lords in the Lowlands, there's chiefs in the
    North ;
There are wild Duniewassals three thousand times three,
Will cry ' Hoigh ! for the bonnets o' Bonnie Dundee.'

" There's brass on the target of barken'd bull-hide ;
There's steel in the scabbard that dangles beside :
The brass shall be burnish'd, the steel shall flash free,
At a toss of the bonnet o' Bonnie Dundee.

  marrows, mates   *barken'd*, hardened

" Away to the hills, to the caves, to the rocks :
Ere I own an usurper, I'll couch with the fox ;
And tremble, false Whigs, in the midst of your glee,
You have not seen the last of my bonnet and me ! "

He waved his proud hand, and the trumpets were
    blown,
The kettle-drums clash'd, and the horsemen rode on,
Till on Ravelston's cliffs and on Clermiston's lee,
Died away the wild war notes o' Bonnie Dundee.

    Come fill up my cup, come fill up my can,
    Come saddle the horses, and call out the men ;
    Come open your gates and let me gae free,
    For it's up with the bonnets o' Bonnie Dundee ! "
                                    Sir Walter Scott.

81   THE REIVER

    WALD God I war baith sound and haill
    Now liftit into Liddisdaill,
    The Mers sould find me beif and kaill ;
        What rak of bread ?
    War I thair liftit, with my lyfe,
    The Devill sould stick me with ane knyfe,
    And evir I come againe to Fyfe,
        Whyll I war dead.
                            Sir David Lyndsay.

rak, matter   *And evir*, before   *whyll*, until

82   THE GABERLUNZIE MAN

THE pawky auld carle cam ower the lea
Wi' mony good-e'ens and days to me,
Saying, " Gudewife, for your courtesie,
    Will you lodge a silly poor man ? "
The night was cauld, the carle was wat,
And down ayont the ingle he sat ;
My dochter's shoulders he 'gan to clap,
    And cadgily ranted and sang.

" O wow ! " quo' he, " were I as free
As first when I saw this countrie,
How blyth and merry wad I be !
    And I wad nevir think lang."
He grew canty, and she grew fain,
But little did her auld minny ken
What thir twa togither were say'n
    When wooing they were sa thrang.

" An' O ! " quo' he, " an' ye were as black
As e'er the crown of your daddy's hat,
'Tis I wad lay thee by my back,
    And awa' wi' me thou sould gang."
" And O ! " quo' she, " an' I were as white
As e'er the snaw lay on the dike,
I'd clead me braw and lady-like,
    And awa' wi' thee I would gang."

          silly, innocent   *cadgily*, cheerily
          thrang, busy   *clead*, clothe

Between the twa was made a plot ;
They raise a wee before the cock,
And wiliIy they shot the lock,
    And fast to the bent are gane.
Up in the morn the auld wife raise,
And at her leisure put on her claiths,
Syne to the servant's bed she gaes,
    To speir for the silly poor man.

She gaed to the bed where the beggar lay,
The strae was cauld, he was away ;
She clapt her hand, cried " Waladay !
    For some of our gear will be gane."
Some ran to coffers and some to kist,
But nought was stown, that could be mist ;
She danced her lane, cried " Praise be blest,
    I have lodg'd a leal poor man.

" Since naething's awa' as we can learn,
The kirn's to kirn and milk to earn ;
Gae but the house, lass, and waken my bairn,
    And bid her come quickly ben."
The servant gaed where the dochter lay,
The sheets were cauld, she was away,
And fast to her goodwife did say,
    " She's aff with the gaberlunzie man."

raise a wee, got up a little   *speir*, ask
strae, straw   *kist*, chest   *her lane*, by herself
leal, true   *kirn*, churn
but the house, to the other room   *gaberlunzie*, beggar

" O fy gar ride and fy gar rin,
And haste ye find these traitors again ;
For she's be burnt, and he's be slain,
   The wearifu' gaberlunzie man."
Some rade upo' horse, some ran afit,
The wife was wud, and out of her wit :
She could na gang, nor yet could she sit,
   But ay she curs'd and she bann'd.

Meantime far 'hind out o'er the lea,
Fu' snug in a glen, where nane could see,
The twa, with kindly sport and glee,
   Cut frae a new cheese a whang :
The priving was gude, it pleas'd them baith,
To lo'e her for ay, he ga'e her his aith.
Quo' she, " To leave thee I will be laith,
   My winsome gaberlunzie man.

" O kend my minny I were wi' you,
Ill-fardly wad she crook her mou' ;
Sic a poor man she'd never trow,
   After the gaberlunzie man."
" My dear," quo' he, " ye're yet ower young,
And hae na learn'd the beggar's tongue,
To follow me frae toun to toun,
   And carry the gaberlunzie on.

" Wi' cauk and keel I'll win your bread,
And spindles and whorles for them wha need,
Whilk is a gentle trade indeed,
   The gaberlunzie to carry, O.

wud, mad   *priving*, tasting
ill-fardly, ill-favouredly   *cauk*, chalk   *keel*, red earth

I'll bow my leg, and crook my knee,
And draw a black clout ower my e'e ;
A cripple or blind they will ca' me,
    While we sall sing and be merry, O."

83   THE TINKER

GIN I was a sturdy tinker
    Trampin' lang roads an' wide,
An' ye was a beggar hizzie
    Cadgin' the country side ;

The meal bags a' your fortune,
    A jinglin' wallet mine,
I wouldna swap for a kingdom
    Ae blink o' my raggit queyn.

The gowd that hings at your lugs, lass,
    I would hammer it for a ring,
Syne, hey for a tinker's waddin'
    An' the lythe dyke-sides o' Spring.

Oh, whiles we would tak' the turnpike
    An' lauch at the Norlan' win',
An' whiles we would try the lown roads
    An' the wee hill-tracks that rin.

Whaur the blue peat reek is curlin'
    An' the mavis whussles rare,
We'd follow the airt we fancied
    Wi' nane that we kent to care.

hizzie, wench   *cadgin',* hawking   *queyn,* maid
lythe, lee-side, sheltered   *lown,* sheltered
                airt, direction

An' ye would get the white siller
   Spaein' the lasses' han's,
An' I would win the brown siller
   Cloutin' the aul' wives' cans.

Whiles wi' a stroop to souder,
   Girdin' at times a cogue ;
But aye wi' you at my elbuck
   To haud me content, you rogue.

We'd wash in the rinnin' water,
   An' I would lave your feet,
An' ye would lowse your apron
   An' I would dry them wi't.

I'd gather yows at gloamin'
   An' ye would blaw the fire
Till the lilt o' the singin' kettle
   Gart baith forget the tire.

An' blithe my cutty luntin'
   We'd crack aboot a' we'd seen,
Wi' mony a twa-han' banter
   Aneth the risin' meen.

Syne in some cosy plantin'
   Wi' fern and heather spread,
An' the green birks for rafters
   The lift would roof your bed.

spaein', telling	*cloutin'*, patching	*stroop*, a kettle's spout
souder, solder		*cogue*, wooden vessel
elbuck, elbow	*yows*, fir-cones	*gart*, made
cutty, short pipe		*luntin'*, smoking
meen, moon	*plantin'*, wood	*lift*, sky

An' when your een grew weary
    Twa stars would tine their licht,
An' saftly in my oxter
    I'd faul' ye for the nicht.

Nae cry frae frichtened mawkin
    Snared in the dewy grass,
Nor eerie oolet huntin'
    Would wauken you then, my lass.

An' when the mists were liftin'
    An' the reid sun raise to peep,
Ye would only cuddle the closer
    An' lauch to me in your sleep.

Wi' a' the warl' to wander
    An' the fine things yet to see,
Will you kilt your coats an' follow
    The lang lang road wi' me?

The open lift an' laughter,
    Is there onything mair you lack?
*A wee heid in the bundle
    That shouds upon my back.*

                                    Charles Murray.

tine, lose	*oxter*, arms	*mawkin*, hare
oolet, owl	*shouds*, swings	

84   HIGHWAYS AND BYWAYS

HIGHWAYS for eident feet,
    That hae their mile to gae ;
But byways when spring is sweet,
    And bloom is on the slae.

Highways till day is dune,
    The girr o' gear to ca' ;
But byways for star and mune,
    And wooers twa by twa.

Highways for wheel and whip,
    Till rigs are stibblet clear ;
But byways for haw and hip,
    When robin's on the brier.

Aye it's on the highways
    The feck o' life maun gang ;
But aye it's frae the byways
    Comes hame the happy sang.
                        Walter Wingate.

eident, careful   *slae*, sloe *girr o' gear*, hoop of wealth
ca', make move   *feck*, greater part

BOOK VI
KING AND COMMONWEAL

85   WHEN ALYSANDYR OUR KING WAS DEDE

WHEN Alysandyr our King was dede
   That Scotland led in luve and le,
Away was sons of ale and brede,
   Of wine and wax, of gamyn and gle ;
Our gold was changyd into lede.
   Christ born into Virginitie
Succour Scotland and remede
   That stad is in perplexytie.

86   SIR PATRICK SPENS

THE king sits in Dunfermline town,
   Drinking the blood-red wine :
" O where will I get a skeely skipper,
   To sail this new ship of mine ? "

O up and spake an eldern knight,
   Sat at the king's right knee :
" Sir Patrick Spens is the best sailor
   That ever sail'd the sea."

Our king has written a braid letter,
   And seal'd it with his hand,
And sent it to Sir Patrick Spens,
   Was walking on the strand.

le, law	*sons*, plenty	*gamyn*, sport
stad, stayed	*skeely*, skilful	

" To Noroway, to Noroway,
    To Noroway o'er the faem ;
The king's daughter of Noroway,
    'Tis thou maun bring her hame."

The first word that Sir Patrick read,
    Sae loud, loud laughèd he ;
The neist word that Sir Patrick read,
    The tear blinded his e'e.

" O wha is this has done this deed,
    And tauld the king o' me,
To send me out at this time of the year
    To sail upon the sea ?

" Be it wind, be it weet, be it hail, be it sleet,
    Our ship must sail the faem ;
The king's daughter of Noroway,
    'Tis we must fetch her hame."

They hoysed their sails on Monenday morn,
    Wi' a' the speed they may ;
They hae landed in Noroway,
    Upon a Wodensday.

They hadna been a week, a week
    In Noroway but twae,
When that the lords o' Noroway
    Began aloud to say :

" Ye Scottishmen spend a' our king's goud,
    And a' our queenis fee !
" Ye lie, ye lie, ye liars loud,
    Fu' loud I hear ye lie !

                    goud, gold

" For I brought as much white monie
  As gane my men and me,
And I brought a half fou o' gude red goud
  Out o'er the sea wi' me.

" Make ready, make ready, my merry men a',
  Our gude ship sails the morn : "
" Now, ever alake ! my master dear,
  I fear a deadly storm !

" I saw the new moon late yestreen,
  Wi' the auld moon in her arm ;
And if we gang to sea, master,
  I fear we'll come to harm."

They hadna sailed a league, a league,
  A league but barely three,
When the lift grew dark, and the wind blew loud,
  And gurly grew the sea.

The ankers brak, and the topmasts lap,
  It was sic a deadly storm,
And the waves came o'er the broken ship,
  Till a' her sides were torn.

" O where will I get a gude sailor,
  To take my helm in hand,
Till I get up to the tall topmast,
  To see if I can spy land ? "

gane, suffice	*half fou*, an eighth of a peck
lift, sky	*gurly*, stormy

" O here am I, a sailor gude,
　　To take the helm in hand,
Till you go up to the tall topmast,
　　But I fear you'll ne'er spy land."

He hadna gane a step, a step,
　　A step but barely ane,
When a bout flew out of our goodly ship,
　　And the salt sea it cam in.

" Gae fetch a web o' the silken claith,
　　Another o' the twine,
And wap them into our ship's side,
　　And let na the sea come in."

They fetched a web o' the silken claith,
　　Another o' the twine,
And they wapped them roun' that gude ship's side,
　　But still the sea cam in.

O laith, laith were our gude Scots lords
　　To weet their cork-heel'd shoon ;
But lang or a' the play was play'd,
　　They wat their hats aboon.

And mony was the feather-bed
　　That flottered on the faem,
And mony was the gude lord's son
　　That never mair cam hame.

The ladies wrang their fingers white,
　　The maidens tore their hair,
A' for the sake of their true loves,
　　For them they'll see nae mair.

　　bout, bolt　　　　*wap,* pack　　　　*flottered,* floated

O lang, lang may the ladies sit,
   Wi' their fans into their hand,
Before they see Sir Patrick Spens
   Come sailing to the strand.

And lang, lang may the maidens sit,
   Wi' their goud kames in their hair,
A' waiting for their ain dear loves,
   For them they'll see nae mair.

Half owre, half owre to Aberdour
   'Tis fifty fathoms deep,
And there lies gude Sir Patrick Spens,
   Wi' the Scots lords at his feet.

87   FREEDOM

A ! FREDOME is a noble thing !
Fredome maiss man to haif liking :
Fredome all solace to man giffis :
He levis at ease that freely levis !
A noble heart may haif nane ease,
Na ellis nocht that may him please,
Gif fredome failye ; for free liking
Is yearnit owre all other thing.
Na he, that ay has levit free,
May nocht knaw weil the propertie,
The anger, na the wrechit dome,
That is couplit to foul thyrldome.

kames, combs	*liking*, pleasure in life
Na ellis nocht, nor anything else	*yearnit*, longed for
dome, doom	*thyrldome*, thralldom

Bot gif he had assayit it,
Than all perquer he suld it wit ;
And suld think fredome mar to prize
Than all the gold in warld that is.

John Barbour.

88   SIR JOHN THE GRAHAM

WHEN they him fand, and gude Wallace him saw,
He lichtit doun, and hynt him fra them a'
In armis up ; behaldand his pale face,
He kissit him, and cry'd full oft : " Alas !
My best brother in warld that ever I had !
My ae fald friend when I was hardest stad !
My hope, my heal, thou was in maist honour !
My faith, my help, strenthiest in stour !
In thee was wit, fredome, and hardiness ;
In thee was truth, manheid, and nobleness ;
In thee was rule, in thee was governance ;
In thee was virtue withouttin variance ;
In thee leaute, in thee was great largnas ;
In thee gentrice, in thee was stedfastnas.

Henry the Minstrel.

89   THE RED HARLAW

Now haud your tongue, baith wife and carle,
And listen, great and sma',
And I will sing of Glenallan's Earl
That fought on the red Harlaw.

all perquer, by heart	*wit*, know	*hynt*, took hold of
ae fald, single-hearted	*stad*, beset	*heal*, health
stour, dust of battle	*leaute*, loyalty	*largnas*, largess

The cronach's cried on Bennachie,
    And doun the Don and a',
And hieland and lawland may mournfu' be
    For the sair field of Harlaw.

They saddled a hundred milk-white steeds,
    They hae bridled a hundred black,
With a chafron of steel on each horse's head,
    And a good knight upon his back.

They hadna ridden a mile, a mile,
    A mile but barely ten,
When Donald came branking down the brae
    Wi' twenty thousand men.

Their tartans they were waving wide,
    The glaives were glancing clear,
The pibrochs rung frae side to side,
    Would deafen ye to hear.

The great Earl in his stirrups stood
    That Highland host to see :
" Now here a knight that's stout and good
    May prove a jeopardie :

" What wouldst thou do, my squire so gay,
    That rides beside my reyne,
Were ye Glenallan's Earl the day,
    And I were Roland Cheyne ?

" To turn the rein were sin and shame,
    To fight were wondrous peril,
What would ye do now, Roland Cheyne,
    Were ye Glenallan's Earl ? "

        branking, swaggering

" Were I Glenallan's Earl this tide,
    And ye were Roland Cheyne,
The spur should be in my horse's side,
    And the bridle upon his mane.

" If they hae twenty thousand blades
    And we twice ten times ten,
Yet they hae but their tartan plaids,
    And we are mail-clad men.

" My horse shall ride through ranks sae rude,
    As through the moorland fern,
Then ne'er let the gentle Norman blude
    Grow cauld for Highland kerne."

Sir Walter Scott.

90   THE BATTLE OF OTTERBOURNE

It fell upon the Lammas tide,
    When the muir-men win their hay,
The doughty Douglas bound him to ride
    Into England, to drive a prey.

He chose the Gordons and the Graemes,
    With them the Lindsays, light and gay ;
But the Jardines wald not with him ride,
    And they rue it to this day.

And he has burned the dales of Tyne,
    And part of Bambrough-shire ;
And three good towers on Reidswire fells,
    He left them all on fire.

bound him, prepared

And he marched up to Newcastle,
   And rode it round about ;
" O wha's the lord of this castle,
   Or wha's the lady o't ? "

But up spake proud Lord Percy then,
   And O but he spake hie !
" I am the lord of this castle,
   My wife's the lady gay."

" If thou'rt the lord of this castle,
   Sae weel it pleases me !
For ere I cross the Border fells,
   The tane o' us shall die."

He took a lang spear in his hand,
   Shod with the metal free,
And for to meet the Douglas there,
   He rode right furiouslie.

" Had we twa been upon the green,
   And never an eye to see,
I wad hae had you, flesh and fell ;
   But your sword sall gae wi' me."

" But gae ye up to Otterbourne,
   And wait there dayis three ;
And if I come not ere three dayis end,
   A fause knight ca' ye me."

" The Otterbourne's a bonnie burn,
   'Tis pleasant there to be ;
But there is nought at Otterbourne,
   To feed my men and me.

    tane, one   *fell*, hide

" The deer rins wild on hill and dale,
　　The birds fly wild from tree to tree ;
But there is neither bread nor kail
　　To fend my men and me.

" Yet I will stay at Otterbourne,
　　Where you shall welcome be ;
And if you come not at three dayis end,
　　A fause lord I'll ca' thee."

" Thither will I come," proud Percy said,
　　" By the might of Our Ladie ! "
" There will I bide thee," said the Douglas,
　　" My troth I plight to thee."

They lighted high on Otterbourne,
　　Upon the bent sae brown ;
They lighted high on Otterbourne,
　　And threw their pallions down.

And he that had a bonnie boy,
　　Sent out his horse to grass ;
And he that had not a bonnie boy,
　　His ain servant he was.

But up then spake a little page,
　　Before the peep of dawn—
" O waken ye, waken ye, my good lord,
　　For Percy's hard at hand."

" Ye lie, ye lie, ye liar loud !
　　Sae loud I hear ye lie ;
For Percy had not men yestreen
　　To dight my men and me.

　　fend, support　　　*pallions*, tents　　*dight*, fight

" But I hae dreamed a dreary dream,
    Beyond the Isle of Skye :
I saw a dead man win a fight,
    And I think that man was I."

He belted on his gude braid sword,
    And to the field he ran ;
But he forgot the helmet good,
    That should have kept his brain.

When Percy wi' the Douglas met,
    I wat he was fu' fain !
They swakked their swords, till sair they swat,
    And the blood ran down like rain.

But Percy, with his good broadsword,
    That could so sharply wound,
Has wounded Douglas on the brow,
    Till he fell to the ground.

Then he called on his little foot-page,
    And said, " Run speedilie,
And fetch my ain dear sister's son,
    Sir Hugh Montgomery."

" My nephew good," the Douglas said,
    " What recks the death of ane !
Last night I dreamed a dreary dream,
    And I ken the day's thy ain.

" My wound is deep ; I fain would sleep ;
    Take thou the vanguard of the three,
And hide me by the braken bush,
    That grows on yonder lily lea.

      swakked, clashed   *swat,* sweated

" O bury me by the braken bush,
    Beneath the blooming brier,
Let never living mortal ken
    That a kindly Scot lies here."

He lifted up that noble lord,
    Wi' the saut tear in his e'e ;
He hid him in the braken bush,
    That his merry men might not see.

The moon was clear, the day drew near,
    The spears in flinders flew,
But mony a gallant Englishman
    Ere day the Scotsmen slew.

The Gordons good, in English blood
    They steep'd their hose and shoon ;
The Lindsays flew like fire about,
    Till all the fray was done.

The Percy and Montgomery met,
    That either of other were fain ;
They swakked swords, and they twa swat,
    And aye the blood ran down between.

" Yield thee, O yield thee, Percy," he said,
    " Or else I vow I'll lay thee low ! "
" To whom must I yield," quoth Earl Percy,
    " Now that I see it must be so ? "

" Thou shalt not yield to lord nor loun,
    Nor yet shalt thou yield to me ;
But yield thee to the braken bush,
    That grows upon yon lily lea ! "

" I will not yield to a braken bush,
  Nor yet will I yield to a brier ;
But I would yield to Earl Douglas,
  Or Sir Hugh Montgomery, if he were here."

As soon as he knew it was Montgomery,
  He struck his sword's point in the ground ;
The Montgomery was a courteous knight,
  And quickly took him by the hand.

This deed was done at Otterbourne
  About the breaking of the day ;
Earl Douglas was buried at the braken bush,
  And the Percy led captive away.

91   A REFORMATION BALLAD

THE Paip, that Pagane full of pryde,
  He hes us blindit lang,
For whair the blind the blind dois gyde
  No wounder baith ga wrang ;
Lyke prince and king he led the ring
  Of all iniquitie :
Hay trix,
Tryme go trix,
Under the grene wood tre.

Bot his abominatioun
  The Lord hes brocht to lycht ;
His Popisch pryde and thriefald crowne
  Almaist hes loste thair mycht.

His plak Pardonis ar bot lardonis
Of new fund vanitie :
Hay trix, etc.

His Cardinallis hes cause to murne,
His Bischoppis borne aback,
His Abbotis gat ane uncouth turne,
When schavelingis went to sack,
With burges wyffis thay led thair lyves,
And fure better nor we :
Hay trix, etc.

His Carmelitis and Jacobinis,
His Dominikis had greit do,
His Cordeleris and Augustinis,
Sanct Frances ordour to ;
Thay sillie Freiris mony yeiris
With babling blerit our e'e :
Hay trix, etc.

The blind Bischop, he culd nocht preiche
For playing with the lassis,
The sillie Freir behuiffit to fleiche
For almous that he assis,
The Curat his Creid he culd nocht reid,
Schame fall the cumpanie :
Hay trix, etc.

plak, buffoonery	*lardonis*, lumps
fure, fared	*blerit*, blinded
behuiffit, behoved	*fleiche*, beg
almous, alms	*assis*, asks

Of lait I saw thir lymmaris stand
Lyke mad men at mischeif,
Thinking to get the upper hand,
Thay luke efter releif.
Bot all in vaine, go tell them plaine,
That day will never be :
Hay trix, etc.

92 KINMONT WILLIE

O HAVE ye na heard o' the fause Sakelde ?
  O have ye na heard o' the keen Lord Scroope ?
How they hae ta'en bauld Kinmont Willie
  On Haribee to hang him up ?

Had Willie had but twenty men,
  But twenty men as stout as he,
Fause Sakelde had never the Kinmont ta'en,
  Wi' eight score in his companie.

They band his legs beneath the steed,
  They tied his hands behind his back,
They guarded him, fivesome on each side,
  And they brought him owre the Liddel-rack.

They led him through the Liddel-rack,
  And also through the Carlisle sands ;
They brought him to Carlisle castle,
  To be at my Lord Scroope's commands.

      thir lymmaris, these villains

' My hands are tied, but my tongue is free,
    And wha will dare this deed avow ?
Or answer by the Border law ?
    Or answer to the bauld Buccleuch ? "

" Now haud thy tongue, thou rank reiver !
    There's never a Scot shall set thee free :
Before ye cross my castle yett,
    I trow ye shall take farewell o' me."

" Fear na ye that, my lord," quo' Willie :
    " By the faith o' my body, Lord Scroope," he said,
" I never yet lodged in a hostelrie,
    But I paid my lawing before I gaed."

Now word is gane to the bauld Keeper,
    In Branksome Ha', where that he lay,
That Lord Scroope has ta'en the Kinmont Willie,
    Between the hours of night and day.

He has ta'en the table wi' his hand,
    He gar'd the red wine spring on hie—
" Now Christ's curse on my head," he said,
    " But avenged of Lord Scroope I'll be !

" O is my basnet a widow's curch ?
    Or my lance a wand of the willow-tree ?
Or my arm a lady's lily hand,
    That an English lord should lightly me ?

reiver, robber	*lawing*, reckoning
basnet, helmet	*curch*, coif

" And have they ta'en him, Kinmont Willie,
 Against the truce of Border tide ?
And forgotten that the bauld Buccleuch
 Is Keeper here on the Scottish side ?

" And have they e'en ta'en him, Kinmont Willie,
 Withouten either dread or fear ?
And forgotten that the bauld Buccleuch
 Can back a steed, or shake a spear ?

" O were there war between the lands,
 As well I wot that there is none,
I would slight Carlisle castle high,
 Though it were builded of marble stone.

" I would set that castle in a lowe,
 And sloken it with English blood ;
There's never a man in Cumberland,
 Should ken where Carlisle castle stood.

" But since nae war's between the lands,
 And there is peace, and peace should be ;
I'll neither harm English lad or lass,
 And yet the Kinmont freed shall be ! "

He has called him forty marchmen bauld,
 I trow they were of his ain name,
Except Sir Gilbert Elliot, called
 The Laird of Stobs, I mean the same.

   lowe, flame   *sloken,* quench

He has called him forty marchmen bauld,
    Were kinsmen to the bauld Buccleuch :
With spur on heel, and splent on spauld,
    And gloves of green, and feathers blue.

There were five and five before them a',
    Wi' hunting-horns and bugles bright :
And five and five came wi' Buccleuch,
    Like warden's men, arrayed for fight.

And five and five, like a mason gang,
    That carried the ladders lang and hie ;
And five and five, like broken men ;
    And so they reached the Woodhouselee.

And as we crossed the Bateable land,
    When to the English side we held,
The first o' men that we met wi',
    Wha should it be but fause Sakelde ?

" Where be ye gaun, ye hunters keen ? "
    Quo' fause Sakelde ; " come, tell to me ! "
" We go to hunt an English stag,
    Has trespassed on the Scots countrie."

" Where be ye gaun, ye marshal men ? "
    Quo' fause Sakelde ; " come tell me true ! "
" We go to catch a rank reiver,
    Has broken faith wi' the bauld Buccleuch."

       splent on spauld, mail on shoulder

" Where are ye gaun, ye mason lads,
   Wi' a' your ladders, lang and hie ? "
" We gang to herry a corbie's nest,
   That wons not far frae Woodhouselee."

" Where be ye gaun, ye broken men ? "
   Quo' fause Sakelde ; " come tell to me ! "
Now Dickie of Dryhope led that band,
   And the never a word of lear had he.

" Why trespass ye on the English side ?
   Row-footed outlaws, stand ! " quo' he ;
The never a word had Dickie to say,
   Sae he thrust the lance through his fause body.

Then on we held for Carlisle toun,
   And at Staneshaw-bank the Eden we crossed ;
The water was great and meikle of spate,
   But the never a horse nor man we lost.

And when we reached the Staneshaw-bank,
   The wind was rising loud and hie ;
And there the laird gar'd leave our steeds,
   For fear that they should stamp and neigh.

And when we left the Staneshaw-bank
   The wind began full loud to blaw ;
But 'twas wind and weet, and fire and sleet,
   When we came beneath the castle wa'.

| *herry*, rob | *corbie*, raven |
| *wons*, dwells | *row-footed*, rough-footed |

We crept on knees, and held our breath,
  Till we placed the ladders against the wa';
And sae ready was Buccleuch himsel'
  To mount the first before us a'.

He has ta'en the watchman by the throat,
  He flung him down upon the lead—
" Had there not been peace between our lands,
  Upon the other side thou hadst gaed !

" Now sound out, trumpets ! " quo' Buccleuch ;
  " Let's waken Lord Scroope right merrilie ! "
Then loud the warden's trumpet blew—
  O wha daur meddle wi' me ?

Then speedily to wark we gaed,
  And raised the slogan ane and a',
And cut a hole through a sheet of lead,
  And so we wan to the castle ha'.

They thought King James and a' his men
  Had won the house wi' bow and spear ;
It was but twenty Scots and ten,
  That put a thousand in sic a steir.

Wi' coulters, and wi' forehammers,
  We gar'd the bars bang merrilie,
Until we cam to the inner prison,
  Where Willie o' Kinmont he did lie.

steir, stir

And when we cam to the lower prison,
    Where Willie o' Kinmont he did lie—
" O sleep ye, wake ye, Kinmont Willie,
    Upon the morn that thou's to die ? "

" O I sleep saft, and I wake aft ;
    It's lang since sleeping was fley'd frae me !
Gie my service back to my wife and bairns,
    And a' gude fellows that speir for me."

Then Red Rowan has hent him up,
    The starkest man in Teviotdale—
" Abide, abide now, Red Rowan,
    Till of my Lord Scroope I take farewell.

" Farewell, farewell, my gude Lord Scroope !
    My gude Lord Scroope, farewell ! " he cried ;
" I'll pay you for my lodging mail,
    When first we meet on the Borderside."

Then shoulder high, with shout and cry,
    We bore him down the ladder lang ;
At every stride Red Rowan made,
    I wot the Kinmont's airns played clang.

" O mony a time," quo' Kinmont Willie,
    " I have ridden horse baith wild and wud ;
But a rougher beast than Red Rowan
    I ween my legs have ne'er bestrode.

saft, light   *fley'd*, frightened   *hent*, taken
mail, rent   *wud*, mad

" And mony a time," quo' Kinmont Willie,
   " I've prick'd a horse out owre the furs ;
But since the day I backed a steed,
   I never wore sic cumbrous spurs ! "

We scarce had won the Staneshaw-bank,
   When a' the Carlisle bells were rung,
And a thousand men on horse and foot,
   Cam wi' the keen Lord Scroope along.

Buccleuch has turned to Eden Water,
   Even where it flowed frae bank to brim,
And he has plunged in wi' a' his band,
   And safely swam them through the stream.

He turned him on the other side,
   And at Lord Scroope his glove flung he—
" If ye like na my visit in merry England,
   In fair Scotland come visit me ! "

All sore astonished stood Lord Scroope,
   He stood as still as rock of stane ;
He scarcely dared to trow his eyes,
   When through the water they had gane.

" He is either himsel' a devil frae hell,
   Or else his mother a witch maun be ;
I wadna have ridden that wan water
   For a' the gowd in Christentie."

furs, furrows   *trow*, believe

93   KILLICRANKIE

WHARE hae ye been sae braw, lad ?
    Whare hae ye been sae brankie-o ?
Whare hae ye been sae braw, lad ?
    Cam ye by Killicrankie-o ?
An ye had been whare I hae been,
    Ye wadna be sae cantie-o ;
An ye had seen what I hae seen,
    On the braes of Killicrankie-o.

I faught at land, I faught at sea,
    At hame I faught my auntie-o ;
But I met the devil and Dundee
    On the braes o' Killicrankie-o.
The bauld Pitcur fell in a furr,
    And Clavers gat a clankie-o,
Or I had fed an Athol gled,
    On the braes o' Killicrankie-o.

O fie, Mackay ! what gart ye lie
    I' the bush ayont the bankie-o ?
Ye'd better kiss'd King Willie's loof,
    Than come to Killicrankie-o.
It's nae shame, it's nae shame—
    It's nae shame to shank ye-o ;
There's sour slaes on Athol braes,
    And deils at Killicrankie-o.

brankie, spruce   *cantie,* jolly
furr, furrow   *clankie,* knock
gled, hawk   *loof,* palm
shank ye, run   *slaes,* sloes

94　KENMURE'S ON AND AWA', WILLIE

O, KENMURE's on and awa', Willie,
　Kenmure's on and awa' ;
And Kenmure's lord's the bravest lord
　That ever Galloway saw.

Success to Kenmure's band, Willie,
　Success to Kenmure's band ;
There's no a heart that fears a Whig
　That rides by Kenmure's hand.

Here's Kenmure's health in wine, Willie,
　Here's Kenmure's health in wine ;
There ne'er was a coward o' Kenmure's blude,
　Nor yet of Gordon's line.

O, Kenmure's lads are men, Willie,
　O, Kenmure's lads are men ;
Their hearts and swords are metal true,
　And that their faes shall ken.

They'll live or die wi' fame, Willie,
　They'll live or die wi' fame ;
And soon wi' sound of victory
　May Kenmure's lads come hame !

There's a rose in Kenmure's cap, Willie,
　A bright sword in his hand—
A hundred Gordons at his side,
　And hey for English land !

Here's him that's far awa', Willie,
   Here's him that's far awa' ;
And here's the flower that I lo'e best,
   The rose that's like the snaw.

Robert Burns.

95   KENMURE
                1715

" THE heather's in a blaze, Willie,
   The White Rose decks the tree,
The Fiery Cross is on the braes,
   And the King is on the sea !

" Remember great Montrose, Willie,
   Remember fair Dundee,
And strike one stroke at the foreign foes
   Of the King that's on the sea.

" There's Gordons in the north, Willie,
   Are rising frank and free,
Shall a Kenmure Gordon not go forth
   For the King that's on the sea ?

" A trusty sword to draw, Willie,
   A comely weird to dree,
For the royal rose that's like the snaw,
   And the King that's on the sea ! "

He cast ae look across his lands,
   Looked over loch and lea,
He took his fortune in his hands,
   For the King was on the sea.

      weird, fate   *dree*, fulfil

Kenmures have fought in Galloway
　　For Kirk and Presbyt'rie,
This Kenmure faced his dying day,
　　For King James across the sea.

It little skills what faith men vaunt,
　　If loyal men they be
To Christ's ain Kirk and Covenant,
　　Or the King that's o'er the sea.

Andrew Lang.

96　　AWA', WHIGS, AWA'

Awa', Whigs, awa' !
　　Awa', Whigs, awa' !
Ye're but a pack o' traitor louns,
　　Ye'll do nae guid at a'.

Our thrissles flourish'd fresh and fair,
　　And bonnie bloom'd our roses ;
But Whigs cam like a frost in June,
　　And wither'd a' our posies.

Our ancient crown's fa'n in the dust—
　　Deil blin' them wi' the stoure o't ;
And write their names in his black beuk
　　Wha gae the Whigs the power o't !

Our sad decay in Church and State
　　Surpasses my descriving ;
The Whigs cam o'er us for a curse,
　　And we hae done wi' thriving.

stoure, dust

Grim vengeance lang has ta'en a nap,
   But we may see him wauken ;
Gude help the day when royal heads
   Are hunted like a maukin !

Robert Burns.

97   O'ER THE WATER TO CHARLIE

    WE'LL o'er the water and o'er the sea,
      We'll o'er the water to Charlie ;
    Come weal, come woe, we'll gather and go,
      And live and die wi' Charlie.

Come boat me o'er, come row me o'er,
   Come boat me o'er to Charlie ;
I'll gie John Ross another bawbee,
   To boat me o'er to Charlie.

I lo'e weel my Charlie's name,
   Tho' some there be abhor him :
But O, to see auld Nick gaun hame,
   And Charlie's faes before him !

I swear and vow by moon and stars,
   And sun that shines so early,
If I had twenty thousand lives,
   I'd die as aft for Charlie.

    We'll o'er the water and o'er the sea,
      We'll o'er the water to Charlie ;
    Come weal, come woe, we'll gather and go,
      And live and die wi' Charlie.

Robert Burns.

wauken, waken   *maukin*, hare

98   LEWIE GORDON

Och hon ! my Highland man,
Och, my bonny Highland man ;
Weel would I my true love ken
Among ten thousand Highland men.

Oh ! send Lewie Gordon hame,
And the lad I daurna name ;
Though his back be at the wa',
Here's to him that's far awa' !

Oh ! to see his tartan trews,
Bonnet blue, and laigh-heel'd shoes ;
Philabeg aboon his knee,
That's the lad that I'll gang wi' !

Och hon ! my Highland man,
Och, my bonny Highland man ;
Weel would I my true love ken
Among ten thousand Highland men.

Alexander Geddes.

99   DRUMOSSIE MOOR

The lovely lass o' Inverness
Nae joy nor pleasure can she see ;
For e'en and morn she cries, " Alas ! "
And aye the saut tear blin's her e'e :

" Drumossie moor—Drumossie day—
    A waefu' day it was to me !
For there I lost my father dear,
    My father dear, and brethren three.

" Their winding sheet the bluidy clay,
    Their graves are growing green to see :
And by them lies the dearest lad
    That ever blest a woman's e'e !

" Now wae to thee, thou cruel lord,
    A bluidy man I trow thou be ;
For mony a heart thou hast made sair
    That ne'er did wrang to thine or thee."

                                        Robert Burns.

100   WAE'S ME FOR PRINCE CHARLIE

A WEE bird cam to our ha' door,
    He warbled sweet and clearly,
And aye the owre-come o' his sang
    Was " Wae's me for Prince Charlie ! "
O ! when I heard the bonnie, bonnie bird,
    The tears cam drappin' rarely,
I took my bannet aff my head,
    For weel I lo'ed Prince Charlie.

Quo' I, " My bird, my bonnie, bonnie bird,
    Is that a tale ye borrow ?
Or is't some words ye've learnt by rote,
    Or a lilt o' dule and sorrow ? "

owre-come, refrain   *Wae's me*, woe is me
                dule, tragedy

" Oh ! no, no, no ! " the wee bird sang,
  " I've flown sin' morning early ;
But sic a day o' wind and rain !—
  Oh ! wae's me for Prince Charlie !

" On hills that are by right his ain,
  He roams a lonely stranger ;
On ilka hand he's pressed by want,
  On ilka side by danger.
Yestreen I met him in the glen,
  My heart near bursted fairly,
For sadly changed indeed was he—
  Oh ! wae's me for Prince Charlie !

" Dark night cam on, the tempest howled
  Out-owre the hills and valleys :
And whaur was't that your prince lay down,
  Whase hame should been a palace ?
He row'd him in a Highland plaid,
  Which covered him but sparely,
And slept beneath a bush o' broom—
  Oh ! wae's me for Prince Charlie ! "

But now the bird saw some redcoats,
  And he shook his wings wi' anger ;
" O this is no a land for me,
  I'll tarry here nae langer."
A while he hovered on the wing,
  Ere he departed fairly :
But weel I mind the fareweel strain
  Was " Wae's me for Prince Charlie ! "

William Glen.

row'd, rolled

101   LADY KEITH'S LAMENT

I MAUN sit in my wee croo house,
    At the rock and the reel to toil fu' dreary ;
I maun think on the day that's gane,
    And sigh and sab till I grow weary.
I ne'er could brook, I ne'er could brook,
    A foreign loon to own or flatter ;
But I will sing a rantin' sang,
    That day our king comes ower the water.

O gin I live to see the day,
    That I hae begg'd, and begg'd frae Heaven,
I'll fling my rock and reel away,
    And dance and sing frae morn till even :
For there is ane I winna name,
    That comes the reignin' byke to scatter ;
And I'll put on my bridal goun,
    That day our king comes ower the water.

I hae seen the gude auld day,
    The day o' pride and chieftain's glory,
When royal Stuarts bare the sway,
    And ne'er heard tell o' Whig nor Tory.
Though lyart be my locks and grey,
    And eild has crook'd me down—what matter !
I'll dance and sing ae other day,
    The day our king comes ower the water.

    byke, hive   *lyart*, white   *eild*, old age

A curse on dull and drawling Whig,
   The whining, ranting, low deceiver,
Wi' heart sae black, and look sae big,
   And canting tongue o' clish-ma-claver !
My father was a gude lord's son,
   My mither was an earl's daughter ;
And I'll be Lady Keith again,
   That day our king comes ower the water.

102   AN OLD SONG

                         1750

         OH, it's hame, hame, hame,
            And it's hame I wadna be,
         Till the Lord calls King James
            To his ain countrie ;
         Bids the wind blaw frae France,
            Till the Firth keps the faem,
         And Loch Garry and Lochiel
            Bring Prince Charlie hame.

         May the lads Prince Charlie led
            That were hard on Willie's track,
         When frae Laffen field he fled,
            Wi' the claymore at his back ;
         May they stand on Scottish soil
            When the White Rose bears the gree,
         And the Lord calls the King
            To his ain countrie !

Bid the seas arise and stand
  Like walls on ilka side,
Till our Highland lad pass through
  With Jehovah for his guide.
Dry up the river Forth,
  As Thou didst the Red Sea,
When Israel cam hame
  To his ain countrie.

                              Andrew Lang.

103   I CANNA SEE THE SERGEANT

I CANNA see the sergeant,
I canna see the sergeant,
I canna—see the—sergeant,
  He's owre far awa'.
Bring the wee chap nearer,
Bring the wee chap nearer,
O bring the—wee chap—nearer—
  He's owre bloomin' sma'.

We canna see the sergeant,
The five foot five inch sergeant,
We canna—see the—sergeant
  For smoke, and shell, and a.—
Now we can see him clearer,
Now we can see him nearer—
Upon the topmost parapet
  He's foremost o' us a'!

We canna see the sergeant,
The sma', stout-hearted sergeant,

We canna—see the—sergeant,
    He's dead and gone awa'.
Bring the wee chap nearer,
Bring the wee chap nearer,
    O, he has grown the dearer
        Now that he's far awa' !

Joseph Lee.

104   ON LEAVE

I HAD auchteen months o' the war,
    Steel and pouther and reek,
Fitsore, weary and wauf—
    Syne I got hame for a week.

Daft-like I entered the toun,
    I scarcely kenned for my ain ;
I sleepit twae days in my bed,
    The third I buried my wean.

The wife sat greetin' at hame
    While I wandered oot to the hill,
My hert as cauld as a stane,
    But my heid gaun roond like a mill.

I wasna the man I had been—
    Juist a gangrel dozin' in fits ;
The pin had faun oot o' the warld,
    And I doddered amang the bits.

auchteen, eighteen   *wauf*, worn-out
wean, child   *greetin'*, weeping
gangrel, vagrant   *doddered*, stumbled

I clamb to the Lammerlaw
   And sat me doun on the cairn ;
The best o' my freends were deid,
   And noo I had buried my bairn ;

The stink o' the gas in my nose,
   The colour o' bluid in my e'e,
And the biddin' o' Hell in my lug
   To curse my Maker and dee.

But up in that gloamin' hour,
   On the heather and thymy sod,
Wi' the sun gaun doun in the West,
   I made my peace wi' God. . . .

      .   .   .

I saw a thoosand hills,
   Green and gowd i' the licht,
Roond and backit like sheep,
   Huddle into the nicht.

But I kenned they werena hills,
   But the same as the mounds ye see
Doun by the back o' the line
   Whaur they bury oor lads that dee.

They were juist the same as at Loos,
   Whaur we happit Andra and Dave.
There was naething in life but death,
   And a' the warld was a grave.

    lug, ear   *gloamin'*, twilight   *happit*, covered

A' the hills were graves,
  The graves o' the deid langsyne,
And somewhere oot in the West
  Was the grummlin' battle-line.
      .   .   .   .   .

But up frae the howe o' the glen
  Came the waft o' the simmer e'en ;
The stink gaed oot o' my nose,
  And I sniffed it, caller and clean.

The smell o' the simmer hills—
  Thyme and hinny and heather,
Jeniper, birk and fern—
  Rose in the lown June weather.

It minded me o' auld days,
  When I wandered barefit there,
Guddlin' troot in the burns,
  Howkin' the tod frae his lair.

If a' the hills were graves
  There was peace for the folk aneath,
And peace for the folk abune,
  And life in the hert o' death. . . .
      .   .   .   .   .

Up frae the howe o' the glen
  Cam the murmur o' wells that creep
To swell the heids o' the burns,
  And the kindly voices o' sheep ;

caller, fresh   *hinny*, honey   *jeniper*, juniper
lown, soft   *guddlin'*, tickling   *howkin'*, digging
                    tod, fox

And the cry o' a whaup on the wing,
  And a plover seekin' its bield—
And oot o' my crazy lugs
  Went the din o' the battlefield.

   .   .   .

I flang me doun on my knees
  And I prayed as my hert wad break;
And I got my answer sune,
  For oot o' the nicht God spake.

As a man that wauks frae a stound
  And kens but a single thocht,
Oot o' the wind and the nicht
  I got the peace that I socht.

Loos and the Lammerlaw,
  The battle was feucht in baith,
Death was roond and abune,
  But life in the hert o' death.

A' the warld was a grave,
  But the grass on the graves was green,
And the stanes were bields for hames,
  And the laddies played atween.

Kneelin' aside the cairn
  On the heather and thymy sod,
The place I had kenned as a bairn,
  I made my peace wi' God.

John Buchan.

| *whaup*, curlew | *stound*, swoon |
| *feucht*, fought | *bields*, shelters |

105   ADDRESS TO THE GERMAN GUN IN THE
      QUADRANGLE OF EDINBURGH COLLEGE

YE grim auld deevil, how's yersel ?
Oft hae I cursed your snoovin' shell,
But since ye've come wi' us tae dwell,
    Let bygones be.
There's much in common, strange to tell,
    'Tween you an' me.

Ye maun hae found it unco queer,
Auld Blood an' Iron, comin' here,
Whaur these grey massive walls austere
    Glower on your muzzle ;
Weel, mair than you are vexed, I fear,
    By that same puzzle.

While doon the street the traffic hums,
While, like the throb o' distant drums,
The myriad voice o' Learnin' bums
    Wi' blended drone ;
Nae doot tae you remembrance comes
    O' days noo flown.

The worm-like maze o' trenches white,
The roarin' day, the unquiet night,
The shell, the soarin' signal light,
    The pitted plain,
The ordered squalor o' the fight
    Come back again.

        snoovin', boring

Though here sits Reason, throned in state,
An' spins her spider-web elate,
Secure frae besom-stroke o' Fate
    In cloistered glory :
Yet grimly here your time you wait—
    Memento Mori !

An' I can aiblins hear you say :
" *Thus was it on anither day ;*
Thus did you mortals preach an' pray
    Sae glib an' cheery,
Till I your douce, weel-ordered way
    Dang tapselteerie !

" *On Learning's mouth I clapped a hand,*
Your sons came forth at my command,
An' all you prayed for, preached an' planned,
    My voice made crumble—
An' noo, nae wiser do ye stand,
    An' nae mair humble ! "

Weel, weel, auld Roosty, bide you there
A captive's lot is hard to bear ;
But tell the sage in ilka chair
    That your dread reign,
The auld, unaltered phrases fair,
    Will bring again !

                W. S. Morrison.

aiblins, perhaps   *tapselteerie*, upside down
           Roosty, Rusty

First published "Student Magazine" 1921

BOOK VII
THE HUMAN COMEDY

AULD LANG SYNE

SHOULD auld acquaintance be forgot,
  And never brought to mind ?
Should auld acquaintance be forgot,
  And auld lang syne ?

  For auld lang syne, my dear,
    For auld lang syne,
  We'll tak a cup o' kindness yet
    For auld lang syne !

And surely you'll be your pint-stoup,
  And surely I'll be mine ;
And we'll tak a cup o' kindness yet
  For auld lang syne !

We twa hae run about the braes,
  And pu'd the gowans fine ;
But we've wandered mony a weary fit
  Sin auld lang syne.

We twa hae paidl'd in the burn,
  Frae morning sun till dine ;
But seas between us braid hae roar'd
  Sin auld lang syne !

pint-stoup, etc., you'll pay for one pint and I'll pay for
  another   *paidl'd*, waded   *dine*, noon

And there's a hand, my trusty fiere,
 And gie's a hand o' thine ;
And we'll tak a right guid-willie waught
 For auld lang syne.

 For auld lang syne, my dear,
  For auld lang syne,
 We'll tak a cup o' kindness yet
  For auld lang syne !

Robert Burns.

107   GREAT FOLK

O would they stay aback frae courts,
An' please themsels wi' countra sports,
It wad for ev'ry ane be better,
The laird, the tenant, and the cotter !
For thae frank, rantin' ramblin' billies,
Fient haet o' them's ill-hearted fellows ;
Except for breakin' o' their timmer,
Or speakin' lightly o' their limmer,
Or shootin' o' a hare or moorcock,
The ne'er a bit they're ill to poor folk.

Robert Burns.

fiere, crony   *guid-willie*, full of goodwill
waught, long draught   *billies*, fellows
Fient haet, devil a one   *limmer*, mistress

108   POOR FOLK

THEY'RE no sae wretched 's ane wad think
Tho' constantly on poortith's brink ;
They're sae accustom'd wi' the sight,
The view o't gies them little fright.

Then chance an' fortune are sae guided,
They're aye in less or mair provided ;
An' tho' fatigued wi' close employment,
A blink o' rest 's a sweet enjoyment.

The dearest comfort o' their lives,
Their grushie weans an' faithfu' wives ;
The prattling things are just their pride,
That sweetens a' their fireside ;
An' whyles twalpennie worth o' nappy
Can mak the bodies unco happy ;
They lay aside their private cares,
To mind the Kirk and State affairs :
They'll talk o' patronage an' priests,
Wi' kindling fury in their breasts ;
Or tell what new taxation's comin',
An' ferlie at the folk in Lon'on.

As bleak-fac'd Hallowmass returns
They get the jovial, ranting kirns,
When rural life, o' ev'ry station,
Unite in common recreation ;

poortith, poverty   *grushie*, growing   *nappy*, ale
ferlie, marvel   *kirns*, harvest-homes

Love blinks, Wit slaps, an' social Mirth
Forgets there's Care upo' the earth.

That merry day the year begins
They bar the door on frosty win's;
The nappy reeks wi' mantling ream,
And sheds a heart-inspiring steam;
The luntin' pipe, an' sneeshin' mill,
Are handed round wi' right guid-will;
The cantie auld folks crackin' crouse,
The young anes rantin' thro' the house,—
My heart has been sae fain to see them,
That I for joy hae barkit wi' them.

Robert Burns.

109   TIBBIE FOWLER

Tibbie Fowler o' the glen,
    There's ower mony wooin' at her;
Tibbie Fowler o' the glen,
    There's ower mony wooin' at her.
        Wooin' at her, pu'in' at her,
            Courtin' her, and canna get her;
        Filthy elf, it's for her pelf
            That a' the lads are wooin' at her.

Ten cam east and ten cam west,
    Ten cam rowin' o'er the water;
Twa cam down the lang dyke-side:
    There's twa-and-thirty wooin' at her.

ream, cream   *luntin'*, smoking
sneeshin' mill, snuff-box   *crackin' crouse*, talking merrily

There's seven but, and seven ben,
　　Seven in the pantry wi' her,
Twenty head about the door :
　　There's ane-and-forty wooin' at her.

She's got pendles in her lugs,
　　Cockle-shells wad set her better !
High-heel'd shoon and siller tags,
　　And a' the lads are wooin' at her.

Be a lassie e'er sae black,
　　Gin she hae the name o' siller,
Set her upon Tintock tap,
　　The wind will blaw a man till her.

Be a lassie e'er sae fair,
　　An' she want the penny siller,
A flie may fell her in the air
　　Before a man be even'd till her.

110   THE LAIRD O' COCKPEN

The laird o' Cockpen, he's proud an' he's great,
His mind is ta'en up wi' the things o' the state ;
He wanted a wife his braw house to keep,
But favour wi' wooin' was fashious to seek.

but and ben, both rooms of a house　　*pendles*, earrings
set, become　　　　　　　　　*even'd till her*, matched with her
　　　　　fashious, troublesome

Doun by the dyke-side a lady did dwell,
At his table-head he thought she'd look well ;
M'Cleish's ae daughter o' Claverse-ha Lee,
A penniless lass wi' a lang pedigree.

His wig was well pouther'd, and as guid as new,
His waistcoat was white, his coat it was blue ;
He put on a ring, a sword, and cock'd hat—
And wha could refuse the laird wi' a' that ?

He took the grey mare, and rade cannilie,
And rapp'd at the yett o' Claverse-ha Lee :
" Gae tell Mistress Jean to come speedily ben,
She's wanted to speak to the laird o' Cockpen."

Mistress Jean was makin' the elder-flower wine :
" And what brings the laird at sic a like time ? "
She put off her apron and on her silk gown,
Her mutch wi' red ribbons, and gaed awa' doun.

And when she cam' ben, he bowed fu' low,
And what was his errand he soon let her know ;
Amazed was the laird when the lady said " Na " ;
And wi' a laigh curtsie she turned awa'.

Dumfounder'd he was, nae sigh did he gie,
He mounted his mare and he rade cannilie ;
And often he thought, as he gaed thro' the glen,
She's daft to refuse the laird o' Cockpen.

Lady Nairne.

yett, gate *ben*, into the room *laigh*, low

III   THE WHISTLE

HE cut a sappy sucker from the mu
He trimmed it, an' he wet it, an' h
    knee ;
He never heard the teuchat when th
    eggs,
He missed the craggit heron nabbin puddocks in the
    seggs,
He forgot to hound the collie at the cattle when they
    strayed,
But you should hae seen the whistle that the wee herd
    made !

He wheepled on't at mornin' an' he tweetled on't at
    nicht,
He puffed his freckled cheeks until his nose sank oot o'
    sicht,
The kye were late for milkin' when he piped them up the
    closs,
The kitlins got his supper syne, an' he was beddit
    boss ;
But he cared na doit nor docken what they did or thocht
    or said,
There was comfort in the whistle that the wee herd
    made.

rodden, rowan   *teuchat*, pewit   *craggit*, long-necked
nabbin' puddocks, catching frogs   *seggs*, sedges
closs, farmyard   *kitlins*, kittens
beddit boss, sent to bed empty   *doit*, a small copper coin
                    docken, dock

played a march to battle, it cam' dirlin' through the
    mist,

Till the halflin' squared his shou'ders an' made up his
    mind to 'list ;

He tried a spring for wooers, though he wistna what it
    meant,

But the kitchen-lass was lauchin' an' he thocht she
    maybe kent ;

He got ream an' buttered bannocks for the lovin' lilt he
    played.

Wasna that a cheery whistle that the wee herd made ?

He blew them rants sae lively, schottisches, reels,
    an' jigs,

The foalie flang his muckle legs an' capered ower
    the rigs,

The grey-tailed futt'rat bobbit oot to hear his ain
    strathspey,

The bawd cam' loupin' through the corn to " Clean
    Pease Strae " ;

The feet o' ilka man an' beast gat youkie when he
    played—

Hae ye ever heard o' whistle like the wee herd made ?

But the snaw it stopped the herdin' an' the winter
    brocht him dool,

When in spite o' hacks an' chilblains he was shod again
    for school ;

dirlin', ringing	*halflin*, hobbledehoy	*kent*, knew
ream, cream	*rigs*, ridges	*futt'rat*, whittret, weasel
bobbit, leaped	*bawd*, hare	*youkie*, restless
	dool, sorrow	

He couldna sough the catechis nor pipe the rule o'
    three,
He was keepit in an' lickit when the ither loons
    got free ;
But he aften played the truant—'twas the only thing he
    played,
For the maister brunt the whistle that the wee herd
    made !

Charles Murray.

112   HALLOWE'EN

UPON that night, when fairies light
    On Cassilis Downans dance,
Or owre the lays, in splendid blaze,
    On sprightly coursers prance ;
Or for Colean the rout is ta'en,
    Beneath the moon's pale beams ;
There, up the Cove, to stray an' rove
    Amang the rocks an' streams
        To sport that night.

Amang the bonnie, winding banks
    Where Doon rins, wimplin', clear,
Where Bruce ance rul'd the martial ranks,
    An' shook his Carrick spear,
Some merry, friendly, countra folks,
    Together did convene,

sough, whistle softly	*catechis*, catechism	*keepit*, kept
lickit, punished	*brunt*, burned	*lays*, pasture fields
rout, road	*wimplin'*, winding	

To burn their nits, an' pou their stocks,
    An' haud their Hallowe'en
            Fu' blythe that night.

The lasses feat, an' cleanly neat,
    Mair braw than when they're fine ;
Their faces blythe fu' sweetly kythe
    Hearts leal, an' warm, an' kin' :
The lads sae trig, wi' wooer-babs
    Weel knotted on their garten,
Some unco blate, an' some wi' gabs
    Gar lasses' hearts gang startin'
            Whyles fast at night.

Then, first and foremost, thro' the kail,
    Their stocks maun a' be sought ance ;
They steek their een, an' graip an' wale,
    For muckle anes an' straught anes,
Poor hav'rel Will fell aff the drift,
    An' wandered through the bow-kail,
An' pou't, for want o' better shift,
    A runt was like a sow-tail,
            Sae bow't that night.

Then, straught or crooked, yird or nane,
    They roar an' cry a' throu'ther ;
The vera wee-things, toddlin', rin,
    Wi' stocks out-owre their shouther ;

nits, nuts	*pou their stocks,* pull their cabbage plants	
feat, spruce	*kythe,* show	*wooer-babs,* love-knots
garten, garters	*gabs,* powers of talk	*steek,* shut
graip, grope	*wale,* choose	*hav'rel,* half-witted
bow-kail, cabbage	*runt,* stock	*yird,* mould
throu'ther, through-other, pell-mell		

An gif' the custock's sweet or sour,
    Wi' joctelegs they taste them ;
Syne coziely, aboon the door,
    Wi' cannie care they've placed them
                 To lie that night.

The lasses staw frae 'mang them a'
    To pou their stalks o' corn :
But Rab slips out, an' jinks about,
    Behint the muckle thorn :
He grippet Nelly hard an' fast ;
    Loud skirl'd a' the lasses ;
But her tap-pickle maist was lost
    When kiutlin in the fause-house
                 Wi' him that night.

The auld guidwife's weel-hoorded nits
    Are round an' round divided,
An' mony lads' an' lasses' fates
    Are there that night decided ;
Some kindle, couthie, side by side,
    An' burn thegither trimly ;
Some start awa' wi' saucy pride
    And jump out-owre the chimlie
                 Fu' high that night.

Jean slips in twa wi' tentie e'e ;
    Wha 'twas she wadna tell ;
But this is Jock, an' this is me,
    She says in to hersel' :

---

custock, pith   *joctelegs*, pocket-knives   *staw*, stole
tap-pickle, a grain at the top of the stalk   *kiutlin*, cuddling
fause-house, an opening in the stack   *tentie*, careful

He bleez'd owre her, an' she owre him,
    As they wad never mair part ;
'Till, fuff ! he started up the lum,
    An' Jean had e'en a sair heart
                To see 't that night.

Poor Willie, wi' his bow-kail runt,
    Was brunt wi' primsie Mallie ;
An' Mallie, nae doubt, took the drunt,
    To be compar'd to Willie ;
Mall's nit lap out wi' pridefu' fling,
    An' her ain fit it brunt it ;
While Willie lap, an' swoor, by jing,
    'Twas just the way he wanted
                To be that night.

Nell had the fause-house in her min',
    She pits hersel' an' Rob in ;
In loving bleeze they sweetly join,
    'Till white in ase they 're sobbin' ;
Nell's heart was dancin' at the view,
    She whisper'd Rob to leuk for't :
Rob, stowlins, prie'd her bonnie mou,
    Fu' cozie in the neuk for't,
                Unseen that night.

But Merran sat behint their backs,
    Her thoughts on Andrew Bell ;
She lea'es them gashin' at their cracks,
    An' slips out by hersel' :

primsie, precise   *drunt*, huff   *ase*, ashes
stowlins, stealthily   *prie'd*, tasted   *gashin'*, gabbling

She thro' the yard the nearest taks,
  An' to the kiln she goes then,
An' darklins graipit for the bauks,
  And in the blue-clue throws then,
          Right fear't that night.

An' aye she win't, an' aye she swat,
  I wat she made nae jaukin ;
'Till something held within the pat—
  Guid Lord ! but she was quaukin !
But whether 'twas the Deil himsel',
  Or whether 'twas a bauk-en',
Or whether it was Andrew Bell,
  She did na wait on talkin'
          To spier that night.

Wee Jenny to her grannie says,
  " Will ye go wi' me, grannie ?
I'll eat the apple at the glass
  I gat frae uncle Johnnie : "
She fuff'd her pipe wi' sic a lunt,
  In wrath she was sae vap'rin',
She notic't na, an aizle brunt
  Her braw new worset apron
          Out thro' that night.

" Ye little skelpie-limmer's face !
  How daur you try sic sportin',
As seek the foul thief onie place,
  For him to spae your fortune ?

---

graipit, groped	*bauks*, rafters
blue-clue, a clue of blue yarn	*win't*, wound
swat, sweated	*jaukin*, trifling	*spier*, inquire
lunt, smoke	*aizle brunt*, cinder burned

Nae doubt but ye may get a sight !
  Great cause ye hae to fear it ;
For mony a ane has gotten a fright,
  An' liv'd an' died deleeret,
      On sic a night.

" Ae hairst afore the Sherra-moor,—
  I mind 't as weel's yestreen,
I was a gilpey then, I'm sure
  I was na past fyfteen ;
The simmer had been cauld an' wat,
  An' stuff was unco green ;
An' aye a rantin' kirn we gat,
  An' just on Halloween
      It fell that night.

" Our stibble-rig was Rab M'Graen,
  A clever, sturdy fallow :
He's sin gat Eppie Sim wi' wean,
  That liv'd in Achmacalla :
He gat hemp-seed, I mind it weel,
  An' he made unco light o't ;
But mony a day was by himsel',
  He was sae sairly frighted
      That vera night."

Then up gat fechtin' Jamie Fleck,
  An' he swoor by his conscience,
That he could saw hemp-seed a peck ;
  For it was a' but nonsense.

deleeret, mad	*hairst,* harvest
gilpey, young girl	*stibble-rig*, chief harvester

The auld guidman raught down the pock,
   An' out a handfu' gied him ;
Syne bad him slip frae 'mang the folk,
   Sometime when nae ane see'd him,
           An' try 't that night.

He marches thro' amang the stacks,
   Tho' he was something sturtin ;
The graip he for a harrow taks,
   An' haurls at his curpin ;
An' every now an' then he says,
   " Hemp-seed, I saw thee,
An' her that is to be my lass,
   Come after me, and draw thee
           As fast this night."

He whistl'd up *Lord Lennox' March*,
   To keep his courage cheery ;
Altho' his hair began to arch,
   He was sae fley'd and eerie :
'Till presently he hears a squeak,
   An' then a grane an' gruntle ;
He by his shouther gae a keek,
   An' tumbl'd wi' a wintle
           Out-owre that night.

He roar'd a horrid murder-shout,
   In dreadfu' desperation !
An' young an' auld came rinnin out,
   To hear the sad narration ;

raught, reached	*pock*, a bag	*sturtin*, staggered
graip, fork	*haurls*, trails	*curpin*, crupper
fley'd, scared	*keek*, look	*wintle*, somersault

He swoor 'twas hilchin Jean M'Craw,
    Or crouchie Merran Humphie,
'Till, stop ! she trotted thro' them a' ;
    An' wha was it but grumphie
        Asteer that night !

Meg fain wad to the barn hae gaen,
    To winn three wechts o' naething ;
But for to meet the Deil her lane,
    She pat but little faith in :
She gies the herd a pickle nits,
    An' twa red-cheekit apples,
To watch, while for the barn she sets,
    In hopes to see Tam Kipples
        That vera night.

She turns the key wi' cannie thraw,
    An' owre the threshold ventures ;
But first on Sawnie gies a ca'
    Syne bauldly in she enters :
A ratton rattled up the wa',
    And she cried, Lord, preserve her !
An' ran thro' midden-hole an' a',
    An' pray'd wi' zeal and fervour,
        Fu' fast that night.

They hoy't out Will, wi' sair advice ;
    They hecht him some fine braw ane ;

hilchin, limping   *crouchie*, hump-backed   *grumphie*, the pig
asteer, astir   *winn*, winnow   *wechts*, close sieves
thraw, twist   *ratton*, rat
midden-hole, the gutter below the dunghill   *hoy't*, urged
            hecht, promised

It chanc'd the stack he faddom't thrice,
   Was timmer-propt for thrawin ;
He taks a swirlie, auld moss-oak,
   For some black, grousome carlin ;
An' loot a winze, an' drew a stroke,
   'Till skin in blypes cam haurlin
               Aff's nieves that night.

A wanton widow Leezie was,
   As canty as a kittlin :
But, och ! that night, amang the shaws,
   She gat a fearfu' settlin' !
She thro' the whins, an' by the cairn,
   An' owre the hill gaed scrievin,
Whare three lairds' lands met at a burn,
   To dip her left sark-sleeve in,
               Was bent that night.

Whyles owre a linn the burnie plays,
   As thro' the glen it wimpl't ;
Whyles round a rocky scaur it strays :
   Whyles in a wiel it dimpl't ;
Whyles glitter'd to the nightly rays,
   Wi' bickerin' dancin' dazzle ;
Whyles cookit underneath the braes,
   Below the spreading hazel,
               Unseen that night.

faddom't, fathomed		*timmer*, timber	
for thrawin, against binding		*swirlie*, twisted	
loot a winze, uttered a curse		*blypes*, shreds	
Aff's nieves, off his fists	*kittlin*, kitten	*shaws*, woods
scrievin, careering	*wiel*, eddy	*cookit*, hid

Amang the brachens, on the brae,
　　Between her an' the moon,
The Deil, or else an outler quey,
　　Gat up an' gae a croon :
Poor Leezie's heart maist lap the hool !
　　Near lav'rock-height she jumpit ;
But mist a fit, an' in the pool
　　Out-owre the lugs she plumpit,
　　　　　　Wi' a plunge that night.

In order, on the clean hearth-stane,
　　The luggies three are ranged,
And ev'ry time great care is ta'en,
　　To see them duly changed :
Auld uncle John, wha wedlock's joys
　　Sin Mar's-year did desire,
Because he gat the toom dish thrice,
　　He heav'd them on the fire
　　　　　　In wrath that night.

Wi' merry sangs, an' friendly cracks,
　　I wat they did na weary ;
An' unco tales, an' funny jokes,
　　Their sports were cheap an' cheery ;
Till butter'd sow'ns, wi' fragrant lunt,
　　Set a' their gabs a-steerin' ;

outler quey, young cow lying in the open
lap the hool, leaped the sheath　　*lav'rock-height*, lark-height
lugs, ears　　　*luggies*, dishes　　*Mar's-year*, 1715
toom, empty　　*unco*, curious　　*sow'ns*, a thin porridge
　　　　　　lunt, steam

Syne, wi' a social glass o' strunt,
  They parted aff careerin'
      Fu' blythe that night.
                              Robert Burns.

113   ROBIN TAMSON'S SMIDDY

My mither ment my auld breeks,
  An' wow ! but they were duddy,
And sent me to get Mally shod
  At Robin Tamson's smiddy ;
The smiddy stands beside the burn
  That wimples through the clachan,
I never yet gae by the door,
  But aye I fa' a-lauchin'.

For Robin was a walthy carle,
  An' had ae bonnie dochter,
Yet ne'er wad let her tak a man,
  Tho' mony lads had socht her ;
But what think ye o' my exploit ?
  The time our mare was shoeing,
I slippit up beside the lass,
  And briskly fell a-wooing.

An' aye she e'ed my auld breeks,
  The time that we sat crackin',
Quo' I, " My lass, ne'er mind the clouts,
  I've new anes for the makin' ;

strunt, liquor	*breeks*, breeches
duddy, ragged	*smiddy*, smithy
crackin', talking	*clouts*, patches

But gin ye'll just come hame wi' me,
    An' lea'e the carle, your father,
Ye'se get my breeks to keep in trim,
    Myself, an' a' thegither."

" 'Deed lad," quo' she, " your offer's fair,
    I really think I'll tak it.
Sae, gang awa', get out the mare,
    We'll baith slip on the back o't :
For gin I wait my father's time,
    I'll wait till I be fifty ;
But na !—I'll marry in my prime,
    An' mak a wife most thrifty."

Wow ! Robin was an angry man,
    At tyning o' his dochter :
Thro' a' the kintra-side he ran,
    An' far an' near he socht her ;
But when he cam to our fire-end,
    An' fand us baith thegither,
Quo' I, " Gudeman, I've ta'en your bairn,
    An' ye may tak my mither."

Auld Robin girn'd an' sheuk his pow.
    " Guid sooth ! " quo' he, " ye're merry ;
But I'll just tak ye at your word,
    An' end this hurry-burry."

tyning, losing	*kintra-side*, countryside
fand, found	*girn'd*, grimaced
sheuk his pow, shook his head	

So Robin an' our auld wife
   Agreed to creep thegither ;
Now, I hae Robin Tamson's pet,
   An' Robin has my mither.
                         Alexander Rodger.

114   BRAID CLAITH

YE wha are fain to hae your name
Wrote i' the bonnie book o' fame,
Let merit nae pretension claim
      To laurell'd wreath,
But hap ye weel, baith back and wame,
      In gude braid claith.

He that some ells o' this may fa',
And slae-black hat on pow like snaw,
Bids bauld to bear the gree awa',
      Wi' a' this graith,
When bienly clad wi' shell fu' braw
      O' gude braid claith.

Waesuck for him wha has nae feck o't !
For he's a gowk they're sure to geck at ;
A chiel that ne'er will be respeckit
      While he draws breath,
Till his four quarters are bedeckit
      Wi' gude braid claith.

hap, cover	*wame*, belly	*braid claith*, broadcloth
fa', chance to own	*gree*, prize	*graith*, accoutrement
bienly, snugly	*Waesuck*, alas	*feck*, quantity
gowk, fool	*geck*, mock	*chiel*, fellow

On Sabbath-days the barber spark,
When he has done wi' scrapin' wark,
Wi' siller broachie in his sark,
    Gangs trigly, faith !
Or to the Meadows, or the Park,
    In gude braid claith.

Weel might ye trow, to see them there,
That they to shave your haffits bare,
Or curl and sleek a pickle hair,
    Would be right laith,
When pacin' wi' a gawsy air
    In gude braid claith.

If ony mettled stirrach grien
For favour frae a lady's een,
He maunna care for bein' seen
    Before he sheath
His body in a scabbard clean
    O' gude braid claith.

For, gin he come wi' coat thread-bare,
A feg for him she winna care,
But crook her bonny mou fu' sair,
    And scauld him baith :
Wooers should aye their travel spare
    Withoot braid claith.

trigly, neatly   *trow*, think
haffits, temples   *laith*, loth
gawsy, complacent   *stirrach*, fellow
grien, wish   *scauld*, scold

Braid claith lends fouk an unco heeze,
Maks mony kail-worms butterflees,
Gies mony a doctor his degrees,
    For little skaith :
In short, you may be what you please,
    Wi' gude braid claith.

For tho' ye had as wise a snout on,
As Shakespeare or Sir Isaac Newton,
Your judgment fouk would hae a doubt on,
    I'll tak' my aith,
Till they could see ye wi' a suit on
    O' gude braid claith.

                 Robert Fergusson.

115   THE ANNUITY

I GAED to spend a week in Fife—
    An unco week it proved to be—
For there I met a waesome wife
    Lamentin' her viduity.
Her grief brak out sae fierce and fell,
I thought her heart wad burst the shell ;
And—I was sae left to mysel'—
    I sell't her an annuity.

The bargain lookit fair enough—
    She just was turned o' saxty-three ;
I couldna guessed she'd prove sae teugh,
    By human ingenuity.

fouk, folk   *unco heeze,* a wonderful lift   *skaith,* trouble

But years have come, and years have gane,
And there she's yet as stieve's a stane—
The limmer's growin' young again,
    Since she got her annuity.

She's crined awa' to bane an' skin,
    But that it seems is nought to me ;
She's like to live—although she's in
    The last stage o' tenuity.
She munches wi' her wizened gums,
An' stumps about on legs o' thrums,
But comes—as sure as Christmas comes—
    To ca' for her annuity.

She jokes her joke, an' cracks her crack,
    As spunkie as a growin' flea—
An' there she sits upon my back,
    A livin' perpetuity.
She hurkles by her ingle side,
An' toasts an' tans her wrunkled hide—
Lord kens how lang she yet may bide
    To ca' for her annuity !

I read the tables drawn wi' care
    For an Insurance Company ;
Her chance o' life was stated there,
    Wi' perfect perspicuity.
But tables here or tables there,
She's lived ten years beyond her share,
An's like to live a dizzen mair,
    To ca' for her annuity.

stieve, hard   *limmer*, woman   *crined*, dwindled
spunkie, spirited   *hurkles*, crouches

I gat the loon that drew the deed—
  We spelled it o'er right carefully ;—
In vain he yerked his souple head,
  To find an ambiguity ;
It's dated—tested—a' complete—
The proper stamp—nae word delete—
And diligence, as on decreet,
  May pass for her annuity.

Last Yule she had a fearfu' hoast—
  I thought a kink might set me free ;
I led her out, 'mang snaw and frost,
  Wi' constant assiduity.
But Deil ma' care—the blast gaed by,
And missed the auld anatomy ;
It just cost me a tooth, forbye
  Discharging her annuity.

I thought that grief might gar her quit—
  Her only son was lost at sea—
But aff her wits behuved to flit,
  An' leave her in fatuity !
She threeps, an' threeps, he's living yet,
For a' the tellin' she can get ;
But catch the doited runt forget
  To ca' for her annuity !

If there's a sough o' cholera
  Or typhus—wha sae gleg as she ?
She buys up baths, an' drugs, an' a',
  In siccan superfluity !

yerked, jerked   _hoast_, cough   _threeps_, repeats
doited runt, crazy remnant   _sough_, suspicion
(2,470)   7

She doesna need—she's fever proof—
The pest gaed o'er her very roof;
She tauld me sae—an' then her loof
    Held out for her annuity.

Ae day she fell—her arm she brak—
    A compound fracture as could be;
Nae leech the cure wad undertak,
    Whate'er was the gratuity.
It's cured!—She handles't like a flail—
It does as weel in bits as hale;
But I'm a broken man mysel'
    Wi' her and her annuity.

Her broozled flesh, and broken banes,
    Are weel as flesh an' banes can be.
She beats the taeds that live in stanes,
    An' fatten in vacuity!
They die when they're exposed to air—
They canna thole the atmosphere;
But her! expose her onywhere—
    She lives for her annuity.

If mortal means could nick her thread,
    Sma' crime it wad appear to me;
Ca't murder, or ca't homicide—
    I'd justify't,—an' do it tae.
But how to fell a withered wife
That's carved out o' the tree o' life—
The timmer limmer daurs the knife
    To settle her annuity.

loof, palm	*broozled*, bloodless	*taeds*, toads
thole, endure	*timmer limmer*, wooden woman	

I'd try a shot.—But whar's the mark ?—
  Her vital parts are hid frae me ;
Her back-bane wanders through her sark
  In an unkenn'd corkscrewity.
She's palsified—an' shakes her head
Sae fast about, ye scarce can see't ;
It's past the power o' steel or lead
  To settle her annuity.

She might be drowned ;—but go she'll not
  Within a mile o' loch or sea ;—
Or hanged—if cord could grip a throat
  O' siccan exiguity.
It's fitter far to hang the rope—
It draws out like a telescope ;
'Twad tak a dreadfu' length o' drop
  To settle her annuity.

Will puzion do't ?—It has been tried ;
  But, be't in hash or fricassee,
That's just the dish she can't abide,
  Whatever kind o' *goût* it hae.
It's needless to assail her doubts,—
She gangs by instinct—like the brutes—
An' only eats an' drinks what suits
  Hersel' an' her annuity.

The Bible says the age o' man
  Threescore an' ten perchance may be ;
She's ninety-four ;—let them wha can
  Explain the incongruity.

She should hae lived afore the Flood—
She's come o' Patriarchal blood—
She's some auld Pagan, mummified
    Alive for her annuity.

She's been embalmed inside and out—
    She's sauted to the last degree—
There's pickle in her very snout
    Sae caper-like an' cruety ;
Lot's wife was fresh compared to her ;
They've Kyanised the useless knir—
She canna decompose—nae mair
    Than her accursed annuity.

The water-drap wears out the rock
    As this eternal jaud wears me ;
I could withstand the single shock,
    But no the continuity.
It's pay me here—an' pay me there—
An' pay me, pay me, evermair ;
I'll gang demented wi' despair—
    I'm *charged* for her annuity !

                                  George Outram.

116   HAME CAM OUR GUDEMAN AT E'EN

HAME cam our gudeman at e'en,
    And hame cam he,
And there he saw a saddle-horse,
    Where nae horse should be :

    jaud, hussy

" And how cam this horse here,
    And how can it be ?
O how cam this horse here
    Without the leave o' me ? "
" A horse ! " quo' she.—" Aye, a horse," quo' he.
    " Ye blind auld doited bodie,
        And blinder may ye be,
    'Tis but a dainty milk-cow
        My mither sent to me."
" A milk-cow ! " quo' he.—" Aye, a milk-cow,"
        quo' she.
    " O far hae I ridden,
        And meikle hae I seen,
    But a saddle on a milk-cow
        Saw I never nane."

Hame cam our gudeman at e'en,
    And hame cam he,
And he spied a pair of jack-boots
    Where nae boots should be :
" What's this now, gudewife,
    What's this I see ?
How cam these boots here
    Without the leave o' me ? "
" Boots ! " quo' she.—" Aye, boots ! " quo' he.
    " Shame fa' yere cuckold face,
        And waur may ye see,
    It's but a pair o' milking-pails
        My mither sent to me."
" Milking-pails ! " quo' he.—" Aye, milking-pails ! "
        quo' she.
    " Far hae I ridden,
        And farer hae I gane,

> But siller spurs on milking-pails
>   Saw I never nane."

Hame cam our gudeman at e'en,
    And hame cam he,
And there he saw a shining sword
    Where nae sword should be ;
" What's this now, gudewife,
    And what's this I see ?
O how cam this sword here
    Without the leave o' me ? "
" A sword ! " quo' she.—" Aye, a sword ! " quo' he.
  " Shame fa' yere cuckold face,
    And waur may ye see,
    It's but a porridge spurtle
    My mither sent to me."
" A spurtle ! " quo' he.—" Aye, a spurtle ! " quo' she.
  " Far hae I ridden,
    And meikle hae I seen,
    But silver-hilted spurtles
    Saw I never nane."

Hame cam our gudeman at e'en,
    And hame cam he,
And there he spied a powdered wig
    Where nae wig should be :
" What's this now, gudewife,
    What's this I see ?
How came this wig here
    Without the leave o' me ? "
" A wig ! " quo' she.—" Aye, a wig ! " quo' he.

spurtle, porridge stick

" Shame fa' yere cuckold face,
  And waur may ye see,
 'Tis nothing but a clocking-hen
  My mither sent to me."
" A clocking-hen ! " quo' he.—" Aye, a clocking-
   hen ! " quo' she.
" Far hae I ridden,
  And meikle hae I seen,
 But powder on a clocking-hen
  Saw I never nane."

Hame cam our gudeman at e'en,
  And hame cam he,
And there he saw a meikle coat
  Where nae coat should be :
" And how cam this coat here,
  And how can it be ?
O how cam this coat here
  Without the leave o' me ? "
" A coat ! " quo' she.—" Aye, a coat ! " quo' he.
 " Ye blind donard bodie,
  And blinder may ye be ;
 It's but a pair o' blankets
  My mither sent to me."
" Blankets ! " quo' he.—" Aye, blankets ! " quo' she.
 " Far hae I ridden,
  And meikle hae I seen ;
 But buttons upon blankets
  Saw I never nane."

Ben went our gudeman,
  And ben went he ;

   clocking-hen, sitting hen

And there he spied a sturdy man
　　Where nae man should be.
" How cam this man here ?
　　And how can it be ?
How cam this man here
　　Without the leave o' me ? "
　" A man ! " quo' she.—" Aye, a man ! " quo' he.
　　" Ye silly blind bodie,
　　　　And blinder may ye be :
　　'Tis a new milking maiden
　　　　My mither sent to me."
" A maid ! " quo' he.—" Aye, a maid ! " quo' she.
　" Far hae I ridden,
　　　And meikle hae I seen ;
　But long-bearded maidens
　　　Saw I never nane."

117 TO A HAGGIS

Fair fa' your honest, sonsie face,
Great chieftain o' the puddin'-race !
Aboon them a' ye tak your place,
　　　　Painch, tripe, or thairm :
Weel are ye wordy of a grace
　　　　As lang 's my arm.

The groaning trencher there ye fill,
Your hurdies like a distant hill,
Your pin wad help to mend a mill
　　　　In time o' need,
While thro' your pores the dews distil
　　　　Like amber bead.

sonsie, jolly　　*Painch*, paunch　　*thairm*, guts
　　　　hurdies, buttocks

His knife see rustic Labour dight,
An' cut you up wi' ready slight,
Trenching your gushing entrails bright
      Like ony ditch ;
And then, O what a glorious sight,
      Warm-reekin', rich !

Then, horn for horn, they stretch an' strive,
Deil tak the hindmost, on they drive,
'Till all their weel-swall'd kytes belyve
      Are bent like drums ;
Then auld guidman, maist like to rive,
      " Bethankit ! " hums.

Is there that owre his French ragout,
Or olio that wad staw a sow,
Or fricassee wad mak her spew,
      Wi' perfect sconner,
Looks down wi' sneering, scornfu' view
      On sic a dinner ?

Poor devil ! see him owre his trash,
As feckless as a wither'd rash,
His spindle shank a guid whip-lash,
      His nieve a nit ;
Thro' bloody flood or field to dash,
      O how unfit !

horn, spoon	*kytes*, bellies	*belyve*, by-and-bye
rive, burst	*staw*, sicken	*sconner*, disgust
feckless, feeble	*rash*, rush	

But mark the rustic, haggis-fed,
The trembling earth resounds his tread,
Clap in his walie nieve a blade,
      He'll mak it whissle ;
An' legs, an' arms, an' heads will sned,
      Like taps o' thrissle.

Ye Pow'rs wha mak mankind your care,
And dish them out their bill o' fare,
Auld Scotland wants nae skinking ware
      That jaups in luggies ;
But, if ye wish her gratefu' pray'r,
      Gie her a Haggis !

                         Robert Burns.

118   WHISTLE, WHISTLE, AULD WIFE

" WHISTLE, whistle, auld wife,
    An' ye'se get a hen."
" I wadna whistle," quo' the wife,
    " Though ye wad gie me ten."

" Whistle, whistle, auld wife,
    An' ye'se get a cock."
" I wadna whistle," quo' the wife,
    " Though ye'd gie me a flock."

" Whistle, whistle, auld wife,
    An' ye'se get a goun."
" I wadna whistle," quo' the wife,
    " For the best ane i' the town."

walie nieve, massive fist   *sned*, shear   *skinking*, watery
jaups in luggies, splashes in bowls   *goun*, gown

" Whistle, whistle, auld wife,
   An' ye'se get a coo."
" I wadna whistle," quo' the wife,
   " Though ye wad gie me two."

" Whistle, whistle, auld wife,
   An' ye'se get a man."
" *Wheeple-whauple*," quo' the wife,
   " I'll whistle gin I can."

119   TAM O' THE LINN

Tam o' the Linn cam' up the gait,
Wi' twenty puddin's on a plate,
And every puddin' had a pin—
" There's wud eneuch here," quo' Tam o' the Linn.

Tam o' the Linn had nae breeks to wear,
He coft him a sheep's-skin to mak' him a pair,
The fleshy side out, the woolly side in—
" It's fine summer cleedin'," quo' Tam o' the Linn.

Tam o' the Linn and a' his bairns,
They fell in the fire in ilk ither's airms ;
" Oh," quo' the bunemost, " I have a het skin "—
" It's hetter below," quo' Tam o' the Linn.

Tam o' the Linn gaed to the moss
To seek a stable to his horse ;
The moss was open, and Tam fell in—
" I've stabled mysel'," quo' Tam o' the Linn.

gait, road	*wud*, wood	*breeks*, breeches
coft, bought	*cleedin'*, clothing	*bunemost*, uppermost
	het, hot	

BOOK VIII
BACCHANALIA

_120_ O, WILLIE BREW'D A PECK O' MAUT

O, WILLIE brew'd a peck o' maut,
   And Rob and Allan cam to see ;
Three blither hearts, that lee-lang night,
   Ye wad na find in Christendie.

We are na fou, we're nae that fou,
   But just a drappie in our e'e ;
The cock may craw, the day may daw,
   And aye we'll taste the barley bree.

Here are we met, three merry boys,
   Three merry boys, I trow, are we ;
And mony a night we've merry been,
   And mony mae we hope to be !

It is the moon—I ken her horn,
   That's blinkin' in the lift sae hie ;
She shines sae bright to wyle us hame,
   But, by my sooth, she'll wait a wee !

Wha first shall rise to gang awa',
   A cuckold coward loon is he !
Wha first beside his chair shall fa',
   He is the king amang us three.

                            Robert Burns.

lee-lang, livelong	_fou_, drunk	_drappie_, little drop
daw, dawn	_bree_, brew	_mae_, more
lift, sky	_wyle_, entice	

121   CONTENTED WI' LITTLE

CONTENTED wi' little, and cantie wi' mair,
Whene'er I foregather wi' sorrow and care,
I gie them a skelp as they're creepin' alang,
Wi' a cog o' gude swats, and an auld Scottish sang.

I whyles claw the elbow o' troublesome thought ;
But man is a soger, and life is a faught :
My mirth and gude humour are coin in my pouch,
And my freedom's my lairdship nae monarch dare touch.

A towmond o' trouble, should that be my fa',
A night o' gude fellowship sowthers it a' :
When at the blithe end o' our journey at last,
Wha the deil ever thinks o' the road he has past !

Blind chance, let her snapper and stoyte on her way,
Be't to me, be't frae me, e'en let the jade gae :
Come ease, or come travail, come pleasure or pain,
My warst word is—Welcome, and welcome again !
                                        Robert Burns.

cantie, jolly   *skelp,* whack
cog o' gude swats, a pot of good new ale
claw, scratch   *soger,* soldier   *faught,* fight
towmond, twelvemonth   *fa',* lot   *sowthers,* solders
          snapper and stoyte, stumble and stagger

122 THE BANKS O' THE DEE

I MET wi' a man on the banks o' the Dee,
An' a merrier body I never did see ;
Though Time had bedrizzled his haffits wi' snaw,
An' Fortune had stown his luckpenny awa',
Yet never a mortal mair happy could be
Than the man that I met on the banks o' the Dee.

When young, he had plenty o' owsen an' kye,
A wide wavin' mailin, an' siller forbye ;
But cauld was his hearth ere his youdith was o'er,
An' he delved on the lands he had lairded before ;
Yet though beggared his ha' an' deserted his lea,
Contented he roamed on the banks o' the Dee.

'Twas heartsome to see the auld body sae gay,
As he toddled adown by the gowany brae,
Sae canty, sae crouse, an' sae pruif against care ;
Yet it wasna through riches, it wasna through lear ;
But I fand out the cause ere I left the sweet Dee—
The man was as drunk as a mortal could be !

George Outram.

123 GUDEWIFE, COUNT THE LAWIN

GANE is the day, and mirk's the night,
But we'll ne'er stray for faut o' light,
For ale and brandy's stars and moon,
And blude-red wine's the risin' sun.

haffits, temples	*owsen*, oxen	*mailin*, farm
youdith, youth	*crouse*, cheerful	*lear*, learning
mirk, dark	*faut*, lack	

Then, gudewife, count the lawin,
The lawin, the lawin ;
Then, gudewife, count the lawin,
And bring a coggie mair.

There's wealth and ease for gentlemen,
And semple-folk maun fecht and fen' ;
But here we're a' in ae accord,
For ilka man that's drunk's a lord.

My coggie is a haly pool,
That heals the wounds o' care and dool ;
And pleasure is a wanton trout—
An' ye drink but deep, ye'll find him out.
    Then, gudewife, count the lawin,
    The lawin, the lawin ;
    Then, gudewife, count the lawin,
    And bring a coggie mair.

                            Robert Burns.

124 GUDE ALE HAUDS MY HEART ABOON

O GUDE ale comes and gude ale goes,
Gude ale gars me sell my hose,
Sell my hose and pawn my shoon,
Gude ale hauds my heart aboon :

coggie, bowl   *semple,* simple
fecht and fen', fight and fend for themselves
haly, holy   *dool,* sorrow   *gars,* makes
    hauds my heart aboon, keeps my heart up

Gude ale keeps me bare and busy,
Brandy makes me dull and dizzy,
Gars me sleep and sough i' my shoon,
Gude ale hauds my heart aboon.

O in the sweetest plums there's stanes,
And in the fairest beef there's banes ;
Rum turns ye rude, wine makes ye pale,
There's life and love and soul in ale :
Gude ale's the medicine oft spae'd of,
The very stuff that life is made of,
Dropt in a receipt from the moon,
To haud men's sinking hearts aboon.

May he rub shoulders wi' the gallows,
Who wad keep gude ale frae gude fallows ;
May he gape wide when suns are south,
And never drink come near his drouth ;
But here's to him, where'er he roam,
Who loves to see the flagons foam,
For he's a king o'er lord and loon—
Gude ale hauds my heart aboon.

TODLEN HAME

WHEN I've a saxpence under my thumb,
Then I'll get credit in ilka town,
But ay when I'm poor they bid me gang by ;
O ! poverty parts good company.
  Todlen hame, todlen hame,
    Couldna my love come todlen hame ?

sough, sigh	*spae'd,* prophesied
drouth, thirst	*todlen,* trotting

Fair fa' the goodwife, and send her gude sale,
She gies us white bannocks to drink her ale,
Syne if that her tippeny chance to be sma',
We'll tak' a good scour o't and ca't awa' :
 Todlen hame, todlen hame,
 As round as a neep come todlen hame.

My kimmer and I lay down to sleep,
And twa pint stoups at our bed's feet ;
And ay when we waken'd, we drank them dry :
What think ye of my wee kimmer and I ?
 Todlen but, and todlen ben,
 Sae round as my love comes todlen hame.

Leez me on liquor, my todlen dow,
Ye're aye sae good-humoured, when weeting your
 mou' ;
When sober, sae sour, ye'll fight with a flee,
That 'tis a blyth sight to the bairns and me,
 When todlen hame, todlen hame,
 When round as a neep you come todlen hame.

126 HOOLIE AND FAIRLY

Down in yon valley a couple did tarry ;
The wife she drank naething but sack and canary :
The gudeman complain'd to her friends right sairly,
O ! gin my wife wad drink hoolie and fairly !

fair fa', good befall	*tippeny*, twopenny ale
neep, turnip	*kimmer*, gossip
but and ben, into the kitchen and the parlour	
leez me, blessings	*dow*, dove
weeting, wetting	*hoolie*, softly

First she drank Crummie, and syne she drank
    Gairie,
And syne she has drucken my bonnie grey mairie,
That carried me through the dub and the glairie :
O ! gin my wife wad drink hoolie and fairly !

She has drucken her hose, she has drucken her
    shoon,
Her snaw-white mutch and her bonnie new goun,
Her sark of the hollans that cover'd her rarely :
O ! gin my wife wad drink hoolie and fairly !

Wad she drink but her ain things I wadna much care,
But she drinks my claes that I canna weel spare ;
At kirk and at market I'm cover'd but barely :
O ! gin my wife wad drink hoolie and fairly !

127   THE ORGIASTS

(1)

O FARE ye weel, my auld wife !
    Sing bum, biberry bum.
O fare ye weel, my auld wife !
    Sing bum.
O fare ye weel, my auld wife,
Thou steerer up o' sturt and strife !
The maut's aboon the meal the nicht
    Wi' some.

dub, pool	*glairie*, mire
claes, clothes	*steerer*, stirrer
sturt, conflict	*maut*, malt

And fare ye weel, my pike-staff !
    Sing bum, biberry bum.
And fare ye weel, my pike-staff !
    Sing bum.
And fare ye weel, my pike-staff—
Nae mair with thee my wife I'll baff !
The maut's aboon the meal the nicht
        Wi' some.

Fu' white white was her winding-sheet !
    Sing bum, biberry bum.
Fu' white white was her winding-sheet !
    Sing bum.
I was ower gladsome far to greet,
I danced my lane, and sang to see 't—
The maut's aboon the meal the nicht
        Wi' some.

(2)

WAS there ere sic a parish, a parish, a parish,
    Was there ere sic a parish as Little Dunkeld ?
They've stickit the minister, hanged the precentor,
    Dung doun the steeple, and drucken the bell !

(3)

WE'RE a' dry wi' the drinkin' o't,
    We're a' dry wi' the drinkin' o't,
The minister kissed the fiddler's wife,
    And he couldna preach for thinkin' o't.

baff, beat	*greet,* weep
stickit, stabbed	*dung,* knocked

A WISH

    I wish I was a Bottle !
O' brandy, rum, or what you please,
    In some frequented hottle,
Where gude souls tak their bread an' cheese ;
    To fill out a gill
For some puir chield that wants a trade—
    Or pass o'er the hass
O' some blythe, rantin', roarin' blade ;
  An' while unscrewed, I'd sit an' brood,
    An' think mysel' weel blessed to ken
  That when I dee'd I'd spend my bluid
    To purchase joy for honest men !
                    George Outram.

        hass, throat

128

A WISH

I WISH I was a Bottle!
O, brandy, rum, or what you please,
In some frequented bottle,
Where gude souls tak their bread an' cheese;
To fill out a gill
For some puir chield that wants a trade—
Or pass o'er the bass
O, some blythe, rattlin', roarin' blade;
An', while unscrew'd, I'd sit an' brood,
An' think mysel' weel blessed to ken
That when I dee'd I'd spend my bluid
To purchase joy for honest men!

George Outram.

lass, throat.

BOOK IX
CHARACTERS

To the Quene

THE Wardraipper of Venus' boure,
To giff a doublett he is als doure,
As it war off ane futt syd frog :
   Madame, ye hev a dangerouss Dog !

When that I schawe to him your markis,
He turnis to me again, and barkis,
As he war wirriand ane hog :
   Madame, ye hev a dangerouss Dog !

When that I schawe to him your wryting,
He girnis that I am red for byting ;
I wald he had ane hevye clog :
   Madame, ye hev ane dangerouss Dog !

When that I speik till him freindlyk,
He barkis lyk ane midden tyk,
War chassand cattell through a bog :
   Madame, ye hev a dangerouss Dog !

als doure, as unwilling
ane futt syd frog, (?) an outer coat reaching to the feet
markis, seals   *wirriand*, worrying   *girnis*, shows his teeth
red for byting, afraid of being bitten   *clog*, muzzle
midden tyk, dunghill hound   *chassand*, chasing

He is ane mastyf, mekle of mycht,
To keip your wardroippe ower nycht
Fra the grytt Sowdan Gog-ma-gog :
    Madame, ye hev a dangerouss Dog !

He is owre mekle to be your messan,
Madame, I red you get a less ane,
His gang garris all your chalmeris schog :
    Madame, ye hev a dangerouss Dog !

                    William Dunbar.

130   AGANIS THE THIEVIS OF LIDDISDALE

THAE thiefis that stealis and tursis hame,
Ilk ane of them has ane to-name :
        Will of the Lawis,
        Hab of the Shawis ;
        To mak bare wa's,
They think na shame.

They spuilye puir men of their packis ;
They leif them nocht on bed nor backis ;
        Baith hen and cock,
        With reel and rock,
        The Lairdis Jock
All with him takis.

They leif not spindle, spoon, nor spit,
Bed, bowster, blanket, serk, nor sheet :

mekle of mycht, great of might   *red*, advise
gang garris, etc., walk makes all your chambers shake
tursis, carries off   *to-name*, nickname   *spuilye,* despoil
rock, distaff   *bowster*, bolster

John of the Park
Ripes kist and ark ;
For all sic wark
He is richt meet.

He is weil kend, John of the Side ;
A greater thief did never ride :
He never tires
For to break byres ;
Owre muir and mires
Owre gude ane guide.

There is ane, callit Clement's Hob,
Fra ilk puir wife reifis her wob,
And all the laif,
Whatever they haif :
The devil resave
Therefor his gob ! . . .

Of stouth thoch now they come gude speed
That neither of men nor God has dreid,
Yit, or I die,
Some sall them see
Hing on a tree
Whill they be deid.

Sir Richard Maitland.

ripes kist, ransacks chest		*Owre*, over
wob, web	*laif*, rest	*gob,* belly
stouth, robbery	*or*, before	*whill,* till

131   EPITAPH ON CAPTAIN MATTHEW
                    HENDERSON

STOP, passenger !—my story's brief,
    And truth I shall relate, man ;
I tell nae common tale o' grief—
    For Matthew was a great man.

If thou uncommon merit hast,
    Yet spurn'd at fortune's door, man,
A look of pity hither cast—
    For Matthew was a poor man.

If thou a noble sodger art,
    That passest by this grave, man,
There moulders here a gallant heart—
    For Matthew was a brave man.

If thou on men, their works and ways,
    Canst throw uncommon light, man,
Here lies wha weel had won thy praise—
    For Matthew was a bright man.

If thou at friendship's sacred ca'
    Wad life itself resign, man,
Thy sympathetic tear maun fa'—
    For Matthew was a kind man !

If thou art staunch without a stain,
    Like the unchanging blue, man,
This was a kinsman o' thy ain—
    For Matthew was a true man.

If thou hast wit, and fun, and fire,
　And ne'er guid wine did fear, man,
This was thy billie, dam, and sire—
　For Matthew was a queer man.

If ony whiggish whingin' sot,
　To blame poor Matthew dare, man,
May dool and sorrow be his lot !
　For Matthew was a rare man.

Robert Burns.

132　　　　　THE MILLER

(1)

O MERRY may the maid be
　Who marries wi' the miller,
For foul day or fair day
　He's ay bringing till her ;
Has ay a penny in his pouch,
　Has something het for supper,
Wi' beef and pease, and melting cheese,
　An' lumps o' yellow butter.

Behind the door stand bags o' meal,
　And in the ark is plenty ;
And good hard cakes his mither bakes,
　And mony a sweeter denty.
A good fat sow, a sleeky cow,
　Are standing in the byre ;
Whilst winking puss, wi' mealy mou,
　Is playing round the fire.

billie, brother　　　　*whingin'*, whining
dool, woe　　　　　　*mou*, mouth

Good signs are these, my mither says,
　　And bids me take the miller ;
A miller's wife's a merry wife,
　　And he's ay bringing till her.
For meal or maut she'll never want
　　Till wood and water's scanty ;
As lang as cocks and cackling hens,
　　She'll ay hae eggs in plenty.

In winter time, when wind and sleet
　　Shake ha-house, barn and byre,
He sits aside a clean hearth stane,
　　Before a rousing fire ;
O'er foaming ale he tells his tale ;
　　And ay to show he's happy,
He claps his weans, and dawtes his wife
　　Wi' kisses warm and sappy.
　　　　　　　　　Sir John Clerk of Pennycuik.

(2)

THE miller's rung did deeds o' weir,
　　For mortal fray it aye was ready ;
The miller kent nor sloth nor fear
　　When he fought for king or bonnie leddy !
His head was pruif o' stane or steel,
　　His skin was teucher than bend-leather ;
He could pu' against his ain mill-wheel,
　　Or snap in bits his horse's tether.
　　　　　　　　　　George Outram

maut, malt	*ha-house*, the hall
weans, children	*dawtes*, fondles
rung, staff	*weir*, war
	teucher, tougher

133   THE PARDONER

My patent Pardons, ye may se,
Cum frae the Cane of Tartarie,
    Weill seal'd with oster-schellis.
Thoch ye have na contritioun,
Ye sall have full remissioun,
    With help of buiks and bellis.

Heir is ane relict, lang and braid,
Of Fine Macoull, the richt chaft blaid.
    With teith and al togidder :
Of Colling's cow heir is ane horne,
For eating of Makconnal's corne
    Wes slane into Balquhidder.

Heir is ane cord baith greit and lang,
Whilk hangit Johne the Armistrang,
    Of gude hemp soft and sound :
Gude halie pepill ! I stand for'd
Wha ever beis hangit with this cord
    Neids never to be drownd.

The culum of Sanct Bryd's cow,
The gruntill of Sanct Antonis sow,
    Whilk buir his halie bell ;
Wha ever he be heiris this bell clink,
Gif me ane ducat for till drink,
    He sall never gang to hell.

                        Sir David Lyndsay.

chaft, jaw   *culum*, tail   *gruntill*, snout
(2,470)   8

134   THE SOUTERS OF SELKIRK

Up wi' the souters of Selkirk,
  And down wi' the Earl of Home ;
And up wi' a' the braw lads
  Wha sew the single-soled shoon !
O ! fye upon yellow and yellow,
  And fye upon yellow and green ;
But up wi' the true blue and scarlet,
  And up wi' the single-soled shoon !

Up wi' the souters of Selkirk—
  Up wi' the lingle and last !
There's fame wi' the days that's comin',
  And glory wi' them that are past :
Up wi' the souters of Selkirk—
  Lads that are trusty and leal ;
And up wi' the men of the Forest,
  And down wi' the Merse to the Deil !

O ! mitres are made for noddles,
  But feet they are made for shoon :
And fame is as sib to Selkirk
  As light is true to the mune :
There sits a souter in Selkirk
  Wha sings as he draws his thread—
There's gallant souters in Selkirk
  As lang's there's water in Tweed.

souters, shoemakers   *shoon*, shoes   *sib*, kin

135 THE EPITAPH OF HABBIE SIMSON,
          PIPER OF KILBARCHAN

> KILBARCHAN now may say alas !
> For she hath lost her game and grace,
> Both *Trixie* and *The Maiden Trace* :
>   But what remead ?
> For no man can supply his place :
>   Hab Simson's dead.
>
> Now who shall play *The Day it Dawis*,
> Or *Hunts Up*, when the cock he craws ?
> Or who can for our kirk-town cause
>   Stand us in stead ?
> On bagpipes now nobody blaws
>   Sen Habbie's dead.
>
> Or who will cause our shearers shear ?
> Wha will bend up the brags of weir,
> Bring in the bells, or good play-meir
>   In time of need ?
> Hab Simson could, what needs you speir,
>   But now he's dead.
>
> So kindly to his neighbours neist
> At Beltan and St. Berchan's feast
> He blew, and then held up his breast,
>   As he were weid ;
> But now we need not him arrest,
>   For Habbie's dead.

remead, remedy
bend up the brags of weir, bear up the brags of war (a game)
play-meir, hobby-horse   *speir*, ask
neist, next   *weid*, mad

At fairs he play'd before the spear-men,
All gaily graithed in their gear, man :
Steel bonnets, jacks, and swords so clear then
    Like ony bead :
Now wha will play before such weir-men
    Sen Habbie's dead ?

At clerk-plays when he wont to come,
His pipe played trimly to the drum ;
Like bikes of bees he gart it hum,
    And tun'd his reed :
Now all our pipers may sing dumb,
    Sen Habbie's dead.

And at horse races many a day,
Before the black, the brown, the grey,
He gart his pipe, when he did play,
    Baith skirl and skreed :
Now all such pastime's quite away
    Sen Habbie's dead.

He counted was a waled wight-man,
And fiercely at football he ran :
At every game the gree he wan
    For pith and speed.
The like of Habbie was na than,
    But now he's dead.

And then, besides his valiant acts,
At bridals he wan many placks ;

graithed, clad   *weir-men,* men of war
waled wight-man, picked strong man
gree, prize   *placks,* small coins

He bobbit ay behind folk's backs
    And shook his head.
Now we want many merry cracks
    Sen Habbie's dead.

He was a convoyer of the bride,
With Kittock hanging at his side ;
About the kirk he thought a pride
    The ring to lead :
But now we may gae but a guide,
    For Habbie's dead.

So well's he keeped his decorum,
And all the stots of *Whip-meg-morum ;*
He slew a man, and wae's me for him,
    And bure the feid !
But yet the man wan hame before him,
    And was not dead.

And when he play'd, the lasses leugh
To see him teethless, auld, and teugh.
He wan his pipes besides Barcleugh,
    Withouten dread !
Which after wan him gear eneugh ;
    But now he's dead.

Ay when he play'd the gaislings gedder'd,
And when he spake the carl bleddered,

cracks, talks   *the ring*, the bridal procession
but, without   *stots*, turnings of a tune
feid, feud   *the gaislings gedder'd*, the goslings gathered
the carl bleddered, the old man babbled

On Sabbath days his cap was fedder'd,
    A seemly weid ;
In the kirk-yeard his mare stood tedder'd,
    Where he lies dead.

Alas ! for him my heart is sair,
For of his spring I gat a skair,
At every play, race, feast, or fair,
    But guile or dread ;
We need not look for piping mair,
    Sen Habbie's dead.

Sir Robert Sempill of Beltrees.

136   THE BEADLE'S LAMENT

NAE mair, auld Sabbath Book, nae mair
Shall we twa tak' the poopit stair ;
Aneth my airm wi' decent care
    Ye've traivelled lang ;
But noo, like bauchles past repair,
    We twa maun gang.

For yon sleek Herd, wi' face o' whey,
Wha cam' last Spring frae yont Glenspey,
Has set his will, has wrocht his wey,
    Wi' laird and cottar ;
Till e'en the Session are as cley,
    And he the potter !

fedder'd, feathered	*weid*, dress
skair, share	*But*, without
poopit, pulpit	*bauchles*, old shoes

He's turned the auld kirk upside-doon ;
Pentit the wa's blue, green, and broun ;
The book-brod, tossled roun' and roun',
    Glowers wi' red, plush on't ;
And in the pews ilk glaiket loon
    Cocks whare he's cushion'd !

The douce precentor, Dauvit Parks,
Nae mair in his bit boxie barks ;
An organ, stuffed wi' water-warks,
    Mak's a' lugs dirl :
And twa-three lads in lang white sarks
    Start aff the skirl.

A braw new Bible has been bocht,—
Revised, to clink wi' Modern Thocht ;
A braw new beadle has been socht,
    Soople and snod ;
And this new Herd, himsel' has wrocht
    A braw new God !

A God wha wadna fricht the craws ;
A God wha never lifts the taws ;
Wha never heard o' Moses' laws,
    On stane or paper ;
A kind o' thowless Great First Cause,
    Skinklin' thro' vapour.

As for the Bible, if you please,
He thinks it's true,—in twa degrees ;

glaiket, foolish-faced   *lugs,* ears   *dirl,* hum
skirl, noise   *soople and snod,* supple and neat
taws, implement of punishment   *thowless,* thoughtless

Some pairt is chalk, some pairt is cheese ;
    But he'll engage
To riddle oot the biggest lees
    Frae ilka page !

The Fall, he thinks, is nocht but fable ;
Adam ne'er delved, nor killed was Abel ;
Men never built the Tower of Babel ;
    Nor lenched an Ark ;
While auld Methuselah's birthday-table
    Clean jumps the mark !

No that he says sic things straucht oot ;
Lord ! he's as sly's Loch Leven troot ;
But here wi' Science, there wi' Doot
    He crams his sermons ;
Thrawin' the plainest text aboot
    To please the Germans.

The auld blue Hell he thinks a haiver ;
The auld black Deil a kintry claver ;
And what is Sin, but saut to savour
    Mankind's wersh luggies ?
While Saunts, if ye'd believe the shaver,
    Are kirk-gaun puggies !

The Lord have mercy on sic teachin'
And on the kirk that tholes sic speech in ;

Thrawin', twisting	*haiver*, piece of nonsense
kintry claver, country fable	*wersh luggies*, tasteless dishes
kirk-gaun puggies, church-going apes	*tholes*, endures

A heathen-man, wi' heathen screechin',
 Were less to blame ;
Satan himsel' would damn sic preachin'
 For very shame !

Oh ! for the days when sinners shook
Aneth the true Herd's righteous crook ;
When men were telt that this auld Book
 Is God's ain Word ;
When texts were stanes waled frae the brook,
 And prayer a sword.

Four ministers I've seen ta'en ower
To yon kirkyaird ; and a' the four
Were men o' prayer, were men o' power,
 In kirk and session ;
Preachers wha nailed ye wi' a glower
 To your transgression.

Oh ! for sic men o' godly zeal ;
Men wha could grab ye, head and heel, .
And slype ye to the Muckle Deil,
 Withoot a qualm ;
The sinner thro' the reek micht squeal,—
 They sang a psalm !

Stout Herds were they, and steeve their creed :
But this chiel drones a wee bit screed,
In which God's will, and what Christ dreed,
 Are things to guess on ;
Yammers for our Eternal need
 A bairn's schule-lesson.

waled, picked	*glower*, glare	*slype*, fling
steeve, firm	*dreed*, suffered	*Yammers*. prattles

(2,470)

8 *a*

A wee schule-lesson dull and dowff ;
Scribbled atween twa games at gowff ;
For at the tee he mak's his howff
    Baith syne and sune :
But wha cares for a beadle's bowff
    Wha's day is dune.

My day is dune ; and richt or wrang
The thocht comes like a waefu' sang ;
This Book and me, we've traivelled lang
    The poopit stair ;
But that's a gate we twa shall gang
    Nae mair, nae mair.

                 Hamish Hendry.

137   THE AUCTIONEER

THERE's nae sic men a-makin' noo
  As ane I kent near Robslaw quarries ;
His een are closed, cauld, cauld his broo,
  He's deen wi' a' life's cares and sharries :
    Daavit Drain o' Hirpletillim,
    Drink never yet was brewed wad fill him ;
    Stout an' swack, broad breist, straucht back,
    Gied strength and swing to Hirpletillim.

At kirk and market, Daavit Drain
  Ower elder, factor, got a hearin' ;

dowff, dreary	*gowff*, golf	*howff*, resort
bowff, bark	*gate*, road	*deen*, done
sharries, troubles	*swack*, massive	

On dootfu' pints to mak' things plain
  He exerceesed the gift o' swearin' :
    Daavit Drain o' Hirpletillim,
     Storm and stour ne'er dang could kill him ;
     Up wi' the lark—fae morn to dark
     Was heard the soun' o' Hirpletillim.

He held things gaun in barn and byre,
  At judgin' stock he own'd nae marrow ;
'Nent horse and nowt he'd never tire,
  His skill confoonit Farrier Harrow :
    Daavit Drain o' Hirpletillim,
     Wi' fear nae soul micht try instil him ;
     Even Ury's laird, wi' feint and gaird,
     Was scarce a match for Hirpletillim.

Bauld Daavit was an unctioneer,
  At plenishin's he flourish't bravely ;
His " Going, gone " rang firm and clear,
  Slow higglers he admonished gravely :
    Daavit Drain o' Hirpletillim,
     What mortal born could e'er ill-will him ?
     But noo he's gane—and 'neath yon stane
     Nae bode can wauken Hirpletillim.
                William Carnie.

stour, dust	*dang*, struck	*marrow*, equal
nowt, cattle		*unctioneer*, auctioneer
plenishin's, sales of furniture		*bode*, bid at an auction

O THOU, wha in the heavens dost dwell,
Wha, as it pleases best Thysel',
Sends ane to heaven, and ten to hell,
        A' for Thy glory,
And no' for ony guid or ill
        They've done afore Thee !

I bless and praise Thy matchless might,
When thousands Thou hast left in night,
That I am here, afore Thy sight,
        For gifts an' grace,
A burning an' a shining light
        To a' this place.

What was I, or my generation,
That I should get sic exaltation ?
I, wha deserve sic just damnation,
        For broken laws,
Sax thousand years 'fore my creation,
        Thro' Adam's cause.

When frae my mither's womb I fell,
Thou might hae plung'd me into hell,
To gnash my gums, to weep and wail,
        In burnin' lake,
Whare damnèd devils roar and yell,
        Chain'd to a stake.

Yet I am here, a chosen sample,
To show Thy grace is great and ample ;

I'm here a pillar o' Thy temple,
    Strong as a rock,
A guide, a buckler, and example
    To a' Thy flock.

But yet, O Lord! confess I must,
At times I'm fash'd wi' fleshly lust;
And sometimes, too, wi' warldly trust,
    Vile self gets in;
But Thou remembers we are dust,
    Defil'd in sin. . . .

Maybe Thou lets this fleshly thorn
Buffet Thy servant e'en and morn,
Lest he owre high and proud should turn,
    That he's sae gifted;
If sae, Thy han' maun e'en be borne,
    Until Thou lift it.

Lord, bless Thy chosen in this place,
For here Thou hast a chosen race!
But God confound their stubborn face,
    And blast their name,
Wha bring Thy elders to disgrace,
    An' open shame. . . .

.   .   .   .   .

But, Lord, remember me and mine,
Wi' mercies temporal and divine,
That I for grace an' gear may shine,
    Excell'd by nane;
An' a' the glory shall be Thine—
    Amen, Amen!

Robert Burns.

139

THE TINKLERS

THE mist lies like a plaid on plain,
The dyke-taps a' are black wi' rain,
A soakit head the clover hings,
On ilka puddle rise the rings.

Sair dings the rain upon the road,—
It dings, an' nae devallin' o'd ;
Adoun the gutter rins a rill
Micht halflins ca' a country mill.

The very roadman's left the road :
The only kind o' beas' abroad
Are dyucks, rejoicin' i' the flood,
An' pyots, clatterin' i' the wud.

On sic a day wha tak's the gate ?
The cadger ? maybe ; but he's late.
The carrier ? na ! he doesna flit
Unless, *D.V.*, the pooers permit.

On sic a day wha tak's the gate ?
The tinkler, an' his tousie mate ;
He foremost, wi' a nose o' flint,
She sour an' sulky, yards ahint.

A blanket, fra her shouthers doun,
Wraps her an' a' her bundles roun' ;
A second rain rins aff the skirt ;
She skelps alang through dub an' dirt.

dings, beats	*devallin'*, ceasing	*pyots*, magpies
gate, road	*D.V.*, Deo volente	*tousie*, dishevelled
ahint, behind	*skelps*, clatters	*dub*, puddle

Her cheeks are red, her een are sma',
Her head wi' rain-draps beadit a' ;
The yellow hair, like wires o' bress,
Springs, thrivin' in the rain, like gress.

Her man an' maister stalks in front,
Silent mair than a tinkler's wont ;
His wife an' warkshop there ahint him,—
This day he caresna if he tint them.

His hands are in his pouches deep,
He snooves alang like ane in sleep,
His only movement's o' his legs,
He carries a' aboon like eggs.

Sma' wecht ! his skeleton an' skin,
And a dour heavy thocht within.
His claes, sae weel wi' weet they suit him,
They're like a second skin aboot him.

They're doun the road, they're oot o' sicht ;
They'll reach the howff by fa' o' nicht,
In Poussie Nancy's cowp the horn,
An' tak' the wanderin' gate the morn.

They'll give their weasands there a weet,
Wi' kindred bodies there they'll meet,
Wi' drookit gangrels o' the clan,
The surgeons o' the pat an' pan.

tint, lost	*snooves*, shuffles	*wecht*, weight
claes, clothes	*howff*, shelter	*cowp*, turn up
weasands, throats	*drookit*, drenched	*gangrels*, tramps

Already on the rain-washed wa'
A darker gloom begins to fa';
Sooms fra the sicht the soakin' plain,—
It's closin' for a nicht o' rain.

James Logie Robertson.

sooms, swims

BOOK X
LITERATURE

THE ORIGIN OF POETRY

WHAT'S a' your jargon o' your schools,
Your Latin names for horns an' stools ;
If honest Nature made you fools,
    What sairs your grammars ?
Ye'd better ta'en up spades and shools,
      Or knappin-hammers.

A set o' dull, conceited hashes,
Confuse their brains in college classes !
They gang in stirks, and come out asses,
    Plain truth to speak ;
And syne they think to climb Parnassus
      By dint o' Greek !

Gie me ae spark o' Nature's fire !
That's a' the learning I desire ;
Then, though I drudge thro' dub and mire
    At pleugh or cart,
My Muse, though hamely in attire,
      May touch the heart.
              Robert Burns.

sairs, serves   *shools*, shovels
knappin, stone-breaking   *stirks*, young bullocks
        dub, puddle

141   HELICON

> THE Muse, nae poet ever fand her,
> Till by himsel' he learn'd to wander,
> Adown some trottin' burn's meander
>   An no think lang ;
> O sweet to stray an' pensive ponder
>   A heart-felt sang !
>
> Robert Burns.

142   DUNBAR TO HIS MASTERS

> O REUEREND Chaucere, rose of rethoris all,
> As in oure tong ane flour imperiall,
>   That raise in Britane evir, who redis rycht,
> Thou bearis of makaris the tryumph riall ;
> Thy fresch anamalit termes celicall
>   This mater coud illumynit have full brycht :
>   Was thou noucht of our Inglisch all the lycht,
> Surmounting eviry tong terrestriall,
>   Alls fer as Mayes morow dois mydnycht ?
>
> O morall Gower, and Lydgate laureate,
> Your sugurit lippis and tongis aureate,
>   Bene to oure eris cause of grete delyte ;
> Your angel mouthis most mellifluate
> Our rude langage has clere illumynate,

fand, found	*makaris,* poets
anamalit, enamelled	*celicall,* heavenly

And faire our-gilt oure speche, that imperfyte
   Stude, or your goldyn pennis schupe to wryte ;
This Ile before was bare, and desolate
   Off rethorike, or lusty fresch endyte.

Thou lytill Quair, be evir obedient,
Humble, subiect, and symple of entent,
   Before the face of eviry connyng wicht :
I knaw what thou of rethorike hes spent ;
Off all hir lusty rosis redolent
   Is nonn in to thy gerland sette on hicht ;
   Eschame thar of, and draw the out of sicht.
Rude is thy wede, disteynit, bare, and rent,
   Wel aucht thou be afferit of the licht.
                  William Dunbar.

143   LAMENT OF THE MAKARIS

   I THAT in heill wes and glaidnes,
   Am trublit now with grit seiknes
   And feblit with infirmitie :
     Timor Mortis conturbat me.

   Our plesance heir is all vain glory,
   This fals world is bot transitory,
   The flesh is brukle, the Feynd is sle :
     Timor Mortis conturbat me.

or, ere	*schupe*, began	*endyte*, writing
Quair, book		*connyng wicht*, connoisseur
eschame thar of, be ashamed thereof		*wede*, garment
afferit, afraid	*heill*, health	*plesance*, pleasure
brukle, frail	*sle*, sly	

The state of man dois change and vary,
Now sound, now seik, now blyth, now sary,
Now dansand mirry, now like to de :
    Timor Mortis conturbat me.

No state in Erd heir standis sicker ;
As with the wind wavis the wicker,
So wavis this warldis vanitie :
    Timor Mortis conturbat me.

Unto the Deth gois all estaitis,
Princis, prelattis and potestaitis,
Bayth rich and pure of all degree :
    Timor Mortis conturbat me.

He taikis the knychtis in to the feild
Enarmit under helme and scheild ;
Victor he is at all mellie :
    Timor Mortis conturbat me.

That strang unmerciful tyrand
Takis on the muderis breist sowkand
The bab, full of benignitie :
    Timor Mortis conturbat me.

He taikis the campioun in the stour,
The capitane closit in the tour,
The lady in bour full of bewtie :
    Timor Mortis conturbat me.

sary, sorry   *sicker,* sure   *mellie,* mêlée
campioun, champion   *stour,* dust

He spairis no lord for his puissance,
Nor clerk for his intelligens ;
His awful straik may no man fle :
  Timor Mortis conturbat me.

Art, magicianis and astrologis,
Rethoris, logicianis and theologis,
Them helpis no conclusionis sle :
  Timor Mortis conturbat me.

In medicyne the most practitianis,
Leichis, surrigianis and phisicianis,
Them self fra Deth may not supple :
  Timor Mortis conturbat me.

I see that makaris amang the laif
Playis heir thair pageant, syne gois to graif ;
Sparit is nocht thair facultie :
  Timor Mortis conturbat me.

He hes done petouslie devour
The noble Chaucer of makaris flouir,
The Monk of Berry, and Gowyir, all thre :
  Timor Mortis conturbat me.

The gude Schir Hew of Eglintoun,
Ettrik, Heryot, and Wyntoun,
He hes tane out of this countrie :
  Timor Mortis conturbat me.

sle, clever	*supple*, rescue
the laif, the rest	*graif*, grave

That scorpioun fell hes done infek
Maister Johine Clerk and James Afflek,
Fra balat-making and tragedie :
    Timor Mortis conturbat me.

Holland and Barbour he has berevit ;
Allace ! that he nocht with us levit
Schir Mungo Lokkart of the Le :
    Timor Mortis conturbat me.

Clerk of Tranent eik he has tane,
That made the Awnteris of Schir Gawane ;
Schir Gilbert Hay endid has he :
    Timor Mortis conturbat me.

He has Blind Hary and Sandy Traill
Slain with his schot of mortal haill,
Whilk Patrik Johnstoun mycht nocht fle :
    Timor Mortis conturbat me.

He has reft Mersar his indyte,
That did in luve so lyfly wryte,
So schort, so quick, of sentens hie :
    Timor Mortis conturbat me.

He has tane Roull of Aberdene,
And gentle Roull of Corstorphyne ;
Twa bettir fallowis did no man sie :
    Timor Mortis conturbat me.

In Dumfermelyne he hes done roune
With Maister Robert Henrisoun ;
Schir John the Ross embrast hes he :
    Timor Mortis conturbat me.

Awnteris, adventures   *in luve,* on love
         done roune, whispered

And he has now tane, last of aw,
Gude gentill Stobo and Quintyne Schaw,
Of whom all wichtis has pitie :
    Timor Mortis conturbat me.

Gude Maistir Walter Kennedy
In poynt of deth lyis veraly ;
Grit rewth it wer that so suld be :
    Timor Mortis conturbat me.

Sen he has all my brether tane,
He will nocht lat me leif allane,
On forss I mon his nixt prey be :
    Timor Mortis conturbat me.

Sen for the deid remeid is none,
Best is that we for deth dispone,
Eftir our deth that leif may we :
    Timor Mortis conturbat me.

                William Dunbar.

144   THERE WAS A LAD WAS BORN IN KYLE

THERE was a lad was born in Kyle,
But whatna day o' whatna style
I doubt it's hardly worth the while
    To be sae nice wi' Robin.
      Robin was a rovin boy
        Rantin rovin, rantin rovin ;
      Robin was a rovin boy,
        Rantin rovin Robin !

rewth, pity   *on forss,* of necessity
       dispone, dispose ourselves

Our monarch's hindmost year but ane
Was five and twenty days begun,
'Twas then a blast o' Janwar win'
    Blew hansel in on Robin.

The gossip keekit in his loof,
Quo' she, " Wha lives will see the proof,
This waly boy will be nae coof—
    I think we'll ca' him Robin.

" He'll hae misfortunes great and sma',
But aye a heart aboon them a' ;
He'll be a credit till us a'
    We'll a' be proud o' Robin." . . .
                   Robert Burns.

145   THEOCRITUS IN SCOTS

THE FISHERS (Idyll xxi.)

'TIS puirtith sooples heid and hand
And gars inventions fill the land ;
And dreams come fast to folk that lie
Wi' nocht atween them and the sky.

Twae collier lads frae near Lasswade,
Auld skeely fishers, fand their bed
Ae simmer's nicht aside the shaw
Whaur Manor rins by Cademuir Law,
Dry flowe-moss made them pillows fine,
And, for a bield to kep the win',

Janwar, January   *hansel*, the first gift in the New Year
keekit, glanced   *loof*, palm   *waly*, sturdy   *coof*, fool

A muckle craig owerhung the burn,
A' thacked wi' blaeberry and fern.
Aside them lay their rods and reels,
Their flee-books and their auncient creels.
The pooches o' their moleskin breeks
Contained unlawfu' things like cleeks,
For folk that fish to fill their wame
Are no fasteedious at the game.
The twae aye took their jaunts thegither ;
Geordie was ane and Tam the ither.
Their chaumer was the mune-bricht sky,
The siller stream their lullaby.

When knocks in touns were chappin' three,
Tam woke and rubbed a blinkin' e'e.
It was the 'oor when troots are boun'
To gulp the May-flee floatin' doun,
Afore the sun is in the glens
And dim are a' the heughs and dens.

TAM : " Short is the simmer's daurk, they say,
But this ane seemed as lang's the day ;
For siccan dreams as passed my sicht
I never saw in Januar' nicht.
If some auld prophet chiel were here
I wad hae curious things to speir."

GEORDIE : " It's conscience gars the nichtmares rin,
Sae, Tam, my lad, what hae ye dune ? "

pooches, pockets   *wame*, belly
chaumer, chamber   *knocks*, clocks

TAM : " Nae ill ; my saul is free frae blame,
        Nor hae I wrocht ower hard my wame,
        For last I fed, as ye maun awn,
        On a sma' troot and pease-meal scone.
        But hear my dreams, for aiblins you
        May find a way to riddle't true. . . .

        " I thocht that I was castin' steady
        At the pule's tail ayont the smiddy,
        Wi' finest gut and sma'est flee,
        For the air was clear and the water wee ;
        When sudden wi' a rowst and swish
        I rase a maist enormous fish . . .
        I struck and heuked the monster shure.
        Guidsakes ! to see him loup in air !
        It was nae saumon, na, nor troot ;
        To the last yaird my line gaed oot,
        As up the stream the warlock ran
        As wild as Job's Leviathan.
        I got him stopped below the linn,
        Whaur verra near I tumbled in,
        Aye prayin' hard my heuk wad haud ;
        And syne he turned a dorty jaud,
        Sulkin' far doun amang the stanes.
        I tapped the butt to stir his banes.
        He warsled here and plowtered there,
        But still I held him ticht and fair,
        The water rinnin' oxter-hie,
        The sweat aye drippin' in my e'e.
        Sae bit by bit I wysed him richt
        And broke his stieve and fashious micht,

aiblins, perhaps   dorty, sulky   oxter-hie, breast-high
wysed, guided   stieve and fashious, strong and troublesome

Til sair fordone he cam to book
And walloped in a shallow crook.
I had nae gad, sae doun my wand
I flang and pinned him on the sand.
I claucht him in baith airms and peched
Ashore—he was a michty wecht ;
Nor stopped till I had got him sure
Amang the threshes on the muir.

"Then, Geordie lad, my een I rowed :
The beast was made o' solid gowd !—
Sic ferlie as was never kenned,
A' glitterin' gowd frae end to end !
I lauched, I grat, my kep I flang,
I danced a step, I sang a sang.
And syne I wished that I micht dee
If wark again was touched by me. . . .

"Wi' that I woke ; nae fish was there—
Juist the burnside and empty muir.
Noo tell me honest, Geordie lad,
Think ye yon daftlike aith will haud ? "

GEORDIE : "Tuts, Tam, ye fule, the aith ye sware
Was like your fish, nae less, nae mair.
For dreams are nocht but simmer rouk,
And him that trusts them hunts the gowk. . . .
It's time we catched some fish o' flesh
Or we will baith gang brekfastless."

John Buchan.

gad, gaff   *peched,* panted   *ferlie,* marvel   *rouk,* mist

VIRGIL IN SCOTS

The Entrance to Hell

(*Æneid* VI. 268–284)

THAY walkit furth so derk oneith they wist
Whidder thay went amyddis dim schaddois thare,
Whare ever is nicht, and never licht doth repare,
Throwout the waste dungeoun of Pluto king,
Thay roid boundis and the gousty ring ;
Siklyke as wha wald throw thick woodis wend,
In obscure light whare none may not be kend,
As Jupiter the king etherial
With erdis skug hydis the hevynnys al,
And the mirk nicht with her vysage gray
From every thing has reft the hew away.

  Befor the portis and first jawis of hel
Lamentacioun and wraikful Thochtis fel
Thare loging had, and thereat dwellis eik
Pale Maledyis that causis man be seik,
The fereful Drede and als unweildy Age,
The felone Hunger with her undantit rage :
There was also the laithly Indigence,
Terribil of schape and schameful her presence ;
The grisly Dede that mony ane has slane,
The hard Laubour and diseisful Pane,

    oneith, scarcely   *siklyke*, just as one
    erdis skug, earth's shadow   *portis*, gates
    wraikful, revengeful   *eik*, also   *Drede*, fear
    laithly, loathsome   *Dede*, death

The slottry Slepe Dedis cousin of kynd,
Inordinat Blithnes of perversit mind :
And in the yett, forganis thaym did stand
The mortal Battel with his dedely brand,
The irne chaimeris of hellis Furies fel,
Witles Discord, that woundring maist cruel.
Womplit and buskit in ane bludy bend,
With snakis hung at every haris end.
And in the myddis of the uttir ward,
With brade branchis sprede over al the sward,
Ane rank elme tre stude, huge, grete and stok auld.
The vulgar pepil in that samyn hauld
Belevis thare vane Dremes makis thare dwelling,
Under ilk leif ful thik they stik and hing.

Gawain Douglas.

147   HORACE IN SCOTS

(1)

Car. III. 15

KIRSTY, ye besom ! auld an' grey,
    Peer Sandy's wrunkled kimmer,
Death's at your elbuck, cease to play
    Baith hame an' furth the limmer.

Ongauns like yours lads weel may fleg
    Fae lasses a' thegither ;

slottry, sluggish	*yett*, gate	*forganis*, over against
irne chalmeris, iron chambers		*woundring*, monster
Womplit, wimpled, folded		*buskit*, arrayed
bend, fillet	*stok auld*, old in trunk	*samyn*, same
elbuck, elbow	*limmer*, wanton	*fleg*, frighten

Tibbie may fling a wanton leg
    Would ill set you her mither.

She Anra's bothy sneck may tirl
    An' loup like ony filly ;
Love stirs her as the pipers' skirl
    Some kiltit Hielan' billie.

Nane pledge or bring you posies noo ;
    Auld wives nae trumps set strummin',
For runts like you the Cabrach woo'—
    It's time your wheel was bummin'.

Charles Murray.

(2)

Epod. II

HAPPY is he, far fae the toon's alairm
Wha wons contentit on his forbears' fairm ;
Whistlin' ahint his owsen at the ploo,
Oonfashed wi' siller lent or int'rest due.
Nae sodger he, that's piped to wark an' meat,
Nae bar'fit sailor, fleyed at wind an' weet,
Schoolboard nor Sessions tempt him fae his hame,
Provost or Bailie never heard his name ;
His business 'tis to sned the larick trees
For lichened hag to stake his early peas,
Or on his plaid amang the braes to lie
Herdin' his sleekit stots an' hummel kye,
Here wi' his whittle nick a sooker saft,
There mark a stooter shank for future graft ;
Whiles fae a skep a dreepin' comb he steals,
Or clips the doddit yowes for winter wheels.

sneck, latch   *runt*, hag   *hag*, branch   *doddit*, hornless

When ower the crafts blythe Autumn lifts her head
Buskit wi' aipples ripe an' roddens red,
He speels the trees the hazel nits to pu',
An' rasps an' aivrins fill his bonnet fu'. . . .
When stormy winter comes an' in its train
Brings drivin' drift an' spates o' plashin' rain,
Wi' dog an' ferret then he's roon the parks
Whaur rabbits in the snaw hae left their marks ;
Or brings wi' smorin' sulphur thuddin' doon
The roostin' pheasant fae the boughs aboon,
Or daunders furth wi' girn an' gun to kill
White hares an' ptarmigan upon the hill.
Wha 'mid sic joys would ever stop to fash
Wi' trystin' queyns, their valinteens an' trash ?
But gin a sonsy wife be his, she'll help
Wi' household jots, the weans she'll clead an' skelp
An'—Buchan kimmers ken the way fu' weel
Or Hielan' hizzies—tenty toom the creel
O' lang hained heath'ry truffs to reist the fire
Against her man's return, fair dead wi' tire,
An' byre-ward clatter in her creeshie brogues,
Syne fae the press the cakes an' kebbuck draw
An' hame-brewed drink nae gauger ever saw—
Plain simple fare ; could partans better please
Or skate or turbot fae the furthest seas,

crafts, small farms	*roddens*, rowans	*speels*, climbs
aivrins, cloudberries	*smorin'*, suffocating	*girn*, snare
fash, trouble	*trystin' queyns*, girls making assignations	
sonsy, comely	*jots*, jobs	*clead*, clothe
skelp, spank	*kimmers*, wives	*hizzies*, hussies
tenty toom, carefully empty		*lang hained*, long stored
truffs, peats	*reist*, bank up	*creeshie*, well-greased
	kebbuck, cheese	*partans*, crabs

Brocht to the market by the trawler's airt,
Hawkit fae barrows or the cadger's cairt ?
Nae frozen dainties, nae importit meat,
Nae foreign galshochs, taste they e'er sae sweet,
But I will match them fast as ye can name
Wi' simple berries that we grow at hame—
Wi' burnside soorocks that ye pu' yoursel',
Wi' buttered brose, an' chappit curly kail,
Wi' mealy puddins fae the new killed mart,
Or hill-fed braxy that the tod has spar'd.
What happier life than this for young or auld ?
To see the blackfaced wethers seek the fauld,
The reekin' owsen fae the fur' set free
Wear slowly hamewith ower the gowan'd lea,
An' gabbin' servants fae the field an' byre
Scorchin' their moleskins at the kitchen fire.

The banker swore 'mid siccan scenes to die,
" Back to the land " was daily his refrain ;
A fortnicht syne he laid his ledgers by,
The nicht he's castin' his accounts again !

Charles Murray.

148   HEINE IN SCOTS

(1)

THE GRAVE OF LOVE
(Die alten bösen Lieder)

Lyrischer Intermezzo 65

THE auld sangs soored and cankered,
Ill dreams that keep me fleyed,—
Let's get a michty coffin,
And stow them a' inside.

galshochs, kickshaws   *tod*, fox   *hamewith*, homeward

There's muckle I maun lay there,
  Though what I daurna tell ;
The coffin maun be bigger
  Than St. Andrews' auld draw-well.

And bring a bier, weel-timmered,
  O' brods baith lang and wide :
Needs be they maun be longer
  Than the auld brig ower the Clyde.

And bring me twal' great giants,
  A' men o' muckle worth—
As strang as William Wallace
  That looks across the Forth.

And they maun tak' the coffin
  And sink it in the wave,
For sic a michty coffin
  Maun hae a michty grave.

D'ye ken what way the coffin
  Maun be sae great and strang ?
It's my love I mean to lay there,
  And the dule I've tholed sae lang.

(2)
THE KINGS FROM THE EAST
(Die heil'gen drei Kön'ge aus Morgenland)

Die Heimkehr 39

THERE were three kings cam' frae the East ;
  They spiered in ilka clachan :

weel-timmered, well-timbered		*brods*, boards
twal', twelve	*dule*, sorrow	*tholed*, borne
spiered, inquired	*ilka clachan*, each village	

" O, which is the way to Bethlehem,
  My bairns, sae bonnily lachin' ? "

O neither young nor auld could tell ;
  They trailed till their feet were weary
They followed a bonny gowden starn
  That shone in the lift sae cheery.

The starn stude ower the ale-hoose byre
  Whaur the stable gear was hingin' ;
The owsen mooed, the bairnie grat,
  The kings begoud their singin'.

(3)

LASSIE, WHAT MAIR WAD YE HAE ?
(Du hast Diamenten und Perlen)
Die Heimkehr 64

O, YOU'RE braw wi' your pearls and your diamonds,
  You've routh o' a' thing, you may say,
And there's nane has got bonnier een, Kate :
  'Od, lassie, what mair wad you hae ?

I've written a hantle o' verses,
  That'll live till the Hendmost Day ;
And they're a' in praise o' your een, Kate ;
  'Od, lassie, what mair wad you hae ?

Your een, sae blue and sae bonny,
  Have plagued me till I am fey ;
'Deed, I hardly think I can live, Kate :
  'Od, lassie, what mair wad you hae ?

Alexander Gray.

lachin', laughing	*gowden starn*, golden star	
lift, sky	*stude*, stood	*owsen*, oxen
grat, wept	*begoud*, began	*routh*, plenty
hantle, number	*Hendmost*, last	*fey*, crazy

BOOK XI
SPORT

WHEN Winter muffles up his cloak,
And binds the mire up like a rock ;
When to the lochs the curlers flock,
      Wi' gleesome speed,
Wha will they station at the cock ?—
        Tam Samson's dead !

He was the king o' a' the core,
To guard, or draw, or wick a bore ;
Or up the rink like Jehu roar
      In time o' need ;
But now he lags on Death's hog-score--
        Tam Samson's dead !

Now safe the stately sawmont sail,
And trouts bedropp'd wi' crimson hail,
And eels weel kenn'd for souple tail,
      And geds for greed,
Since, dark in Death's fish-creel, we wail
        Tam Samson dead !

cock, mark   *core*, company
to guard, or draw, etc. (in curling), to defend a stone, to send
    it into a better position, and to drive it through an
    opening
hog-score, the line which a stone must pass to be in play
sawmont, salmon   *geds*, pikes

Rejoice, ye birring paitricks a' ;
Ye cootie moorcocks, crousely craw ;
Ye maukins, cock your fud fu' braw,
        Withouten dread ;
Your mortal fae is now awa'—
        Tam Samson's dead !

That waefu' morn be ever mourn'd
Saw him in shootin' graith adorn'd,
While pointers round impatient burn'd,
        Frae couples freed ;
But, och ! he gaed and ne'er return'd :
        Tam Samson's dead !

                     Robert Burns.

150   BALLADE OF THE TWEED

THE ferox rins in rough Loch Awe,
   A weary cry frae ony toun ;
The Spey, that loups o'er linn and fa',
   They praise a' ither streams aboon ;
   They boast their braes o' bonny Doon :
Gie *me* to hear the ringing reel,
   Where shilfas sing and cushats croon
By fair Tweed-side, at Ashiesteel !

There's Ettrick, Meggat, Ail, and a',
   Where trout swim thick in May and June ;

paitricks, partridges	*cootie*, leg-feathered
maukins, hares	*fud*, tail
graith, attire	*couples*, leashes
loups, leaps	*shilfas*, chaffinches
cushats, wood-doves	

Ye'll see them tak in showers o' snaw
    Some blinking, cauldrife April noon :
    Rax ower the palmer and march-broun,
And syne we'll show a bonny creel,
    In spring or simmer, late or soon,
By fair Tweed-side, at Ashiesteel !

There's mony a water, great or sma',
    Gaes singing in his siller tune,
Through glen and heugh, and hope and shaw,
    Beneath the sun-licht or the moon :
    But set us in our fishing-shoon
Between the Caddon-burn and Peel,
    And syne we'll cross the heather broun
By fair Tweed-side, at Ashiesteel !

Envoy

Deil take the dirty, trading loon
    Wad gar the water ca' his wheel,
And drift his dyes and poisons doun
    By fair Tweed-side at Ashiesteel !

                Andrew Lang.

151   IN PRAISE OF TWEED

Let ither anglers chuse their ain,
    And ither waters tak' the lead ;
O' Hielan' streams we covet nane,
    But gie to us the bonnie Tweed !
And gie to us the cheerfu' burn
    That steals into its valley fair—
The streamlets that at ilka turn
    Sae saftly meet an' mingle there.

    cauldrife, chilly   *creel*, basket

The lanesome Talla and the Lyne,
  An' Manor wi' its mountain rills,
An' Etterick, whose waters twine
  Wi' Yarrow frae the Forest hills ;
An' Gala too, and Teviot bright,
  An' mony a stream o' playfu' speed ;
Their kindred valleys a' unite
  Amang the braes o' bonnie Tweed.

There's no a hole abune the Crook,
  Nor stane nor gentle swirl aneath,
Nor drumlie rill nor faëry brook,
  That daunders thro' the flowery heath,
But ye may fin' a subtle troot,
  A' gleamin' ower wi' starn an' bead,
An' mony a sawmon sooms about
  Below the bields o' bonnie Tweed.

Frae Holylee to Clovenford,
  A chancier bit ye canna hae
So gin ye tak' an angler's word,
  Ye'd through the whins an' ower the brae.
An' work awa' wi' cunnin' hand
  Yer birzy hackles, black and reid ;
The saft sough o' a slender wand
  Is meetest music for the Tweed !

                    Thomas Tod Stoddart.

drumlie, dark, swollen   *daunders*, meanders
starn, speck of colour   *sooms*, swims   *birzy*, bristling
hackles, the feathers at the foot of an artificial fly

152   FISHER JAMIE

Puir Jamie's killed.   A better lad
    Ye wadna find to busk a flee
Or burn a pule or wield a gad
    Frae Berwick to the Clints o' Dee.

And noo he's in a happier land—
    It's Gospel truith and Gospel law
That Heaven's yett maun open stand
    To folk that for their country fa'.

But Jamie will be ill to mate ;
    He lo'ed nae music, kenned nae tunes
Except the sang o' Tweed in spate,
    Or Talla loupin' ower its linns.

I sair misdoot that Jamie's heid
    A croun o' gowd will never please ;
He liked a kep o' dacent tweed
    Whaur he could stick his casts o' flees.

If Heaven is a' that man can dream
    And a' that honest herts can wish,
It maun provide some muirland stream,
    For Jamie dreamed o' nocht but fish.

And weel I wot he'll up and speir
    In his bit blate and canty way,
Wi' kind Apostles standin' near
    Whae in their time were fishers tae.

busk, dress   pule, pool   gad, gaff   yett, gate
speir, ask   blate and canty, shy and friendly

He'll offer back his gowden croun
    And in its place a rod he'll seek,
And bashfu'-like his herp lay doun
    And speir a leister and a cleek.

For Jims had aye a poachin' whim ;
    He'll sune grow tired, wi' lawfu' flee
Made frae the wings o' cherubim
    O' castin' ower the Crystal Sea.

I picter him at gloamin' tide
    Steekin' the backdoor o' his hame
And hastin' to the waterside
    To play again the auld auld game ;

And syne wi' saumon on his back
    Catch't clean against the Heavenly law,
And Heavenly byliffs on his track,
    Gaun linkin' doun some Heavenly shaw.

                        John Buchan.

153   JUVENIS AND PISCATOR

Juv.   Canny Fisher Jamie, comin' hame at e'en,
        Canny Fisher Jamie, whaur hae ye been ?

Pisc.   Mony lang miles, laddie, ower the Kips sae
        green.

Juv.   Fishin' Leithen Water ?

Pisc.   Nay, laddie, nay,
        Just a wee burnie rinnin' doun a brae,
        Fishin' a wee burnie nae bigger than a sheugh.

leister, salmon spear   *steekin'*, shutting
linkin', stealing   *shaw*, wood   *sheugh*, ditch

Juv. Gat ye mony troots, Jamie ?

Pisc. I gat eneugh—
Eneugh to buy my baccy, snuff, and pickle tea,
And lea' me tippence for a gill, and that's eneugh
for me.

154 POACHING *IN EXCELSIS*

(" Two men were fined £120 apiece for poaching a white
rhinoceros."—*South African Press.*)

I'VE poached a pickle paitricks when the leaves were
turnin' sere,
I've poached a twa-three hares an' grouse, an' mebbe
whiles a deer,
But ou, it seems an unco thing, an' jist a wee mysterious,
Hoo any mortal could contrive tae poach a rhinocerious.

I've crackit wi' the keeper, pockets packed wi' pheasants'
eggs,
An' a ten-pun' saumon hangin' doun in baith my trouser
legs,
But eh, I doot effects wud be a wee thing deleterious
Gin ye shuld stow intil yer breeks a brace o' rhinocerious.

I mind hoo me an' Wullie shot a Royal in Braemar,
An' brocht him doun tae Athol by the licht o' mune an'
star.
An' eh, Sirs ! but the canny beast contrived tae fash an'
weary us—
Yet staigs maun be but bairn's play beside a rhinocerious.

pickle, small quantity of   *paitricks*, partridges
unco, strange   *crackit*, talked

I thocht I kent o' poachin' jist as muckle's ither men,
But there is still a twa-three things I doot I dinna ken;
An' noo I cannot rest, my brain is growin' that deleerious
Tae win awa' tae Africa an' poach a rhinocerious.

G. K. Menzies.

155   A SONG OF LIFE AND GOLF

THE thing they ca' the stimy o't,
    I find it ilka where !
Ye 'maist lie deid—an unco shot—
    Anither's ba' is there !
Ye canna win into the hole,
    However gleg ye be,
And aye, where'er ma ba' may roll,
    Some limmer stimies me !

Chorus—Somebody stimying me,
            Somebody stimying me,
        The grass may grow, the ba' may row,
            Some limmer stimies me !

I lo'ed a lass, a bonny lass,
    Her lips an' locks were reid ;
Intil her heart I couldna pass :
    Anither man lay deid !
He cam' atween me an' her heart,
    I turned wi' tearfu' e'e ;
I couldna loft him, I maun part,
    The limmer stimied me !

win awa', get away   ba', ball
limmer, rascal   row, roll

I socht a kirk, a bonny kirk,
   Wi' teind, an' glebe, an' a' ;
A bonny yaird to feed a stirk,
   An' links to ca' the ba' !
Anither lad he cam' an' fleeched—
   A convartit U.P.—
An' a' in vain ma best I preached,
   That limmer stimied me !

It's aye the same in life an' gowf ;
   I'm stimied, late an' ear' ;
This world is but a weary howf,
   I'd fain be itherwhere.
But whan auld deith wad hole ma corp,
   As sure as deith ye'll see
Some coof has played the moudiewarp,
   Rin in, an' stimied me !

    Chorus (if thought desirable).
                 Andrew Lang.

teind, stipend	*stirk*, a cattle beast	*ca'*, drive
fleeched, pled	*howf*, place	*coof*, fool
	moudiewarp, mole	

BOOK XII
NATURE

O PERFITE Light, whilk shed away
   The darkenes from the light,
And set a ruler ou'r the day,
   Ane other ou'r the night—

Thy glorie when the day foorth flies,
   Mair vively does appear,
Nor at midday unto our eyes
   The shining sun is cleare.

The shadow of the earth anon
   Removes and drawes by ;
Syne in the East, when it is gone,
   Appeares a clearer sky :

Whilk sune perceives the little larks,
   The lapwing and the snyp,
And tunes their sangs like Nature's clarks,
   Ou'r medow, muir, and stryp.

They dread the day fra they it see,
   And from the sight of men,
To seats and covers fast they flee,
   As lyons to their den.

Our hemisphere is poleist clean
   And lightened more and more,
While every thing be clearly seen,
   Whilk seemed dim before :

vively, vividly   *stryp*, rill

Except the glistering astres bright,
  Which all the night were cleere,
Offusked with a greater light,
  Na langer does appeare.

The golden globe incontinent
  Sets up his shining head,
And ou'r the earth and firmament
  Displayes his beams abraid.

For joy the birds with boulden throts
  Aganis his visage sheen,
Takes up their kindlie musicke notes
  In woods and gardens green.

Upbraids the carefull husbandman,
  His corns and vines to see ;
And every tymous artisan
  In buith works busilie.

The pastor quits the slothfull sleep
  And passis forth with speede,
His little camow-nosed sheepe
  And rowting kye to feede.

The passenger, from perils sure
  Gangs gladly forth the way :
Brief, everie living creature
  Takes comfort of the day.

astres, stars   *offusked*, obfuscated, darkened
boulden, swelling   *upbraids*, uprises   *buith*, booth
camow-nosed flat-nosed   *rowting kye*, lowing cows

The dew upon the tender crops,
  Like pearles white and round,
Or like to melted silver drops,
  Refreshes all the ground.

The misty rouke, the clouds of raine
  From tops of mountaines skails,
Cleare are the highest hills and plaine,
  The vapors takes the vales.

Begaried is the saphire pend
  With spraings of scarlet hue,
And preciously from end till end
  Damasked white and blue.

The ample heaven of fabric sure
  In cleannes does surpas
The crystall and the silver pure,
  Or clearest poleist glass.

The time sa tranquil is and still,
  That na where sall ye find—
Saif on ane high and barren hill—
  Ane aire of piping wind.

All trees and simples great and small,
  That balmie leaf do bear,
Nor they were painted on a wall
  Na mair they move or steir.

rouke, vapour   *skails*, disperses
begaried, variegated   *pend*, arch
spraings, streaks   *damasked*, inlaid
              simples, herbs

Calm is the deep and purpour sea,
　　Yea, smoother nor the sand ;
The wavis that wolt'ring wont to be,
　　Are stable like the land.

Sa silent is the cessile air,—
　　That every cry and call,
The hills, and dales, and forest fair
　　Againe repeates them all.

The rivers fresh, the caller streams
　　Ou'r rockes can softlie rin,
The water cleare like crystall seems,
　　And makes a pleasant din.

The flourishes and fragrant flowers,
　　Throw Phœbus' fost'ring heit,
Refresh'd with dew and silver showres,
　　Casts up ane odour sweet.

The clogged, busie humming bees,
　　That never thinks to drowne,
On flowers and flourishes of trees,
　　Collects their liquor browne.

The sunne maist like a speedie post
　　With ardent course ascends,
The beautie of the heavenlie host
　　Up to our zenith tends.

cessile, yielding　　　　　　*flourishes*, blossoms

Nocht guided by na Phaeton,
  Nor trained in a chyre,
But by the High and Haly One,
  Whilk does all where empire.

The burning beams down from his face
  Sa fervently can beat,
That man and beast now seeks a place
  To save them fra the heat. . . .

The herds beneath some leafie tree,
  Amids' the flowers they lie ;
The stable ships upon the sea
  Tends up their sails to dry. . . .

Back from the blue paymented whin,
  And from ilk plaister wall,
The hot reflexing of the sunne
  Inflams the aire and all.

The labourers that timelie raise,
  All wearie, faint, and weake
For heat, down to their houses gais,
  Noon-meate and sleepe to take.

The caller wine in cave is sought,
  Men's brothing breists to cule ;
The water cauld and cleare is brought,
  And sallets steip't in ule.

chyre, chariot   *tends*, stretch
paymented whin, pavemented whinstone
brothing breists, sweating breasts
sallets, salads   *ule*, oil

Some plucks the honie plum and peare,
    The cherrie and the peache ;
Some likes the reamand London beer,
    The bodie to refresh.

Forth of their skeps some raging bees
    Lyes out and will not cast ;
Some other swarmes hives on the trees
    In knots togidder fast.

The corbies, and the kekling kais
    May scarce the heate abide ;
Hawks prunyeis on the sunnie braes
    And wedder's back and side.

With gilded eyes and open wings,
    The cock his courage shawes,
With claps of joy his breast he dings,
    And twentie times he crawes.

The dow with whistling wings sa blue,
    The winds can fast collect,
His purpour pennes turnes mony hue
    Against the sunne direct.

Now noone is went, gane is midday,
    The heat does slake at last,
The sunne descends downe west away,
    Fra three of clock be past.

reamand, foaming   *skeps*, hives
kekling kais, cackling jackdaws
prunyeis, preen   *wedder*, wether
        dow, dove

The rayons of the sunne we see
   Diminish in their strength,
The shade of everie tower and tree
   Extended is in length.

Great is the calme, for everie where
   The wind is sitten downe ;
The reek thrawes right up in the air
   From everie tower and towne.

The mavis and the philomene,
   The stirling whistles loud,
The cushats on the branches green
   Full quietly they crowd.

The gloaming comes, the day is spent,
   The sunne goes out of sight,
And painted is the occident
   With purpour sanguine bright.

Our west horizon circuler,
   Fra time the sunne be set,
Is all with rubies (as it were)
   Or rosis reid ourfret.

What pleasure were to walke and see,
   Endlang a river cleare,
The perfite form of everie tree
   Within the deepe appeare.

O, then it were a seemlie thing,
   While all is still and calme,
The praise of God to play and sing
   With cornet and with shalme !

stirling, starling   *ourfret*, embroidered

All labourers drawes hame at even,
    And can till other say,
Thankes to the gracious God of heaven,
    Whilk sent this summer day.

Alexander Hume.

157   PROCUL NEGOTIIS

Now when the dog-day heats begin
To birsle and to peel the skin,
May I lie streekit at my ease
Beneath the caller shady trees
(Far frae the din o' Borrowstown),
Where water plays the haughs bedown ;
To jouk the simmer's rigour there,
And breathe a while the caller air,
'Mang herds, and honest cottar fouk,
That till the farm and feed the flock ;
Careless o' mair, wha never fash
To lade their kist wi' useless cash,
But thank the gods for what they've sent
O' health eneugh, and blythe content,
And pith that helps them to stravaig
Ower ilka cleugh and ilka craig ;
Unkenn'd to a' the weary granes
That aft arise frae gentler banes,
On easy chair that pamper'd lie,
Wi' baneful viands gustit high,
And turn and fauld their weary clay,
To rax and gaunt the live-lang day.

Robert Fergusson.

birsle, scorch   *streekit*, stretched   *jouk*, escape
stravaig, wander   *cleugh*, ravine   *granes*, groans
gustit, tasted   *fauld*, fold   *rax*, stretch   *gaunt*, yawn

A WINTER DAY

So busteously Boreas his bugill blew,
The deer full dern doune in the dalis drew ;
Smal birdis flokand throw thik ronnis thrang
In chyrming and with cheping changit thair sang,
Seekand hidlis and hirnis them to hyde
Fra feirfull thudis of the tempestuous tyde.
The wattir-lynnis routtis, and every lynde
Whyslyt and brayt of the swouchand wynde.
Puir laboraris and byssy husband-men
Went wet and wery draglyt in the fen ;
The silly scheip and thair lytill hyrd-groomis
Lurkis undir lee of bankis, wodys, and broomys ;
And othir dauntit greater bestial
Within thair stabillis sesyt into stall,
Sic as mulis, horsis, oxen, and ky,
Fed tuskit boaris, and fat swyne in sty,
Sustenit war by mannis governance,
On harvest and on symmeris purveyance.
Widewhair with force so Eolus schouttis schyll
In this congealyt sessoune scharp and chyll,
The caller air, penetrative and pure,
Dasying the bluide in every creature,
Made seik warm stovis and bien firis hot,
In double garment cled and wyly-coat,
With mychty drink, and meatis comfortive,
Agayne the stormie wynter for to strive.

Gawain Douglas.

dern, secretly   *ronnis*, bushes   *chyrming*, chirping
hidlis and hirnis, holes and corners   *routtis*, roar
lynde, linden   *swouchand*, howling   *sesyt*, tethered
Widewhair, far and wide   *schyll*, shrilly   *dasying*, benumbing

159   THE SPATE

The Auld Brig of Ayr speaks :—

CONCEITED gowk ! puff'd up wi' windy pride !
This mony a year I've stood the flood an' tide ;
And tho' wi' crazy eild I'm sair forfairn,
I'll be a brig, when ye're a shapeless cairn !
As yet ye little ken about the matter,
But twa-three winters will inform ye better.
When heavy, dark, continu'd a'-day rains,
Wi' deep'ning deluges o'erflow the plains :
When from the hills where springs the brawling Coil,
Or stately Lugar's mossy fountains boil,
Or where the Greenock winds his moorland course,
Or haunted Garpal draws his feeble source,
Arous'd by blust'ring winds an' spotting thowes,
In mony a torrent down his snaw-broo rowes ;
While crashing ice, borne on the roaring spate,
Sweeps dams, an' mills, an' brigs, a' to the gate ;
And from Glenbuck, down to the Ratton-key,
Auld Ayr is just one lengthened tumbling sea—
Then down ye'll hurl (deil nor ye never rise !)
And dash the gumlie jaups up to the pouring skies.
                                    Robert Burns.

gowk, fool   *eild*, old age   *forfairn*, worn out
thowes, thaws   *snaw-broo*, snow-broth
rowes, rolls   *spate*, flood   *hurl*, crash
          gumlie jaups, muddy splashes

160

A BORDER BURN

Ah, Tam ! gie me a Border burn
That canna rin without a turn,
And wi' its bonnie babble fills
The glens amang oor native hills.
How men that ance have ken'd aboot it
Can leeve their after lives without it,
I canna tell, for day and nicht
It comes unca'd-for to my sicht.
I see't this moment, plain as day,
As it comes bickerin' o'er the brae,
Atween the clumps o' purple heather,
Glistenin' in the summer weather,
Syne divin' in below the grun',
Where, hidden frae the sicht and sun,
It gibbers like a deid man's ghost
That clamours for the licht it's lost,
Till oot again the loupin' limmer
Comes dancin' doon through shine and shimmer
At headlang pace, till wi' a jaw
It jumps the rocky waterfa',
And cuts sic cantrips in the air,
The picture-pentin' man's despair ;
A rountree bus' oot o'er the tap o't,
A glassy pule to kep the lap o't,
While on the brink the blue harebell
Keeks o'er to see its bonnie sel',
And sittin' chirpin' a' its lane
A water-waggy on a stane.

jaw, twist	*rountree,* rowan
keeks, looks	*water-waggy,* wagtail

Ay, penter lad, thraw to the wund
Your canvas, this is holy grund :
Wi' a' its highest airt acheevin',
The picter's deed, and this is leevin'.

J. B. Selkirk.

161   THE BUSH ABOON TRAQUAIR

WILL ye gang wi' me and fare
    To the bush aboon Traquair ?
Owre the high Minchmuir we'll up and awa',
    This bonnie summer noon,
    While the sun shines fair aboon,
And the licht sklents saftly doun on holm and ha'.

    And what wad ye do there,
        At the bush aboon Traquair ?
A long dreich road, ye had better let it be ;
        Save some auld skrunts o' birk
        I' the hill-side lirk,
There's nocht i' the warld for man to see.

    But the blythe lilt o' yon air,
        " The Bush aboon Traquair "—
I need nae mair, it's eneuch for me :
        Owre my cradle its sweet chime
        Cam soughin' frae auld time ;
Sae tide what may, I'll awa' and see.

sklents, slants	*dreich*, dull
skrunts o' birk, stunted birches	*lirk*, fold

And what saw ye there,
    At the bush aboon Traquair ?
Or what did ye hear that was worth your heed ?
    I heard the cushies croon
    Thro' the gowden afternoon,
And the Quair burn singing doun to the vale o' Tweed.

    And birks saw I, three or four,
    Wi' grey moss bearded owre,
The last that are left o' the birken shaw ;
    Whar mony a simmer e'en
    Fond lovers did convene,
Thae bonnie, bonnie gloamins that are lang awa'.

    Frae mony a butt and ben,
    By muirland, holm, and glen,
They cam ane hour to spen' on the green-wood sward ;
    But lang hae lad an' lass
    Been lying 'neath the grass,
The green, green grass o' Traquair kirkyard.

    They were blest beyond compare
    When they held their trysting there,
Amang thae greenest hills shone on by the sun ;
    And then they wan a rest,
    The lownest and the best,
I' Traquair kirkyard when a' was dune.

    Now the birks to dust may rot,
    Names o' luvers be forgot,
Nae lads and lasses there ony mair convene ;

cushies, wood pigeons   *butt and ben*, cot-house
        lownest, most sheltered

But the blythe lilt o' yon air
Keeps the bush aboon Traquair
And the luve that ance was there aye fresh and green.
                              John Campbell Shairp.

162   A NORTHERN MIDSUMMER MORN

YONDIR doun dwynis the evin sky away,
And upspringis the bricht dawing of the day
In till ane uthir place nocht fer in sunder,
Whilk to behold was plesance and half wonder.
Further quenching gan the sternes ane by ane,
That now is left but Lucifer allane.
And furthirmore, to blasin this new day
Whay micht discryve the birdis blissful lay ?
Belyve on wing the bissy lark upsprang,
To salute the bricht morow with hir sang :
Sone ower the feildis schynes the licht clere,
Welcum to pilgryme baith and lauborere :
Tyte on his hindis gaif the greif ane cry—
" Awake on fute, go tyl our husbandry " :
And the herd callis furth upon his page
To drive the catell to thare pasturage :
The hindis wiffe clepis up Katherine and Gyl ;
" Ya, dame," said they, " God wot with ane gude will."
The dewye grene powderit with dasyis gay
Schew on the swarde ane cullour dapil gray :
The mysty vapouris spryngand up ful swete,
Maist comfortabil to glad al mannis sprete :

dwynis, sinks   *fer in sunder*, far asunder   *sternes*, stars
blasin, blazon   *discryve*, describe   *belyve*, soon
tyte, quickly   *hindis*, servants   *greif*, grieve, steward
                       clepis, calls

Thareto the birdis singis in thare schawis,
As menstralis playis, *The jolly day now dawis.*

>   *Gawain Douglas.*

163   MOORLAND PEACE

WHAUR braid the briery muirs expand,
A waefu' an' a weary land,
The bumblebees, a gowden band,
      Are blithely hingin' ;
An' there the canty wanderer fand
      The laverock singin'.

Trout in the burn grow great as herr'n,
The simple sheep can find their fair'n ;
The wind blaws clean about the cairn
      Wi' caller air ;
The muircock an' the barefit bairn
      Are happy there.

>   *R. L. Stevenson.*

164   GENIUS LOCI

                  (1)

            TWEED AND TILL

TWEED said to Till,
" What gars ye rin sae still ? "—
Till said to Tweed,
" Though ye rin wi' speed,
      And I rin slaw,
Where ye droun ae man,
      I droun twa."

gowden, golden   *canty*, quiet   *laverock*, lark
caller, fresh   *barefit*, barefoot
(2,470)   10

(2)

THE BRAES O' MENSTRIE

O ALVA hills is bonny,
    Dalycoutry hills is fair ;
But to think on the braes o' Menstrie,
    It maks my heart fu' sair.

(3)

OH, GIN I WERE A DOO

OH, gin I were a doo,
I wad flee awa' the noo
Wi' my neb to the Lomonds an' my wings wavin'
        steady,
    An' I wadna rest a fit,
    Till at gloamin' I wad sit
Wi' ither neebor doos on the lums o' Balgeddie.

(4)

MANOR WATER

THERE stand three mills on Manor Water,
    A fourth at Posso cleugh ;
Gin heather bells were corn and bear,
    They wad get grist eneugh.

(5)

BUCHLYVIE

BARON of Buchlyvie,
May the foul fiend drive ye,
And a' tae pieces rive ye,
    For buildin' sic a toun,

Where there's neither horse meat nor man's
    meat,
    Nor a chair to sit doon.

(6)

EDINBURGH CASTLE

EDINBURGH castle, towne and tower,
   God grant ye sink for sin !
And that for the black denner
   Yerl Douglas gat therein.

BOOK XIII
FRIENDLY BEASTS

"Gude day, now, bonnie Robin,
   How lang hae ye been here ?"
"I've been a bird about this bush
   This mair than twenty year.

"But now I am the sickest bird
   That ever sat on brier ;
And I wad mak' my testament,
   Gudeman, if ye wad hear.

"Gar tak' this bonnie neb o' mine,
   That picks upon the corn ;
And gie't to the Duke o' Hamilton,
   To be a hunting horn.

"Gar tak' thae bonnie feathers o' mine,
   The feathers o' my neb ;
And gie to the Lady Hamilton
   To fill a feather bed.

"Gar tak' this gude richt leg of mine,
   And mend the brig o' Tay ;
It will be a post and pillar gude,
   It will neither bow nor sway.

neb, beak

"And tak' this other leg of mine,
    And mend the brig o' Weir ;
It will be a post and pillar gude,
    It will neither bow nor steer.

"Gar tak' thae bonnie feathers o' mine,
    The feathers o' my tail ;
And gie to the lads o' Hamilton
    To be a barn-flail.

"And tak' thae bonnie feathers o' mine,
    The feathers o' my breast ;
And gie them to the bonnie lad
    Will bring to me a priest."

Now in there cam' my Lady Wren,
    Wi' mony a sigh and groan :
"O what care I for a' the lads,
    If my ain lad be gone !"

Then Robin turn'd him round about,
    E'en like a little king ;
"Gae pack ye out at my chamber-door,
    Ye little cutty-quean."

166   THE WATCHERS

"O WHERE were ye, my milk-white steed,
    That I hae coft sae dear,
That wadna watch and waken me
    When there was maiden here ? "

steer, move   *cutty-quean*, light of love   *coft*, bought

" I stamped wi' my foot, master,
　And gard my bridle ring,
But na kin thing wald waken ye,
　Till she was past and gane."

" And wae betide ye, my gay goss-hawk,
　That I did love sae dear,
That wadna watch and waken me
　When there was maiden here."

" I clapped wi' my wings, master,
　And aye my bells I rang,
And aye cry'd, Waken, waken, master,
　Before the ladye gang."

" But haste and haste, my gude white steed,
　To come the maiden till,
Or a' the birds of gude green wood
　Of your flesh shall have their fill."

" Ye need na burst your gude white steed
　Wi' racing o'er the howm ;
Nae bird flies faster through the wood
　Than she fled through the broom."

167　THE HERRING LOVES THE MERRY
MOONLIGHT

THE herring loves the merry moonlight,
　The mackerel loves the wind,
But the oyster loves the dredging sang,
　For they come of a gentle kind.
Sir Walter Scott.

　gard, made　　*howm,* riverside meadow

THE TWA DOGS

'Twas in that place o' Scotland's isle,
That bears the name o' auld King Coil,
Upon a bonnie day in June,
When wearing thro' the afternoon,
Twa dogs, that were na thrang at hame,
Forgather'd ance upon a time.

The first I'll name, they ca'd him Cæsar,
Was keepit for "his Honour's" pleasure ;
His hair, his size, his mouth, his lugs,
Shew'd he was nane o' Scotland's dogs ;
But whalpit some place far abroad,
Whare sailors gang to fish for cod.

His lockèd, letter'd, braw brass collar
Shew'd him the gentleman and scholar ;
But tho' he was o' high degree,
The fient a pride—nae pride had he ;
But wad hae spent an hour caressin',
Even wi' a tinkler-gypsy's messan.
At kirk or market, mill or smiddie,
Nae tawted tyke, tho' e'er sae duddie,
But he wad stan't, as glad to see him,
And stroan't on stanes an' hillocks wi' him.

The tither was a ploughman's collie,
A rhyming, ranting, raving billie,

thrang, busy	*lugs*, ears	*messan*, mongrel
smiddie, smithy	*tawted tyke*, unkempt cur	
duddie, ragged	*billie*, fellow	

Wha for his friend an' comrade had him,
And in his freaks had Luath ca'd him,
After some dog in Highland sang,
Was made lang-syne—Lord knows how lang.

He was a gash an' faithfu' tyke,
As ever lap a sheugh or dyke.
His honest, sonsie, baws'nt face,
Aye gat him friends in ilka place.
His breast was white, his tousie back
Weel clad wi' coat o' glossy black ;
His gaucie tail, wi' upward curl,
Hung owre his hurdies wi' a swirl.

Nae doubt but they were fain o' ither,
An' unco pack an' thick thegither ;
Wi' social nose whyles snuff'd and snowkit ;
Whyles mice an' moudieworts they howkit ;
Whyles scour'd awa' in lang excursion,
An' worry'd ither in diversion.

Robert Burns.

169   THE AULD MAN'S MEAR'S DEAD

THE auld man's mear's dead ;
The puir body's mear's dead ;
The auld man's mear's dead,
A mile aboon Dundee.

sheugh, ditch   *dyke,* stone wall   *sonsie,* pleasant
baws'nt, white-marked   *tousie,* shaggy   *gaucie,* joyous
hurdies, buttocks   *fain,* glad   *pack an' thick,* confidential
moudieworts, moles   *howkit,* dug   *mear,* mare

There was hay to ca', and lint to lead,
A hunder hotts o' muck to spread,
And peats and truffs and a' to lead—
          And yet the jaud to dee !

She had the fiercie and the fleuk,
The wheezloch and the wanton yeuk ;
On ilka knee she had a breuk—
          What ail'd the beast to dee ?

She was lang-tooth'd and blench-lippit,
Heam-hough'd and haggis-fittit,
Lang-neckit, chandler-chaftit,
          And yet the jaud to dee !

170 THE AULD FARMER'S NEW YEAR MORN-
          ING SALUTATION TO HIS AULD MARE
          MAGGIE,

ON GIVING HER THE ACCUSTOMED RIPP OF CORN TO
          HANSEL IN THE NEW YEAR

A GUID New Year I wish thee, Maggie !
Hae, there's a ripp to thy auld baggie :
Tho' thou's howe-backit, now, an' knaggie,
          I've seen the day,
Thou could hae gaen like ony staggie
          Out-owre the lay.

hotts, loads	*truffs*, turfs	*jaud*, wretch
yeuk, itch	*ripp*, handful	*howe-backit*, hollow-backed
knaggie, knobby	*staggie*, young horse	*lay*, lea

Tho' now thou's dowie, stiff, an' crazy,
An' thy auld hide's as white's a daisy,
I've seen thee dappl't, sleek, and glaizie,
    A bonny grey :
He should been tight that daur't to raize thee,
    Ance in a day.

Thou ance was i' the foremost rank,
A filly buirdly, steeve, an' swank,
An' set weel down a shapely shank
    As e'er tread yird ;
An' could hae flown out-owre a stank,
    Like ony bird.

It's now some nine-an'-twenty year,
Sin' thou was my guid-father's meere ;
He gied me thee, o' tocher clear,
    An' fifty mark ;
Tho' it was sma', 'twas weel-won gear,
    An' thou was stark.

When first I gaed to woo my Jenny,
Ye then was trottin' wi' your minnie :
Tho' ye was trickie, slee, an' funnie,
    Ye ne'er was donsie !
But hamely, tawie, quiet, an' cannie,
    An' unco sonsie.

That day, ye pranc'd wi' muckle pride,
When we bure hame my bonnie bride :

glaizie, shiny	*tight*, prepared	*raize*, smite
buirdly, stately	*steeve*, firm	*swank*, lithe
yird, earth	*stank*, moat	*tocher*, dowry
stark, strong	*donsie*, vicious	*tawie*, docile
	sonsie, pleasant	

An' sweet and gracefu' she did ride,
    Wi' maiden air !
Kyle-Stewart I could hae bragget wide,
    For sic a pair.

Tho' now ye dow but hoyte and hobble,
An' wintle like a saumont-coble,
That day ye was a jinker noble,
    For heels an' win' !
An' ran them till they a' did wauble,
    Far, far behin' !

When thou an' I were young an' skeigh,
An' stable-meals at fairs were dreigh,
How thou wad prance an' snore, an' skreigh,
    An' tak the road ;
Town's-bodies ran, an' stood abeigh,
    An' ca't thee mad.

When thou was corn't, an' I was mellow,
We took the road aye like a swallow :
At brooses thou had ne'er a fellow,
    For pith an' speed ;
But ev'ry tail thou pay't them hollow,
    Whare'er thou gaed.

The sma' droop-rumpl't, hunter cattle,
Might aiblins waur't thee for a brattle ;

bragget, challenged *dow,* can *hoyte,* stagger
jinker, dodger *skeigh,* skittish *dreigh,* dull
abeigh, aloof *brooses,* wedding races
droop-rumpl't, short-rumped
waur't thee, etc., have beat thee in a spurt

But sax Scotch miles thou try't their mettle,
  An' gar't them whaizle :
Nae whip nor spur, but just a wattle
  O' saugh or hazel.

Thou was a noble fittie-lan',
As e'er in tug or tow was drawn :
Aft thee an' I, in aught hours gaun,
  On guid March weather,
Hae turn'd sax rood beside our han',
  For days thegither.

Thou never braing't, and fetch't, an' fliskit,
But thy auld tail thou wad hae whiskit,
An' spread abreed thy weel-filled brisket,
  Wi' pith and pow'r,
'Till spritty knowes wad rair't and risket
  An' slypet owre.

When frosts lay lang, an' snaws were deep,
An' threaten'd labour back to keep,
I gied thy cog a wee-bit heap
  Aboon the timmer ;
I kenn'd my Maggie wad na sleep
  For that, or simmer.

whaizle, wheeze
fittie-lan', the near horse of the hindmost pair in the plough
gaun, going   *braing't*, pulled wildly
fetch't, stopped suddenly   *fliskit*, capered
spritty knowes, rooty hillocks
rair't and risket, have roared and cracked
slypet, fallen smoothly   *cog*, dish
timmer, edge   *or*, ere

In cart or car thou never reestit ;
The steyest brae thou wad hae fac't it ;
Thou never lap, nor sten't, an' breastit,
      Then stood to blaw ;
But just thy step a wee thing hastit,
      Thou snoov't awa'.

My pleugh is now thy bairn-time a' ;
Four gallant brutes as e'er did draw ;
Forbye sax mae, I've sell't awa'.
      That thou hast nurst :
They drew me thretteen pund an' twa,
      The vera warst.

Mony a sair darg we twa hae wrought,
An' wi' the weary warl' fought !
An' mony an anxious day, I thought
      We wad be beat !
Yet here to crazy age we're brought,
      Wi' something yet.

An' think na, my auld, trusty servan',
That now perhaps thou's less deservin',
An' thy auld days may end in starvin',
      For my last fow,
A heapit stimpart, I'll reserve ane
      Laid by for you.

We've worn to crazy years thegither ;
We'll toyte about wi' ane anither ;

reestit, reared	*steyest*, steepest	*sten't*, sprang
snoov't, jogged	*bairn-time*, progeny	*darg*, day's work
fow, bushel	*stimpart*, quarter-peck	*toyte*, totter

Wi' tentie care I'll flit thy tether,
        To some hain'd rig,
Whare ye may nobly rax your leather,
        Wi' sma' fatigue.

                                Robert Burns.

171 THE EWIE WI' THE CROOKIT HORN

OH, were I able to rehearse
My ewie's praise in proper verse,
I'd sound it out as loud and fierce
        As ever piper's drone could blaw.
            My ewie wi' the crookit horn !
            A' that kend her would hae sworn
            Sic a ewie ne'er was born
                Hereabouts nor far awa'.

I never needit tar nor keel
To mark her upo' hip or heel ;
Her crookit hornie did as weel
        To ken her by amang them a'.

She never threaten'd scab nor rot,
But keepit aye her ain jog-trot ;
Baith to the fauld and to the cot,
        Was never sweir to lead nor ca'.

A better nor a thriftier beast,
Nae honest man need e'er hae wish'd ;
For, silly thing, she never miss'd
        To hae ilk year a lamb or twa.

flit, change   *hain'd rig*, reserved patch
rax your leather, fill your belly
keel, red earth   *sweir*, unwilling

The first she had I gae to Jock,
To be to him a kind o' stock ;
And now the laddie has a flock
    Of mair than thretty head and twa.

The neist I gae to Jean ; and now
The bairn's sae braw, has faulds sae fu',
That lads sae thick come her to woo,
    They're fain to sleep on hay or straw.

Cauld nor hunger never dang her,
Wind or rain could never wrang her ;
Ance she lay an ouk and langer
    Forth aneath a wreath o' snaw.

When other ewies lap the dyke,
And ate the kale for a' the tyke,
My ewie never play'd the like,
    But teezed about the barn wa'.

I lookit aye at even for her,
Lest mishanter should come ower her,
Or the foumart micht devour her,
    Gin the beastie bade awa'.

Yet, last ouk, for a' my keeping,
(Wha can tell o't without greeting ?)
A villain cam', when I was sleeping,
    Staw my ewie, horn and a'.

dang, afflicted	*ouk*, week
for a', in spite of	*mishanter*, mishap
foumart, polecat	*greeting*, weeping
	staw, stole

I socht her sair upon the morn,
And down aneath a bush o' thorn
I got my ewie's crookit horn,
 But my ewie was awa'.

O gin I had the loon that did it,
I hae sworn as weel as said it,
Although the laird himsel' forbid it,
 I sall gie his neck a thraw.

I never met wi' sic a turn
As this sin' ever I was born :
My ewie wi' the crookit horn,
 Silly ewie, stown awa'.

O ! had she died o' croup or cauld,
As ewies do when they grow auld,
It wad na been, by monyfauld,
 Sae sair a heart to nane o's a'.

For a' the claith that we hae worn,
Frae her and hers sae aften shorn,
The loss o' her we could hae borne,
 Had fair strae-death ta'en her awa'.

But thus, poor thing, to lose her life
Aneath a bluidy villain's knife,
I'm really fleyt that our gudewife
 Will never win aboon't ava.

O ! a' ye bards benorth Kinghorn,
Call your muses up and mourn

sair, anxiously   *thraw*, twist
strae-death, death on straw   *fleyt*, afraid

Our ewie wi' the crookit horn,
    Stown frae's, and fell'd and a' !
        Our ewie wi' the crookit horn !
        Wha had kend her might hae sworn
        Sic a ewie ne'er was born
            Hereabouts nor far awa'.
                                John Skinner.

172   MY HOGGIE

WHAT will I do gin my hoggie die ?
    My joy, my pride, my hoggie !
My only beast, I had nae mae,
    And vow but I was vogie !

The lee-lang night we watch'd the fauld,
    Me and my faithfu' doggie ;
We heard nought but the roaring linn,
    Amang the braes sae scroggie ;

But the houlet cry'd frae the castle wa',
    The blitter frae the boggie,
The tod reply'd upon the hill,
    I trembl'd for my hoggie.

When day did daw, and cocks did craw,
    The morning it was foggie ;
An unco tyke lap o'er the dyke,
    And maist has kill'd my hoggie.
                                Robert Burns.

fell'd, killed	*hoggie,* lamb	*vogie,* vain
scroggie, scrubby	*houlet,* owl	*blitter,* snipe
tod, fox	*unco tyke,* strange dog	*maist,* almost

173   ## THE DEATH AND DYING WORDS OF POOR MAILIE,

THE AUTHOR'S ONLY PET YOWE

As Mailie, an' her lambs thegither,
Were ae day nibblin' on the tether,
Upon her cloot she coost a hitch,
An' owre she warsl'd in the ditch :
There, groaning, dying, she did lie,
While Hughoc he cam' doytin by.
Wi' glowrin' een an' lifted han's,
Poor Hughoc like a statue stan's ;
He saw her days were near-hand ended,
But, wae's my heart ! he could na mend it !
He gapèd wide, but naething spak—
At length poor Mailie silence brak.

" O thou, whase lamentable face
Appears to mourn my woefu' case !
My dying words attentive hear,
An' bear them to my master dear.

" Tell him, if e'er again he keep
As muckle gear as buy a sheep,
O, bid him never tie them mair
Wi' wicked strings o' hemp or hair !
But ca' them out to park or hill,
An' let them wander at their will ;
So may his flock increase, and grow
To scores o' lambs, an' packs o' woo' !

yowe, ewe	*cloot*, hoof	*warsl'd*, floundered
doytin', sauntering	*ca'*, drive	

" Tell him he was a master kin',
An' aye was guid to me and mine ;
An' now my dying charge I gie him,
My helpless lambs I trust them wi' him.

" O, bid him save their harmless lives,
Frae dogs, an' tods, an' butchers' knives !
But gie them guid cow-milk their fill,
Till they be fit to fend themsel' ;
An' tent them duly, e'en an' morn,
Wi' teats o' hay, an' ripps o' corn.

" An' may they never learn the gaets
Of ither vile, wanrestfu' pets !
To slink thro' slaps, an' reave an' steal,
At stacks o' pease, or stocks o' kail,
So may they, like their great forbears,
For mony a year come thro' the shears :
So wives will gie them bits o' bread,
An' bairns greet for them when they're dead.

" My poor toop-lamb, my son an' heir.
O, bid him breed him up wi' care !
An' if he live to be a beast,
To pit some havins in his breast !
An' warn him, what I winna name,
To stay content wi' yowes at hame :
An' no to rin an' wear his cloots,
Like ither menseless, graceless brutes.

tods, foxes	*fend*, look after	*teats*, small quantities
ripps, handfuls	*gaets*, ways	*slaps*, breaches
toop, tup	*havins*, manners	*yowes*, ewes
	menseless, shameless	

"An' niest, my yowie, silly thing,
Gude keep thee frae a tether string!
O, may thou ne'er forgather up
Wi' ony blastit, moorland toop,
But aye keep mind to moop an' mell
Wi' sheep o' credit like thysel'!

"And now, my bairns, wi' my last breath
I lea'e my blessin' wi' you baith:
An' when you think upo' your mither,
Mind to be kin' to ane anither.

"Now, honest Hughoc, dinna fail
To tell my master a' my tale;
An' bid him burn this cursed tether,
An', for thy pains, thou'se get my blether."

This said, poor Mailie turn'd her head,
And clos'd her een amang the dead.

Robert Burns.

174 POOR MAILIE'S ELEGY

LAMENT in rhyme, lament in prose,
Wi' saut tears trickling down your nose;
Our Bardie's fate is at a close,
          Past a' remead;
The last sad cape-stane o' his woes;
          Poor Mailie's dead!

moop, nibble   *mell,* meddle   *blether,* bladder

It's no the loss o' warl's gear,
That could sae bitter draw the tear,
Or mak' our Bardie, dowie, wear
        The mourning weed :
He's lost a friend and neibour dear
        In Mailie dead.

Thro' a' the toun she trotted by him ;
A lang half-mile she could descry him ;
Wi' kindly bleat, when she did spy him,
        She ran wi' speed :
A friend mair faithfu' ne'er cam' nigh him,
        Than Mailie dead.

I wat she was a sheep o' sense,
An' could behave herself wi' mense :
I'll say't, she never brak a fence,
        Thro' thievish greed.
Our Bardie, lanely, keeps the spence
        Sin' Mailie's dead.

Or, if he wanders up the howe,
Her living image in her yowe
Comes bleating to him, owre the knowe,
        For bits o' bread ;
An' down the briny pearls rowe
        For Mailie dead.

She was nae get o' moorland tips,
Wi' tawted ket, an' hairy hips ;

mense, tact   *spence*, parlour   *rowe*, roll
get, issue   *tips*, tups   *tawted ket*, matted fleece

For her forbears were brought in ships
    Frae yont the Tweed :
A bonnier fleesh ne'er cross'd the clips
    Than Mailie dead.

Wae worth the man wha first did shape
That vile wanchancie thing—a rape !
It mak's guid fellows girn and gape,
    Wi' chokin' dread ;
An' Robin's bonnet wave wi' crape,
    For Mailie dead.

O, a' ye bards on bonnie Doon !
An' wha on Ayr your chanters tune !
Come, join the melancholious croon
    O' Robin's reed !
His heart will never get aboon
    His Mailie dead !
               Robert Burns.

175   TO A LOUSE,

ON SEEING ONE ON A LADY'S BONNET AT CHURCH

HA ! whare ye gaun, ye crowlin ferlie !
Your impudence protects you sairly :
I canna say but ye strunt rarely,
    Owre gauze and lace ;
Tho', faith, I fear ye dine but sparely
    On sic a place.

fleesh, fleece	*clips*, shears	*wanchancie*, dangerous
girn, grin		*aboon*, over
crowlin ferlie, crawling marvel		*strunt*, swagger

Ye ugly, creepin', blastit wonner,
Detested, shunn'd, by saunt an' sinner,
How dare ye set your fit upon her,
   Sae fine a lady !
Gae somewhere else, and seek your dinner
   On some poor body.

Swith, in some beggar's haffet squattle ;
There ye may creep, and sprawl, and sprattle,
Wi' ither kindred, jumping cattle,
   In shoals and nations ;
Whare horn nor bane ne'er daur unsettle
   Your thick plantations.

Now haud you there ! ye're out o' sight,
Below the fatt'rels, snug an' tight ;
Na, faith ye yet ! ye'll no be right
   'Till ye've got on it,
The vera tapmost, tow'ring height
   O' Miss's bonnet.

My sooth ! right bauld ye set your nose out,
As plump and grey as ony grozet ;
O for some rank, mercurial rozet,
   Or fell, red smeddum,
I'd gie you sic a hearty doze o't,
   Wad dress your droddum !

I wad na been surpris'd to spy
You on an auld wife's flannen toy ;

haffet, temples *fatt'rels*, falderals *grozet*, gooseberry
rozet, rosin   *smeddum*, powder *droddum*, breech
    flannen toy, flannel cap

Or aiblins some bit duddie boy,
      On's wyliecoat ;
But Miss's fine Lunardi ! fie !
      How daur ye do't ?

O Jenny, dinna toss your head,
An' set your beauties a' abroad !
Ye little ken what cursèd speed
      The blastie's makin' !
Thae winks and finger-ends, I dread,
      Are notice takin' !

O wad some Power the giftie gie us
To see oursels as ithers see us !
It wad frae mony a blunder free us,
      An' foolish notion !
What airs in dress an' gait wad lea'e us,
      An' ev'n devotion !

          Robert Burns.

176   TO A MOUSE,

ON TURNING HER UP IN HER NEST WITH THE PLOUGH,
NOVEMBER 1785

WEE, sleekit, cow'rin', tim'rous beastie,
Oh, what a panic's in thy breastie !
Thou need na start awa' sae hasty,
      Wi' bickering brattle !
I wad be laith to rin an' chase thee,
      Wi' murd'ring pattle !

aiblins, maybe   *duddie,* ragged   *wyliecoat,* underclothes
Lunardi, a bonnet in the shape of a balloon
  abread, abroad   *bickering brattle,* hurrying scamper
          pattle, plough stick

I'm truly sorry man's dominion
Has broken nature's social union,
An' justifies that ill opinion
      Which makes thee startle
At me, thy poor earth-born companion,
        An' fellow-mortal !

I doubt na, whyles, but thou may thieve ;
What then ? poor beastie, thou maun live !
A daimen icker in a thrave
      'S a sma' request :
I'll get a blessin' wi' the lave,
        And never miss 't !

Thy wee bit housie, too, in ruin !
Its silly wa's the win's are strewin' !
An' naething, now, to big a new ane,
      O' foggage green !
An' bleak December's winds ensuin',
        Baith snell and keen !

Thou saw the fields laid bare an' waste,
An' weary winter comin' fast,
An' cozie here, beneath the blast,
      Thou thought to dwell,
'Till crash ! the cruel coulter past
        Out thro' thy cell.

That wee bit heap o' leaves an' stibble
Has cost thee mony a weary nibble !

daimen icker, odd ear	*thrave*, twenty-four sheaves	
lave, remainder	*foggage*, grass	*snell*, sharp
	stibble stubble	

Now thou 's turn'd out, for a' thy trouble,
      But house or hald,
To thole the winter's sleety dribble,
      An' cranreuch cauld !

But, Mousie, thou art no thy lane,
In proving foresight may be vain :
The best-laid schemes o' mice an' men,
      Gang aft agley,
An' lea's us nought but grief and pain
      For promis'd joy !

Still thou art blest, compar'd wi' me !
The present only toucheth thee :
But, och ! I backward cast my e'e,
      On prospects drear !
An' forward, tho' I canna see,
      I guess an' fear !
                Robert Burns.

177   THE MISANTHROPE

I wish I was a Brute Beast !
To live in some sequestered vale,
    Frae friends and loves remote placed,
An' ne'er see man, an' wag my tail !
    To chow on a knowe

But, without	*hald*, holding	*thole*, endure
cranreuch, hoar frost	*agley*, awry	*chow*, chew
	knowe, hillock	

A' the herbs, an' flowers, an' grassy blades,
    An' tread on the head
O' gowans never touched wi' spades :
    I'd never see a friendly face,
        Sae nae friend wad prove fause to me ;
    I'd never ken the human race,
        Nor ever curse humanity !

George Outram.

BOOK XIV
ENCHANTMENTS

TAM O' SHANTER

WHEN chapman billies leave the street,
And drouthy neebors neebors meet ;
As market-days are wearin' late,
An' folk begin to tak' the gate ;
While we sit bousing at the nappy,
An' gettin' fou and unco happy,
We think na on the lang Scots miles,
The mosses, waters, slaps, and styles,
That lie between us and our hame,
Whare sits our sulky, sullen dame,
Gathering her brows like gathering storm,
Nursing her wrath to keep it warm.

This truth fand honest Tam o' Shanter,
As he frae Ayr ae night did canter
(Auld Ayr, wham ne'er a town surpasses,
For honest men an' bonny lasses).

O Tam ! hadst thou but been sae wise,
As ta'en thy ain wife Kate's advice !
She tauld thee weel thou wast a skellum,
A bletherin', blusterin', drunken blellum ;
That frae November till October,
Ae market-day thou was na sober ;

chapman billies, pedlars	*drouthy*, thirsty	*gate*, road
nappy, ale	*slaps*, passes	*fand*, found
skellum, good-for-nothing	*blellum*, babbler	

That ilka melder wi' the miller
Thou sat as lang as thou had siller ;
That ev'ry naig was ca'd a shoe on,
The smith and thee gat roarin' fou on ;
That at the Lord's house, ev'n on Sunday,
Thou drank wi' Kirkton Jean till Monday.
She prophesy'd that, late or soon,
Thou wad be found, deep drown'd in Doon !
Or catch'd wi' warlocks in the mirk,
By Alloway's auld haunted kirk.
Ah, gentle dames ! it gars me greet
To think how mony counsels sweet,
How mony lengthen'd, sage advices,
The husband frae the wife despises !

But to our tale :—Ae market-night,
Tam had got planted unco right ;
Fast by an ingle, bleezing finely,
Wi' reaming swats, that drank divinely ;
An' at his elbow, Souter Johnie,
His ancient, trusty, drouthy crony ;
Tam lo'ed him like a vera brither ;
They had been fou for weeks thegither.
The night drave on wi' sangs an' clatter ;
An' aye the ale was growing better :
The landlady and Tam grew gracious,
Wi' favours secret, sweet, and precious ;
The Souter tauld his queerest stories ;
The landlord's laugh was ready chorus :

melder, meal-grinding   *ca'd*, driven
mirk, dark   *greet*, weep
reaming swats, foaming new ale *Souter*, shoemaker

The storm without might rair and rustle—
Tam didna mind the storm a whistle.

Care, mad to see a man sae happy,
E'en drown'd himsel' amang the nappy !
As bees flee hame wi' lades o' treasure,
The minutes wing'd their way wi' pleasure :
Kings may be blest, but Tam was glorious,
O'er a' the ills o' life victorious !

But pleasures are like poppies spread,
You seize the flow'r, its bloom is shed !
Or like the snowfall in the river,
A moment white—then melts for ever ;
Or like the borealis race,
That flit ere you can point their place ;
Or like the rainbow's lovely form,
Evanishing amid the storm.—
Nae man can tether time or tide ;
The hour approaches Tam maun ride ;
That hour, o' night's black arch the key-stane,
That dreary hour he mounts his beast in ;
An' sic a night he tak's the road in,
As ne'er poor sinner was abroad in.

The wind blew as 'twad blawn its last ;
The rattling show'rs rose on the blast ;
The speedy gleams the darkness swallow'd ;
Loud, deep, and lang the thunder bellow'd :
That night, a child might understand,
The Deil had business on his hand.

rair, roar

Weel mounted on his grey mare, Meg—
A better never lifted leg—
Tam skelpit on thro' dub an' mire,
Despising wind, an' rain, an' fire ;
Whiles holding fast his guid blue bonnet ;
Whiles crooning o'er some auld Scots sonnet ;
Whiles glow'ring round wi' prudent cares,
Lest bogles catch him unawares ;
Kirk-Alloway was drawing nigh,
Where ghaists an' houlets nightly cry.

By this time he was cross the ford,
Whare in the snaw the chapman smoor'd ;
An' past the birks and meikle stane,
Whare drunken Charlie brak's neck-bane ;
An' thro' the whins, an' by the cairn,
Whare hunters fand the murder'd bairn ;
An' near the thorn, aboon the well,
Whare Mungo's mither hang'd hersel'.
Before him Doon pours a' his floods ;
The doublin' storm roars thro' the woods ;
The lightnings flash frae pole to pole ;
Near and more near the thunders roll ;
When, glimmerin' thro' the groanin' trees,
Kirk-Alloway seem'd in a bleeze ;
Thro' ilka bore the beams were glancin' ;
An' loud resounded mirth and dancin'.

Inspirin' bold John Barleycorn !
What dangers thou canst mak' us scorn !

skelpit, thrashed   *glow'ring*, staring   *houlets*, owls
smoor'd, smothered   *ilka bore*, each chink

Wi' tippenny, we fear nae evil ;
Wi' usquabae, we'll face the Devil !
The swats sae ream'd in Tammie's noddle,
Fair play, he car'd na deils a boddle.
But Maggie stood, right sair astonish'd,
Till, by the heel an' hand admonish'd,
She ventur'd forward on the light ;
An', wow ! Tam saw a unco sight !

Warlocks an' witches in a dance ;
Nae cotillion brent new frae France,
But hornpipes, jigs, strathspeys, an' reels
Put life an' mettle in their heels :
At winnock-bunker in the east,
There sat Auld Nick, in shape o' beast ;
A towzie tyke, black, grim, an' large,
To gie them music was his charge ;
He screw'd the pipes and gart them skirl,
Till roof and rafters a' did dirl.
Coffins stood round, like open presses,
That shaw'd the dead in their last dresses ;
And (by some dev'lish cantraip sleight)
Each in its cauld hand held a light :
By which heroic Tam was able
To note upon the haly table,
A murderer's banes in gibbet airns ;
Twa span-lang, wee, unchristen'd bairns ;

tippenny, ale	*usquabae*, whisky
boddle, farthing	*unco*, marvellous
brent, brand	*winnock-bunker*, window-seat
towzie tyke, shaggy dog	*dirl*, ring
presses, cupboards	*cantraip sleight*, magic art

A thief, new-cutted frae a rape—
Wi' his last gasp his gab did gape ;
Five tomahawks wi' bluid red-rusted,
Five scimitars wi' murder crusted ;
A garter which a babe had strangled ;
A knife a father's throat had mangled,
Whom his ain son o' life bereft,
The grey hairs yet stack to the heft ;
Wi' mair o' horrible an' awfu',
Which ev'n to name wad be unlawfu'.

As Tammie glowr'd, amaz'd, an' curious,
The mirth an' fun grew fast an' furious :
The piper loud an' louder blew,
The dancers quick an' quicker flew ;
They reel'd, they set, they cross'd, they cleekit,
'Till ilka carlin swat and reekit,
An' coost her duddies to the wark,
An' linket at it in her sark !

Now Tam ! O Tam ! had thae been queans
A' plump an' strappin' in their teens ;
Their sarks, instead o' creeshie flannen,
Been snaw-white seventeen hunder linen !
Thir breeks o' mine, my only pair,
That ance were plush, o' guid blue hair,
I wad hae gi'en them aff my hurdies,
For ae blink o' the bonnie burdies !

gab, mouth   *cleekit*, clasped   *carlin*, beldam
swat and reekit, sweated and steamed   *coost*, cast
duddies, rags   *creeshie*, greasy   *hurdies*, buttocks
                       burdies, maids

But withered beldams, auld an' droll,
Rigwoodie hags, wad spean a foal,
Lowping an' flinging on a crummock,
I wonder didna turn thy stomach.

But Tam kenn'd what was what fu' brawlie,
There was ae winsome wench an' wawlie,
That night enlisted in the core
Lang after kenn'd on Carrick shore ;
(For mony a beast to dead she shot,
An' perish'd mony a bonnie boat,
An' shook baith meikle corn an' bear,
An' kept the country-side in fear).
Her cutty sark, o' Paisley harn,
That, while a lassie, she had worn,
In longitude tho' sorely scanty,
It was her best, an' she was vauntie. . . .
Ah ! little kenn'd thy reverend Grannie,
That sark she coft for her wee Nannie,
Wi' twa pund Scots ('twas a' her riches),
Wad ever grac'd a dance of witches !

But here my Muse her wing maun cour ;
Sic flights are far beyond her pow'r ;
To sing how Nannie lap an' flang
(A souple jade she was, an' strang),
An' how Tam stood, like ane bewitch'd,
An' thought his very een enrich'd ;

Rigwoodie, ancient (?)   *spean*, wean   *crummock*, stick
wawlie, choice   *core*, company   *bear*, barley
cutty sark, short shift   *harn*, cloth   *vauntie*, proud
coft, bought

Ev'n Satan glowr'd, an' fidg'd fu' fain,
An' hotched an' blew wi' might an' main :
'Till first ae caper, syne anither,
Tam tint his reason a' thegither,
An' roars out, " Weel done, Cutty-sark ! "
An' in an instant a' was dark :
An' scarcely had he Maggie rallied,
When out the hellish legion sallied.

    As bees bizz out wi' angry fyke,
When plunderin' herds assail their byke ;
As open pussie's mortal foes,
When, pop ! she starts before their nose ;
As eager runs the market-crowd,
When " Catch the thief ! " resounds aloud ;
So Maggie runs, the witches follow,
Wi' mony an eldritch screech an' hollow.

    Ah, Tam ! ah, Tam ! thou 'lt get thy fairin',
In hell they 'll roast thee like a herrin' !
In vain thy Kate awaits thy comin' !
Kate soon will be a woefu' woman !
Now, do thy speedy utmost, Meg,
An' win the key-stane o' the brig ;
There, at them thou thy tail may toss,
A running stream they darena cross ;
But ere the key-stane she could make,
The fient a tail she had to shake !
For Nannie, far before the rest,
Hard upon noble Maggie prest,

fidg'd fu' fain, fidgeted most fondly
hotched, jerked   *tint*, lost   *fyke*, fret
byke, hive   *pussie*, the hare   *eldritch*, uncanny

An' flew at Tam wi' furious ettle ;
But little wist she Maggie's mettle—
Ae spring brought off her master hale,
But left behind her ain grey tail :
The carlin claught her by the rump,
An' left poor Maggie scarce a stump.

Now, wha this tale o' truth shall read,
Ilk man and mother's son take heed :
Whene'er to drink you are inclin'd,
Or cutty-sarks run in your mind,
Think ! ye may buy the joys o'er dear—
Remember Tam o' Shanter's mare.

Robert Burns.

179   ADDRESS TO THE DEIL

" O Prince ! O Chief of many thronèd pow'rs,
That led th' embattled seraphim to war ! "—MILTON.

O THOU ! whatever title suit thee,
Auld Hornie, Satan, Nick, or Clootie,
Wha in yon cavern grim and sootie,
                    Closed under hatches,
Spairges about the brunstane cootie,
                    To scaud poor wretches !

Hear me, Auld Hangie, for a wee,
An' let poor damnèd bodies be ;
I'm sure sma' pleasure it can gie,
                    E'en to a deil,
To skelp an' scaud poor dogs like me,
                    An' hear us squeel.

ettle, intention   *claught*, seized   *Clootie*, Hoofie
spairges, splashes   *cootie*, dish   *scaud*, scald
(2,470)   11 *a*

Great is thy power, an' great thy fame ;
Far kenn'd and noted is thy name :
An' tho' yon lowin' heugh 's thy hame,
    Thou travels far :
An', faith ! thou 's neither lag nor lame,
    Nor blate nor scaur.

Whyles, ranging like a roaring lion,
For prey, a' holes an' corners tryin' ;
Whyles on the strong-wing'd tempest flyin'
    Tirlin the kirks ;
Whyles, in the human bosom pryin',
    Unseen thou lurks.

I 've heard my reverend grannie say,
In lanely glens ye like to stray ;
Or where auld ruin'd castles, grey,
    Nod to the moon,
Ye fright the nightly wand'rer's way
    Wi' eldritch croon.

When twilight did my grannie summon,
To say her prayers, douce, honest woman !
Aft yont the dyke she 's heard you bummin',
    Wi' eerie drone ;
Or, rustlin', thro' the boor-trees comin',
    Wi' heavy groan.

Ae dreary, windy, winter night,
The stars shot down wi' sklentin light,

lowin' heugh, flaming hollow		*blate*, bashful
scaur, timid	*tirlin*, shaking	*boor-trees*, elders
	sklentin, slanting	

Wi' you, mysel', I gat a fright :
    Ayont the lough,
Ye, like a rash-bush, stood in sight,
    Wi' waving sough.

The cudgel in my nieve did shake,
Each bristl'd hair stood like a stake,
When wi' an eldritch, stoor, " quaick—quaick "
    Amang the springs,
Awa' ye squatter'd, like a drake,
    On whistling wings.

Let warlocks grim, an' wither'd hags,
Tell how wi' you, on ragweed nags,
They skim the muirs an' dizzy crags,
    Wi' wicked speed ;
And in kirk-yards renew their leagues
    Owre howkit dead.

Thence, countra wives wi' toil an' pain,
May plunge an' plunge the kirn in vain :
For, oh ! the yellow treasure 's taen
    By witching skill ;
An' dawtit, twal-pint hawkie 's gaen
    As yell 's the bill.

Thence, mystic knots mak' great abuse
On young guidmen, fond, keen, an' crouse ;

rash-bush, tuft of rushes   *sough*, sigh   *nieve*, fist
stoor, harsh   *howkit*, dug up   *kirn*, churn
dawtit, petted   *twal-pint hawkie*, twelve-pint cow
yell, dry   *bill*, bull

When the best wark-lume i' the house,
          By cantraip wit,
Is instant made no worth a louse,
          Just at the bit.

When thowes dissolve the snawy hoord,
An' float the jinglin' icy boord,
Then water-kelpies haunt the foord,
          By your direction ;
An' 'nighted trav'llers are allur'd
          To their destruction.

An' aft your moss-traversing spunkies
Decoy the wight that late an' drunk is :
The bleezin, curst mischievous monkeys
          Delude his eyes,
Till in some miry slough he sunk is,
          Ne'er mair to rise.

When Masons' mystic word an' grip
In storms an' tempests raise you up,
Some cock or cat your rage maun stop,
          Or, strange to tell !
The youngest brother ye wad whip
          Aff straught to hell.

Lang syne in Eden's bonnie yard,
When youthfu' lovers first were pair'd,
An' all the soul of love they shar'd,
          The raptur'd hour,
Sweet on the fragrant, flow'ry sward,
          In shady bow'r :

wark-lume, tool   *cantraip,* magic   *thowes,* thaws
hoord, hoard   *boord,* surface
spunkies, will-o'-the-wisps   *yard,* garden

Then you, ye auld, sneck-drawing dog !
Ye came to Paradise incog.,
An' play'd on man a cursed brogue
    (Black be your fa' !),
An' gied the infant warld a shog,
    Maist ruin'd a'.

D'ye mind that day, when in a bizz,
Wi' reekit duds, an' reestit gizz,
Ye did present your smoutie phiz
    'Mang better folk,
An' sklented on the man of Uzz
    Your spitefu' joke ?

An' how ye gat him i' your thrall
An' brak him out o' house an' hall,
While scabs an' botches did him gall,
    Wi' bitter claw,
And lows'd his ill-tongu'd, wicked scaul,
    Was warst ava ?

But a' your doings to rehearse,
Your wily snares an' fechtin fierce,
Sin' that day Michael did you pierce,
    Down to this time,
Wad ding a Lallan tongue, or Erse,
    In prose or rhyme.

sneck-drawing, plotting   *brogue*, trick
shog, shake   *reested gizz*, scorched wig
smoutie, smutty   *sklented*, squinted
lows'd, loosed   *scaul*, scold
ding, beat   *Lallan*, Lowland

An' now, Auld Cloots, I ken ye're thinkin',
A certain Bardie's rantin', drinkin',
Some luckless hour will send him linkin'
    To your black pit ;
But, faith ! he'll turn a corner jinkin',
    An' cheat you yet.

But, fare you weel, Auld Nickie-Ben !
O wad ye tak' a thought an' men' !
Ye aiblins might—I dinna ken—
    Still hae a stake :
I'm wae to think upo' yon den,
    Ev'n for your sake !

Robert Burns.

180   THE FALSE KNIGHT UPON THE ROAD

" O WHARE are ye gaun ? "
    Quo' the fause knicht upon the road :
" I'm gaun to the scule,"
    Quo' the wee boy, and still he stude.

" What is that upon your back ? "
    Quo' the fause knicht upon the road :
" Atweel it is my bukes,"
    Quo' the wee boy, and still he stude.

" What's that ye've got in your arm ? "
    Quo' the fause knicht upon the road :
" Atweel it is my peit,"
    Quo' the wee boy, and still he stude.

linkin', hasting	*jinkin'*, dodging	*wae*, sad
scule, school	*stude*, stood	*bukes*, books
	peit, peat	

" Wha's aucht thae sheep ? "
    Quo' the fause knicht upon the road :
" They are mine and my mither's,"
    Quo' the wee boy, and still he stude.

" How mony o' them are mine ? "
    Quo' the fause knicht upon the road :
" A' they that hae blue tails,"
    Quo' the wee boy, and still he stude.

" I wiss ye were on yon tree,"
    Quo' the fause knicht upon the road :
" And a gude ladder under me,"
    Quo' the wee boy, and still he stude.

" And the ladder for to break,"
    Quo the fause knicht upon the road :
" And you for to fa' down,"
    Quo' the wee boy, and still he stude.

" I wiss ye were in yon sie,"
    Quo' the fause knicht upon the road :
" And a gude bottom under me,"
    Quo' the wee boy, and still he stude.

" And the bottom for to break,"
    Quo' the fause knicht upon the road :
" *And ye to be drowned,*"
    Quo' the wee boy, and still he stude.

aucht, owns   *sie*, sea   *bottom*, ship

181   THE WEE WEE MAN

As I was walking all alane
    Atween a water and a wa',
O there I met a wee wee man,
    And he was the least I ever saw :

His legs were scarce a shathmont lang,
    And thick and thimber was his thie ;
Atween his brows there was a span,
    And atween his shoulders there was three.

He took up a mickle stane,
    And flang't as far as I could see ;
Though I had been a Wallace wight
    I could na lift it to my knee.

" O wee wee man, but thou be strang,
    O tell me where thy dwelling be ? "
" My dwelling 's down at yon bonnie bower,
    O will you gang wi' me and see ? "

On we lap, and awa' we rode,
    Till we came to yon bonnie green ;
We lighted down to bait our horse,
    And out there came a lady fine.

Four-and-twenty at her back,
    And they were a' clad out in green ;
Though the king of Scotland had been there,
    The warst o' them might hae been his queen.

shathmont, six inches   *thimber*, massive   *lap*, leapt

And on we lap, and awa' we rade,
    Till we came to yon bonnie ha',
Whare the roof was o' the beaten gowd,
    And the floor was o' the cristal a' :

And there were harpings loud and sweet,
    And ladies dancing jimp and sma' ;
But in the twinkling of an eye
    My wee wee man was clean awa'.

182   THE WATER O' WEARIE'S WELL

THERE cam' a bird out o' a bush,
    On water for to dine,
An' sighing sair, says the king's daughter,
    " O wae's this heart o' mine ! "

He's ta'en a harp into his hand,
    He's harped them all asleep,
Except it was the king's daughter,
    Who one wink couldna get.

He's luppen on his berry-brown steed,
    Ta'en 'er on behind himsell,
Then baith rade down to that water
    That they ca' Wearie's Well.

" Wade in, wade in, my lady fair,
    No harm shall thee befall ;
Oft times I've watered my steed
    Wi' the water o' Wearie's Well."

The first step that she stepped in,
  She stepped to the knee ;
And sighend says this lady fair,
  " This water 's nae for me."

" Wade in, wade in, my lady fair,
  No harm shall thee befall ;
Oft times I've watered my steed
  Wi' the water o' Wearie's Well."

The next step that she stepped in,
  She stepped to the middle ;
" O," sighend says this lady fair,
  " I've wat my gowden girdle."

" Wade in, wade in, my lady fair,
  No harm shall thee befall ;
Oft times have I watered my steed
  Wi' the water o' Wearie's Well."

The next step that she stepped in,
  She stepped to the chin ;
" O," sighend says this lady fair,
  " They sud gar twa loves twin."

" Seven king's daughters I've drowned there,
  In the water o' Wearie's Well,
And I'll make you the eight o' them,
  And ring the common bell."

" Since I am standing here," she says,
  " This dowie death to die,
One kiss o' your comely mouth
  I'm sure wad comfort me."

                    twin, separate

He louted him o'er his saddle-bow,
    To kiss her cheek and chin ;
She's ta'en him in her arms twa,
    And thrown him headlong in.

"Since seven king's daughters ye've drowned
      here,
    In the water o' Wearie's Well,
I'll make you bridegroom to them a',
    An' ring the bell mysell."

And aye she warsled, and aye she swam,
    And she swam to dry lan' ;
She thanked God most cheerfully
    The dangers she o'ercame.

183   THOMAS THE RHYMER

TRUE Thomas lay on Huntlie bank,
    A ferlie he spied wi' his e'e,
And there he saw a lady bright
    Come riding down by the Eildon Tree.

Her shirt was o' the grass-green silk,
    Her mantle o' the velvet fine,
At ilka tett of her horse's mane
    Hang fifty siller bells and nine.

True Thomas, he pulled aff his cap,
    And louted low down to his knee :
"All hail, thou mighty Queen of Heaven !
    For thy peer on earth I never did see."

louted, bowed	*warsled*, struggled
ferlie, wonder	*tett*, lock

" O no, O no, Thomas," she said,
    " That name does not belang to me ;
I am but the queen of fair Elfland,
    That am hither come to visit thee.

" Harp and carp, Thomas," she said,
    " Harp and carp along wi' me,
And if ye dare to kiss my lips,
    Sure of your bodie I will be."

" Betide me weal, betide me woe,
    That weird shall never daunton me ; "
Syne he has kissed her rosy lips,
    All underneath the Eildon Tree.

" Now, ye maun go wi' me," she said,
    " True Thomas, ye maun go wi' me,
And ye maun serve me seven years,
    Thro' weal or woe, as may chance to be."

She mounted on her milk-white steed,
    She's ta'en True Thomas up behind,
And aye whene'er her bridle rung
    The steed flew swifter than the wind.

O they rade on, and farther on—
    The steed gaed swifter than the wind—
Until they reached a desert wide,
    And living land was left behind.

" Light down, light down, now, True Thomas,
    And lean your head upon my knee ;
Abide and rest a little space,
    And I will show you ferlies three.

            carp, sing

" O see not ye yon narrow road,
  So thick beset with thorns and briers ?
That is the path of righteousness,
  Tho' after it but few inquires.

" And see not ye that braid braid road,
  That lies across that lily leven ?
That is the path of wickedness,
  Tho' some call it the road to heaven.

" And see not ye that bonnie road
  That winds about the fernie brae ?
That is the road to fair Elfland,
  Where thou and I this night maun gae.

" But, Thomas, ye maun hold your tongue,
  Whatever ye may hear or see,
For, if you speak word in Elflyn land,
  Ye'll ne'er get back to your ain countrie."

O they rade on, and farther on,
  And they waded thro' rivers aboon the knee,
And they saw neither sun nor moon,
  But they heard the roaring of the sea.

It was mirk mirk night, and there was nae stern
    light,
  And they waded thro' red blude to the knee ;
For a' the blude that's shed on earth
  Rins thro' the springs o' that countrie.

  leven, lawn   *mirk*, dark   *stern*, star

Syne they came on to a garden green,
   And she pu'd an apple frae a tree ;
" Take this for thy wages, True Thomas,
   It will give thee tongue that can never lie."

" My tongue is mine ain," True Thomas said ;
   " A gudely gift ye wad gie to me !
I neither dought to buy nor sell,
   At fair or tryst where I may be.

" I dought neither speak to prince or peer,
   Nor ask of grace from fair ladie : "
" Now hold thy peace," the lady said,
   " For as I say, so must it be."

He has gotten a coat of the even cloth,
   And a pair of shoes of velvet green,
And till seven years were gane and past
   True Thomas on earth was never seen.

184   TAM LIN

" O I FORBID you, maidens a',
   That wear gowd on your hair,
To come or gae by Carterhaugh,
   For young Tam Lin is there.

" There's nane that gaes by Carterhaugh,
   But they leave him a wad,
Either their rings or green mantles,
   Or else their maidenhead."

dought, would be able   *even,* smooth   *wad,* pledge

Janet has kilted her green kirtle
   A little aboon her knee,
And she has braided her yellow hair
   A little aboon her bree,
And she's awa' to Carterhaugh
   As fast as she can hie.

When she cam' to Carterhaugh,
   Tam Lin was at the well ;
And there she fand his steed standing,
   But away was himsel'.

She hadna pu'd a double rose,
   A rose but only twa,
Till up then started young Tam Lin,
   Says, " Lady, thou's pu' nae mae.

" Why pu's thou the rose, Janet ?
   And why breaks thou the wand ?
Or why comes thou to Carterhaugh,
   Withouten my command ? "

" Carterhaugh it is my ain ;
   My daddie gave it me :
I'll come and gang by Carterhaugh,
   And ask nae leave at thee."

Janet has kilted her green kirtle
   A little aboon her knee,
And she has snooded her yellow hair
   A little aboon her bree,
And she is to her father's ha'
   As fast as she can hie.

               bree, brow

Four and twenty ladies fair
   Were playing at the ba' :
And out then cam' the fair Janet,
   Ance the flower amang them a'.

Four and twenty ladies fair
   Were playing at the chess,
And out then cam' the fair Janet,
   As green as onie glass.

Out then spak' an old grey knight,
   Lay o'er the castle wa',
And says, " Alas ! fair Janet, for thee,
   But we'll be blamed a' ! "

" Haud yere tongue, ye auld-faced knight,
   Some ill death may ye die !
Father my bairn on whom I will,
   I'll father nane on thee."

Out then spak' her father dear,
   And he spak' meek and mild :
" And ever, alas ! sweet Janet," he says,
   " I think thou gaes wi' child."

" If that I gae wi' child, father,
   Mysel' maun bear the blame ;
There's ne'er a laird about your ha'
   Shall get the bairn's name.

" If my love were an earthly knight,
   As he's an elfin grey,
I wadna gie my ain true-love
   For nae lord that ye hae.

" The steed that my true-love rides on
    Is lighter than the wind ;
Wi' siller he is shod before,
    Wi' burning gowd behind."

Janet has kilted her green kirtle
    A little aboon her knee,
And she has snooded her yellow hair
    A little aboon her bree,
And she's awa' to Carterhaugh
    As fast as she can hie.

When she cam' to Carterhaugh
    Tam Lin was at the well,
And there she fand his steed standing,
    But away was himsel'.

She hadna pu'd a double rose,
    A rose but only twa,
When up then started young Tam Lin,
    Says, " Lady, thou pu's nae mae.

" Why pu's thou the rose, Janet,
    Amang the groves sae green,
And a' to kill the bonnie babe,
    That we gat us between ? "

" O tell me, tell me, Tam Lin," she says,
    " For 's sake that died on tree,
If e'er ye was in holy chapel,
    Or Christendom did see ? "

" Roxburgh he was my grandfather,
　　Took me with him to bide,
And ance it fell upon a day
　　That wae did me betide.

" And ance it fell upon a day,
　　A cauld day and a snell,
When we were frae the hunting come,
　　That frae my horse I fell ;
The Queen o' Fairies she caught me,
　　In yon green hill to dwell.

" And pleasant is the fairy land,
　　But, an eerie tale to tell,
Aye, at the end of seven years,
　　We pay a tiend to hell ;
I am sae fair and fu' o' flesh,
　　I'm feared it be mysel'.

" But the night is Hallowe'en, lady,
　　The morn is Hallowday ;
Then win me, win me, and ye will,
　　For weel I wat ye may.

" Just at the mirk and midnight hour,
　　The fairy folk will ride ;
And they that wad their true-love win
　　At Miles Cross they maun bide."

" But how shall I thee ken, Tam Lin,
　　Or how my true-love know,
Amang sae mony unco knights,
　　The like I never saw ? "

snell, sharp　　　　*tiend*, tithe　　　　*unco*, strange

" O first let pass the black, lady,
    And syne let pass the brown ;
But quickly run to the milk-white steed,
    Pu' ye his rider down.

" For I'll ride on the milk-white steed,
    And ay nearest the town ;
Because I was an earthly knight,
    They gie me that renown.

" My right hand will be gloved, lady,
    My left hand will be bare ;
Cocked up shall my bonnet be,
    And kaim'd down shall my hair ;
And thae's the tokens I gie thee,
    Nae doubt I will be there.

" They'll turn me in your arms, lady,
    Into an esk and adder ;
But hold me fast, and fear me not,
    I am your bairn's father.

" They'll turn me to a bear sae grim,
    And then a lion bold ;
But hold me fast, and fear me not,
    As ye shall love your child.

" Again they'll turn me in your arms,
    To a red-het gaud of airn ;
But hold me fast, and fear me not,
    I'll do to you nae harm.

kaim'd, combed   *esk*, eft   *gaud of airn*, goad of iron

" And last they'll turn me in your arms,
  Into the burning gleed,
Then throw me into well water ;
  O throw me in wi' speed !

" And then I'll be your ain true-love,
  I'll turn a naked knight ;
Then cover me wi' your green mantle,
  And cover me out o' sight."

Gloomy, gloomy was the night,
  And eerie was the way,
As fair Janet in her green mantle
  To Miles Cross she did gae.

About the middle o' the night,
  She heard the bridles ring ;
The lady was as glad at that
  As any earthly thing.

First she let the black pass by,
  And syne she let the brown ;
But quickly she ran to the milk-white steed,
  And pu'd the rider down.

Sae weel she minded what he did say,
  And young Tam Lin did win ;
Syne covered him wi' her green mantle,
  As blythe's a bird in Spring.

Then out spak' the Queen o' Fairies,
  Out of a bush o' broom :
" Them that has gotten young Tam Lin,
  Has gotten a stately groom."

                    gleed, fire

Out then spak' the Queen o' Fairies,
   And an angry woman was she :
" Shame betide her ill-faured face,
   And an ill death may she die !
For she's ta'en awa' the bonniest knight
   In a' my companie.

" But had I ken'd, Tam Lin," she says,
   " What now this night I see,
I wad hae ta'en out thy twa grey een,
   And put in twa een o' tree."

185 THE WITCH'S BALLAD

O, I HAE come from far away,
   From a warm land far away,
A southern land across the sea,
With sailor-lads about the mast,
Merry and canny, and kind to me.

And I hae been to yon town
   To try my luck in yon town ;
Nort, and Mysie, Elspie too.
Right braw we were to pass the gate,
Wi' gowden clasps on girdles blue.

Mysie smiled wi' miminy mouth,
   Innocent mouth, miminy mouth ;
Elspie wore a scarlet gown,
Nort's grey eyes were unco gleg.
My Castile comb was like a crown.

ill-faured, ill-favoured   *unco gleg*, curiously sharp

We walked abreast all up the street,
   Into the market up the street ;
Our hair with marigolds was wound,
Our bodices with love-knots laced,
Our merchandise with tansy bound.

Nort had chickens, I had cocks,
   Gamesome cocks, loud-crowing cocks ;
Mysie ducks, and Elspie drakes,—
For a wee groat or a pound ;
We lost nae time wi' gives and takes.

Lost nae time, for well we knew,
   In our sleeves full well we knew,
When the gloaming came that night,
Duck nor drake, nor hen nor cock
Would be found by candle-light.

And when our chaffering all was done,
   All was paid for, sold and done,
We drew a glove on ilka hand,
We sweetly curtsied each to each,
And deftly danced a saraband.

The market-lasses looked and laughed
   Left their gear, and looked and laughed ;
They made as they would join the game,
But soon their mithers, wild and wud,
With whack and screech they stopped the same.

Sae loud the tongues o' randies grew,
   The flytin' and the skirlin' grew,

wud, mad	*randies*, viragoes
flytin', scolding	*skirlin'*, shrieking

At all the windows in the place,
Wi' spoons or knives, wi' needle or awl,
Was thrust out every hand and face.

And down each stair they thronged anon,
  Gentle, semple, thronged anon ;
Souter and tailor, frowsy Nan,
The ancient widow young again,
Simpering behind her fan.

Without a choice, against their will,
  Doited, dazed, against their will,
The market lassie and her mither,
The farmer and his husbandman,
Hand in hand dance a' thegither.

Slow at first, but faster soon,
  Still increasing, wild and fast,
Hoods and mantles, hats and hose,
Blindly doffed and cast away,
Left them naked, heads and toes.

They would have torn us limb from limb,
  Dainty limb from dainty limb ;
But never one of them could win
Across the line that I had drawn
With bleeding thumb a-widdershin.

But there was Jeff the provost's son,
  Jeff the provost's only son ;
There was Father Auld himsel',
The Lombard frae the hostelry,
And the lawyer Peter Fell.

Souter, shoemaker   doited, stupid
  a-widdershin, against the course of the sun

All goodly men we singled out,
  Waled them well, and singled out,
And drew them by the left hand in ;
Mysie the priest, and Elspie won
The Lombard, Nort the lawyer carle,
I mysel' the provost's son.

Then, with cantrip kisses seven,
  Three times round with kisses seven,
Warped and woven there spun we
Arms and legs and flaming hair,
Like a whirlwind on the sea.

Like a wind that sucks the sea,
  Over and in and on the sea,
Good sooth it was a mad delight ;
And every man of all the four
Shut his eyes and laughed outright.

Laughed as long as they had breath,
  Laughed while they had sense or breath ;
And close about us coiled a mist
Of gnats and midges, wasps and flies,
Like the whirlwind shaft it rist.

Drawn up I was right off my feet ;
  Into the mist and off my feet ;
And, dancing on each chimney-top,
I saw a thousand darling imps
Keeping time with skip and hop.

  Waled, picked   *cantrip*, witch

And on the provost's brave ridge-tile,
  On the provost's grand ridge-tile,
The Blackamoor first to master me.
I saw, I saw that winsome smile,
The mouth that did my heart beguile,
And spoke the great Word over me,
In the land beyond the sea.

I called his name, I called aloud,
  Alas! I called on him aloud;
And then he filled his hand with stour,
And he threw it towards me in the air;
My mouse flew out, I lost my pow'r!

My lusty strength, my power were gone;
  Power was gone, and all was gone.
He will not let me love him more!
Of bell and whip and horse's tail
He cares not if I find a store.

But I am proud if he is fierce!
  I am as proud as he is fierce;
I'll turn about and backward go,
If I meet again that Blackamoor,
And he'll help us then, for he shall know
I seek another paramour.

And we'll gang once more to yon town,
  Wi' better luck to yon town;
We'll walk in silk and cramoisie,
And I shall wed the provost's son;
My lady of the town I'll be!

stour, dust   *cramoisie*, crimson

For I was born a crowned king's child,
   Born and nursed a king's child,
King o' a land ayont the sea,
Where the Blackamoor kissed me first,
And taught me art and glamourie.

Each one in her wame shall hide
   Her hairy mouse, her wary mouse,
Fed on madwort and agramie,—
Wear amber beads between her breasts,
And blind-worm's skin about her knee.

The Lombard shall be Elspie's man,
   Elspie's gowden husband-man ;
Nort shall take the lawyer's hand ;
The priest shall swear another vow,
We'll dance again the saraband !

William Bell Scott.

186 THE LAILY WORM AND THE MACHREL OF THE SEA

" I was but seven year auld
   When my mither she did dee ;
My father married the ae warst woman
   The warld did ever see.

" For she has made me the laily worm,
   That lies at the fit o' the tree,
An' my sister Masery she's made
   The machrel of the sea.

glamourie, witchcraft   *wame,* belly   *laily,* loathly
fit, foot   *machrel,* mackerel

" An' every Saturday at noon
    The machrel comes to me,
An' she takes my laily head
    An' lays it on her knee,
She kaims it wi' a siller kaim,
    An' washes 't in the sea.

" Seven knights hae I slain,
    Sin' I lay at the fit of the tree,
An' ye war na my ain father,
    The eighth ane ye should be." . . .

He sent for his lady,
    As fast as send could he :
" Whar is my son that ye sent frae me,
    And my daughter, Lady Masery ? "

" Your son is at our king's court,
    Serving for meat an' fee,
An' your daughter's at our queen's court,
    The queen's maiden to be."

" Ye lee, ye lee, ye ill woman,
    Sae loud as I hear ye lee ;
My son's the laily worm,
    That lies at the fit o' the tree,
And my daughter, Lady Masery,
    Is the machrel of the sea ! "

She has tane a siller wan',
    An' gi'en him strokes three,
And he's started up the bravest knight
    That ever your eyes did see.

kaim, comb   *sin'*, since   *lee*, lie

She has ta'en a small horn,
    An' loud an' shrill blew she.
An' a' the fish came her untill
    But the machrel of the sea :
" Ye shapeit me ance an unseemly shape,
    An' ye's never mare shape me."

He has sent to the wood
    For whins and for hawthorn.
An' he has ta'en that gay lady,
    An' there he did her burn.

187   THE DAEMON LOVER

" O WHERE hae ye been, my long, long love,
    These seven long years and more ? "
" O I'm come to seek my former vows,
    That ye promised me before."

" Awa' wi' your former vows," she says,
    " For they will breed but strife ;
Awa' wi' your former vows," she says,
    " For I am become a wife.

" I am married to a ship-carpenter,
    A ship-carpenter he's bound ;
I wadna he kenn'd my mind this nicht
    For twice five hundred pound."

He turn'd him round and round about,
    And the tear blinded his e'e :
" I wad never hae trodden on Irish ground
    If it hadna been for thee.

" I might hae had a noble lady,
  Far, far beyond the sea ;
I might hae had a noble lady,
  Were it no for the love o' thee."

" If ye might hae had a noble lady,
  Yoursel' ye had to blame ;
Ye might hae taken the noble lady,
  For ye kenn'd that I was nane."

" O fause are the vows o' womenkind,
  But fair is their fause bodie :
I wad never hae trodden on Irish ground,
  Were it no for the love o' thee."

" If I was to leave my husband dear,
  And my wee young son also,
O what hae ye to tak' me to,
  If with you I should go ? "

" I hae seven ships upon the sea,
  The eighth brought me to land ,
With mariners and merchandise,
  And music on every hand.

" The ship wherein my love sall sail
  Is glorious to behowd ;
The sails sall be o' the finest silk,
  And the mast o' beaten gowd."

She has taken up her wee young son,
  Kiss'd him baith cheek and chin ;
" O fare ye weel, my wee young son,
  For I'll never see you again ! "

She has put her foot on gude ship-board,
    And on ship-board she has gane,
And the veil that hangit ower her face
    Was a' wi' gowd begane.

She hadna sail'd a league, a league,
    A league but barely two,
Till she minded on her husband she left
    And her wee young son also.

" O haud your tongue o' weeping," he says,
    " Let a' your follies a-bee ;
I'll show where the white lilies grow
    On the banks o' Italie."

She hadna sailed a league, a league,
    A league but barely three,
Till grim, grim grew his countenance
    And gurly grew the sea.

" What hills are yon, yon pleasant hills,
    The sun shines sweetly on ? "
" O yon are the hills o' Heaven," he said,
    " Where you will never won."

" O whaten-a mountain is yon," she said,
    " Sae dreary wi' frost and snow ? "
" O yon is the mountain o' Hell," he said,
    " Where you and I will go.

" But haud your tongue, my dearest dear,
    Let a' your follies a-bee,
I'll show where the white lilies grow,
    In the bottom o' the sea."

     begane, covered   *gurly*, stormy

And aye as she turn'd her round about,
 Aye taller he seem'd to be ;
Until that the tops o' that gallant ship
 Nae taller were than he.

He strack the top-mast wi' his hand,
 The fore-mast wi' his knee ;
And he brake that gallant ship in twain,
 And sank her in the sea.

188   LADY ANN

FAIR Lady Ann walked from her bower
 Down by the greenwood side,
The sweet flowers sprang, and wild birds sang,
 The simmer was in pride.
Among the flowers that lady went,
 As white as was the swan ;
And she thought on her love and sighed,
 The gentle Lady Ann.

Out of the wood came three bonnie boys,
 As naked as they were born,
And they did sing and play at the ba',
 Beneath a milk-white thorn.
" A seven lang years would I stand here,
 All noon, and night, and dawn,
And all for one of thae bonnie boys,"
 Quo' gentle Lady Ann.

Then up and spake the eldest boy :
 " Now listen, thou fair ladie—
O we lay a' at ae milk-white breast,
 And nursed were on ae knee ;

Ae sweet lip smiled on us as we smiled,
    And there was a snaw-white han',
As gentle and kin', and fair as thine,
    That watched us, Lady Ann."

" O come to me, thou lily-white boy,
    The bonniest of the three !
O come, O come, thou lily-white boy,
    My little bower-boy to be !
I'll cleed thee all in silk and gold,
    And nurse thee on my knee."
" Oh mother, oh mother, when I was thine,
    Sic love I couldna see."

                    Allan Cunningham.

189   THE WIFE OF USHER'S WELL

THERE lived a wife at Usher's Well,
    And a wealthy wife was she ;
She had three stout and stalwart sons,
    And sent them o'er the sea.

They hadna been a week from her,
    A week but barely ane,
When word came back to the carline wife
    That her three sons were gane.

They hadna been a week from her,
    A week but barely three,
When word came to the carline wife
    That her sons she'd never see.

cleed, clothe   *carline wife*, old woman

" I wish the wind may never cease,
    Nor fashes in the flood,
Till my three sons come hame to me,
    In earthly flesh and blood ! "

It fell about the Martinmas,
    When nights are lang and mirk,
The carline wife's three sons cam' hame,
    And their hats were o' the birk.

It neither grew in syke nor ditch,
    Nor yet in ony sheugh ;
But at the gates o' Paradise
    That birk grew fair eneugh.

" Blow up the fire, my maidens !
    Bring water from the well !
For a' my house shall feast this night,
    Since my three sons are well."

And she has made to them a bed,
    She's made it large and wide ;
And she's ta'en her mantle her about,
    Sat down at the bedside.

    .   .   .   .   .

Up then crew the red red cock,
    And up and crew the grey ;
The eldest to the youngest said,
    " 'Tis time we were away."

The cock he hadna craw'd but ance,
    And clapped his wings at a',
When the youngest to the eldest said,
    " Brother, we must awa'."

fashes, disturbances   *syke*, trench   *sheugh*, hollow

" The cock doth craw, the day doth daw,
    The channerin' worm doth chide ;
Gin we be missed out o' our place,
    A sair pain we maun bide.

" Fare ye weel, my mother dear !
    Fareweel to barn and byre !
And fare ye weel, the bonnie lass
    That kindles my mother's fire."

190   KILMENY

BONNIE Kilmeny gaed up the glen ;
But it wasna to meet Duneira's men,
Nor the rosy monk of the isle to see,
For Kilmeny was pure as pure could be.
It was only to hear the yorlin sing,
And pu' the cress-flower round the spring ;
The scarlet hypp and the hind-berrye,
And the nut that hung frae the hazel tree ;
For Kilmeny was pure as pure could be.
But lang may her minny look o'er the wa' ;
And lang may she seek i' the green-wood shaw ;
Lang the laird o' Duneira blame,
And lang, lang greet or Kilmeny come hame !

When many a day had come and fled,
When grief grew calm, and hope was dead,
When mess for Kilmeny's soul had been sung,
When the bedesman had pray'd and the dead-bell
    rung,

channerin', fretting   *yorlin*, yellow-hammer
hind-berrye, wild rasp   *minny*, mother   *greet*, weep

Late, late in a gloamin' when all was still,
When the fringe was red on the westlin' hill,
The wood was sere, the moon i' the wane,
The reek o' the cot hung over the plain,
Like a little wee cloud in the world its lane ;
When the ingle lowed wi' an eiry leme—
Late, late in the gloamin' Kilmeny came hame !

" Kilmeny, Kilmeny, where have you been ?
Lang hae we sought baith holt and dean ;
By linn, by ford, and green-wood tree,
Yet you are halesome and fair to see.
Where gat ye that joup o' the lily sheen ?
That bonnie snood o' the birk sae green ?
And these roses, the fairest that ever were seen ?
Kilmeny, Kilmeny, where have you been ? "

Kilmeny look'd up wi' a lovely grace,
But nae smile was seen on Kilmeny's face ;
As still was her look, and as still was her e'e,
As the stillness that lay on the emerant lea,
Or the mist that sleeps on a waveless sea.
For Kilmeny had been she knew not where,
And Kilmeny had seen what she could not declare ;
Kilmeny had been where the cock never crew,
Where the rain never fell, and the wind never blew.
But it seemed as the harp of the sky had rung,
And the airs of heaven played round her tongue,
When she spake of the lovely forms she had seen,
And a land where sin had never been ;

reek, smoke	*its lane*, alone	*lowed*, burned
eiry leme, eerie gleam		*dean*, glen
joup, petticoat	*snood*, hair-band	*emerant*, emerald

A land of love and a land of light,
Withouten sun, or moon, or night ;
Where the river swa'd a living stream,
And the light a pure celestial beam ;
The land of vision, it would seem,
A still, an everlasting dream.

And O, her beauty was fair to see,
But still and steadfast was her e'e !
Such beauty bard may never declare,
For there was no pride nor passion there ;
And the soft desire of maiden's een
In that mild face could never be seen.
Her seymar was the lily flower,
And her cheek the moss-rose in the shower ;
And her voice like the distant melodye
That floats along the twilight sea.
But she loved to raike the lanely glen,
And keeped afar frae the haunts of men ;
Her holy hymns unheard to sing,
To suck the flowers, and drink the spring :
But wherever her peaceful form appeared,
The wild beasts of the hill were cheered ;
The wolf played blythely round the field,
The lordly byson lowed, and kneeled ;
The dun deer wooed with manner bland,
And cowered aneath her lily hand.
And when at eve the woodlands rung,
When hymns of other worlds she sung
In ecstasy of sweet devotion,
O, then the glen was all in motion !

    swa'd, swelled   *seymar*, robe   *raike*, range

The wild beasts of the forest came,
Broke from their bughts and faulds the tame,
And goved around, charmed and amazed ;
Even the dull cattle crooned and gazed,
And murmured, and looked with anxious pain
For something the mystery to explain.
The buzzard came with the throstle-cock ;
The corby left her houf in the rock ;
The blackbird alang wi' the eagle flew ;
The hind cam' tripping o'er the dew ;
The wolf and the kid their raike began,
And the tod, and the lamb, and the leveret ran ;
The hawk and the hern attour them hung,
And the merle and the mavis forhooyed their young ;
And all in a peaceful ring were hurled :
It was like an eve in a sinless world !

When a month and a day had come and gane,
Kilmeny sought the green-wood wene ;
There laid her down on the leaves sae green,
And Kilmeny on earth was never mair seen.
But O ! the words that fell frae her mouth
Were words of wonder, and words of truth !
But all the land were in fear and dread,
For they kendna whether she was living or dead.
It wasna her hame, and she couldna remain ;
She left this world of sorrow and pain,
And returned to the land of thought again.

James Hogg.

bughts, pens   *goved*, mooned   *houf*, haunt
tod, fox   *attour*, above   *forhooyed*, forsook
                  wene, nook

PROUD MAISIE

PROUD Maisie is in the wood,
    Walking so early ;
Sweet Robin sits on the bush,
    Singing so rarely :

" Tell me, thou bonny bird,
    When shall I marry me ? "
" When six braw gentlemen
    Kirkyard shall carry ye."

" Who makes the bridal bed,
    Birdie, say truly ? "
" The grey-headed sexton
    That delves the grave duly.

" The glow-worm o'er grave and stone
    Shall light thee steady ;
The owl from the steeple sing :
    ' Welcome, proud lady.' "

                                    Sir Walter Scott.

BOOK XV
LACRIMAE RERUM

192   THE BONNIE BROUKIT BAIRN

    MARS is braw in crammasy,
    Venus in a green silk goun,
    The auld mune shak's her gowden feathers,
    Their starry talk's a wheen o' blethers,
    Nane for thee a thochtie sparin',
    Earth, thou bonnie broukit bairn !
    —But greet, an' in your tears ye'll droun
    The haill clanjamfrie !

                  C. M. Grieve.

193   THE FLOWERS OF THE FOREST

I'VE heard the lilting at our yowe-milking,
    Lasses a-lilting before the dawn o' day ;
But now they are moaning in ilka green loaning :
    " The Flowers of the Forest are a' wede away."

At buchts, in the morning, nae blythe lads are scorn-
        ing ;
    The lasses are lonely, and dowie, and wae ;
Nae daffin', nae gabbin', but sighing and sabbing :
    Ilk ane lifts her leglen, and hies her away.

crammasy, crimson   *wheen o' blethers*, pack of nonsense
broukit, pale-faced   *greet*, weep   *clanjamfrie*, collection
yowe, ewe   *loaning*, lane   *wede*, withered
buchts, sheepfolds   *daffin'*, romping   *leglen*, milk-pail

In hairst, at the shearing, nae youths now are jeering,
  The bandsters are lyart, and runkled and grey ;
At fair or at preaching, nae wooing, nae fleeching :
  The Flowers of the Forest are a' wede away.

At e'en, in the gloaming, nae swankies are roaming
  'Bout stacks wi' the lasses at bogle to play,
But ilk ane sits drearie, lamenting her dearie :
  The Flowers of the Forest are a' wede away.

Dule and wae for the order sent our lads to the Border ;
  The English, for ance, by guile won the day ;
The Flowers of the Forest, that foucht aye the fore-
    most,
  The prime o' our land, are cauld in the clay.

We'll hear nae mair lilting at the yowe-milking,
  Women and bairns are heartless and wae ;
Sighing and moaning on ilka green loaning ;
  " The Flowers of the Forest are a' wede away."
                                        Jean Elliot.

194   IT WAS A' FOR OUR RIGHTFU' KING

It was a' for our rightfu' king,
  We left fair Scotland's strand ;
It was a' for our rightfu' king
  We e'er saw Irish land,
    My dear,—
  We e'er saw Irish land.

hairst, harvest	*bandsters*, binders	*lyart*, grizzled
runkled, wrinkled	*fleeching*, flattering	
swankies, smart lads	*bogle*, hide-and-seek	*dule*, sorrow

Now a' is done that men can do,
  And a' is done in vain ;
My love and native land farewell,
  For I maun cross the main,
      My dear,—
  For I maun cross the main.

He turned him right, and round about,
  Upon the Irish shore ;
And gae his bridle-reins a shake,
  With adieu for evermore,
      My dear,—
  With adieu for evermore.

The soger from the wars returns,
  The sailor frae the main ;
But I hae parted frae my love,
  Never to meet again,
      My dear,—
  Never to meet again.

When day is gane, and night is come,
  And a' folk bound to sleep ;
I think on him that's far awa',
  The lee-lang night, and weep,
      My dear,—
  The lee-lang night, and weep.

                         Robert Burns.

    lee-lang, livelong

195　　　　　　DURISDEER

WE'LL meet nae mair at sunset, when the weary day is
　　　dune,
Nor wander hame thegither, by the lee licht o' the
　　　mune !
I'll hear your step nae longer amang the dewy corn,
For we'll meet nae mair, my bonniest, either at eve or
　　　morn.

The yellow broom is waving, abune the sunny brae,
And the rowan berries dancing, where the sparkling
　　　waters play.
Tho' a' is bright and bonnie, it's an eerie place to me,
For we'll meet nae mair, my dearest, either by burn or
　　　tree.

　　　　　　　　　　　　　　　Lady John Scott.

196　　　　　　JOHN O' LORN

MY plaid is on my shoulder and my boat is on the shore,
　　And it's all bye wi' auld days and you ;
Here's a health and here's a heartbreak, for it's hame,
　　my dear, no more,
　　To the green glens, the fine glens we knew !

'Twas for the sake o' glory, but oh ! woe upon the wars,
　　That brought my father's son to sic a day ;
I'd rather be a craven wi' nor fame nor name nor scars,
　　Than turn an exile's heel on Moidart Bay.

And you, in the daytime, you'll be here, and in the mirk,
  Wi' the kind heart, the open hand and free ;
And far awa' in foreign France, in town or camp or kirk,
  I'll be wondering if you keep a thought for me.

But never more the heather nor the bracken at my knees,
  I'm poor John o' Lorn, a broken man ;
For an auld Hielan' story I must sail the swinging seas,
  A chief without a castle or a clan.

My plaid is on my shoulder and my boat is on the shore,
  And it's all bye wi' auld days and you :
Here's a health and here's a heartbreak, for it's hame,
        my dear, no more,
    To the green glens, the fine glens we knew !

Neil Munro.

197   ETTRICK

  WHEN we first rade down Ettrick,
  Our bridles were ringing, our hearts were dancing,
  The waters were singing, the sun was glancing,
  An' blithely our voices rang out thegither,
  As we brushed the dew frae the blooming heather,
    When we first rade down Ettrick.

  When we next rade down Ettrick
  The day was dying, the wild birds calling,
  The wind was sighing, the leaves were falling,
  An' silent an' weary, but closer thegither,
  We urged our steeds thro' the faded heather,
    When we next rade down Ettrick.

mirk, dark

When I last rade down Ettrick,
The winds were shifting, the storm was waking,
The snow was drifting, my heart was breaking,
For we never again were to ride thegither,
In sun or storm on the mountain heather,
When I last rade down Ettrick.

Lady John Scott.

198   LAMMERMUIR

HAPPY the craw
That biggs in the Trotten shaw,
And drinks o' the Water o' Dye—
For nae mair may I.

199   THE PIOBRACH O' KINREEN

Och, hey! Kinreen o' the Dee,
Kinreen o' the Dee,
Kinreen o' the Dee—
Och, hey! Kinreen o' the Dee.

I'll blaw up my chanter
I've sounded fu' weel,
To mony a ranter
In mony a reel,
An' poured a' my heart i' the win'bag wi' glee:
Och, hey! Kinreen o' the Dee.
For licht was the lauchter on bonny Kinreen,
An' licht was the fit-fa' that danced o'er the green,
An' licht were the hearts a', and lichtsome the eyne.
Och, hey! Kinreen o' the Dee.

biggs, builds

The auld hoose is bare noo,
        A cauld hoose to me ;
The hearth is nae mair noo
        The centre o' glee ;
Nae mair for the bairnies the bield it has been :
        Och, hey ! for bonny Kinreen.
The auld folk, the young folk, the wee anes an' a',
A hunder years' hame birds are harried awa'—
Are harried an' hameless whatever winds blaw.
        Och, hey ! Kinreen o' the Dee.

Fareweel, my auld plew-lan' !
        I'll never mair plew it ;
Fareweel, my auld plew, an'
        The auld yaud that drew it !
Fareweel, my auld kail-yard, ilk bush an' ilk tree !
        Och, hey ! Kinreen o' the Dee ;
Fareweel, the auld braes that my han' keepit green ;
Fareweel, the auld ways where we wandered unseen,
Ere the licht o' my hearth cam' to bonny Kinreen.
        Och, hey ! Kinreen o' the Dee. . . .

Though little the thing be
        Oor ain we can ca',
That little we cling by
        The mair that it's sma'.
Though puir was oor hame, and though wild was the
        scene,
'Twas the hame o' oor hearts, it was bonny Kinreen ;
And noo we maun leave it, baith grey head and bairn ;
Maun leave it to fatten the deer o' Knock Cairn,
An' a' frae Lochlee to the Morven o' Gairn.

    bield, shelter   *plew*, plough   *yaud*, jade

Och, hey ! Kinreen o' the Dee,
Kinreen o' the Dee,
Kinreen o' the Dee—
Sae fareweel for ever, Kinreen o' the Dee !
William Forsyth.

200 LUCY'S FLITTIN'

'Twas when the wan leaf frae the birk tree was fa'in',
And Martinmas dowie had wound up the year,
That Lucy rowed up her wee kist wi' her a' in't,
    And left her auld maister and neebours sae dear.
For Lucy had served in the Glen a' the simmer ;
    She cam' there afore the flower bloom'd on the pea :
An orphan was she, and they had been kind till her ;
    Sure that was the thing brocht the tear to her e'e.

She gaed by the stable where Jamie was stan'in' ;
    Richt sair was his kind heart that flittin' to see.
" Fare-ye-weel, Lucy ! " quo' Jamie, and ran in :
    The gatherin' tears trickled fast frae his e'e.
As down the burn-side she gaed slow wi' the flittin',
    Fare-ye-weel, Lucy ! was ilka bird's sang ;
She heard the craw sayin't, high on the tree sittin',
    And robin was chirpin't the brown leaves amang.

" Oh, what is't that pits my puir heart in a flutter ?
    And what gars the tears come sae fast to my e'e ?
If I wasna ettled to be ony better,
    Then what gars me wish ony better to be ?

rowed, packed	*kist*, box	*flittin'*, removal
ettled, intended	*gars*, makes	

I'm just like a lammie that loses its mither ;
   Nae mither or friend the puir lammie can see :
I fear I hae tint my puir heart a'thegither ;
   Nae wonder the tear fa's sae fast frae my e'e.

" Wi' the rest o' my claes I hae rowed up the ribbon,
   The bonnie blue ribbon that Jamie gae me :
Yestreen, when he gae me't, and saw I was sabbin',
   I'll never forget the wae blink o' his e'e.
Though now he said naething but ' Fare-ye-weel,
      Lucy ! '
   It made me I could neither speak, hear, nor see :
He couldna say mair, but just ' Fare-ye-weel, Lucy ! '
   Yet that will I mind till the day that I dee."

William Laidlaw.

201   CRAIGO WOODS

CRAIGO WOODS, wi' the splash o' the cauld rain
     beatin'
   I' the back end o' the year,
When the clouds hang laigh wi' the weicht o' their load
     o' greetin'
   And the autumn wind 's asteer ;
Ye may stand like ghaists, ye may fa' i' the blast that's
     cleft ye
   To rot i' the chilly dew,
But when will I mind on aucht since the day I left ye
   Like I mind on you—on you ?

tint, lost	*laigh*, low
weicht, weight	*greetin'*, weeping
asteer, astir	*aucht*, anything

Craigo Woods, i' the licht o' September sleepin'
    And the saft mist o' the morn,
When the hairst climbs to yer feet, an' the sound o'
        reapin'
    Comes up frae the stookit corn,
And the braw reid puddock-stules are like jewels
        blinkin'
    And the bramble happs ye baith,
O what do I see, i the lang nicht, lyin' an' thinkin'
    As I see yer wraith—yer wraith ?

There's a road to a far-aff land, an' the land is yonder
    Whaur a' men's hopes are set ;
We dinna ken foo lang we maun hae to wander,
    But we'll a' win to it yet ;
An' gin there's woods o' fir an' the licht atween them,
    I winna speir its name,
But I'll lay me doon by the puddock-stules when I've
        seen them,
    An' I'll cry " I'm hame—I'm hame ! "

                                    Violet Jacob.

202   DEATH AND FRIENDSHIP

        IT's an owercome sooth for age an' youth,
            And it brooks wi' nae denial,
        That the dearest friends are the auldest friends,
            And the young are just on trial.

hairst, harvest   *stookit*, in sheaves
puddock-stules, toadstools   *happs*, covers
foo, how   *speir*, ask   *owercome*, adage

There's a rival bauld wi' young an' auld,
    And it's him that has bereft me ;
For the surest friends are the auldest friends,
    And the maist o' mines hae left me.

There are kind hearts still, for friends to fill
    And fools to take and break them ;
But the nearest friends are the auldest friends,
    And the grave's the place to seek them.
                                    R. L. Stevenson.

203   THE WILD GEESE

" O TELL me what was on yer road, ye roarin' norlan'
    Wind,
As ye cam' blawin' frae the land that's niver frae my
    mind ?
My feet they traivel England, but I'm deein' for the
    north."
" My man, I heard the siller tides rin up the Firth o'
    Forth."

" Aye, Wind, I ken them weel eneuch, and fine they fa'
    an' rise,
And fain I'd feel the creepin' mist on yonder shore that
    lies,
But tell me, ere ye passed them by, what saw ye on the
    way ? "
" My man, I rocked the rovin' gulls that sail abune the
    Tay."

" But saw ye naething, leein' Wind, afore ye cam' to
Fife ?
There's muckle lyin' 'yont the Tay that's mair to me nor
life."
" My man, I swept the Angus braes ye ha'ena trod for
years."
" O Wind, forgi'e a hameless loon that canna see for
tears ! "

" And far abune the Angus straths I saw the wild geese
flee,
A lang, lang skein o' beatin' wings, wi' their heids towards the sea,
And aye their cryin' voices trailed ahint them on the
air—"
" O Wind, hae maircy, haud yer whisht, for I daurna
listen mair ! "

Violet Jacob.

204 THE PARTING

There surely sud been mair fracaw ;
 A wee bit present, tak' and gie,
 A passin' dimness in the e'e,
  And he's awa'.

For thirty years I've ca'd him frien' ;
 And mony a simmer tryst we set,
 And swappit rhymes when neist we met,
  On a' we'd seen.

haud yer whisht, hold your peace   *neist*, next

And now his stars in yonder sky
 Are no' the stars we used to ken ;
 Yet there his lave o' life he'll spen'—
  And here am I.

How simply can the thing be dune !
 Yet there was nae delusion there—
 We kent that we wad meet nae mair
  This yird abune !

In letters—shortening ilka year—
 Awhile our auld langsynes we'll tell ;
 And sune be auld langsyne oursel'—
  Him there, me here.
      Walter Wingate.

205   A MILE AN' A BITTOCK

A MILE an' a bittock, a mile or twa,
Abune the burn, ayont the law,
Davie an' Donal' an' Cherlie an' a',
 An' the mune was shinin' clearly !

Ane went hame wi' the ither, an' then
The ither went hame wi' the ither twa men,
An' baith wad return him the service again,
 An' the mune was shinin' clearly !

The clocks were chappin' in house an' ha',
Eleeven, twal, an' ane an' twa ;
An' the guidman's face was turnt to the wa',
 An' the mune was shinin' clearly !

lave, rest	*yird*, earth	*ayont*, beyond
law, hill	*chappin'*, striking	

A wind got up frae affa the sea,
It blew the stars as clear's could be,
It blew in the een of a' o' the three,
    An' the mune was shinin' clearly !

Noo, Davie was first to get sleep in his head,
" The best o' frien's maun twine," he said ;
" I'm weariet, an' here I'm awa' to my bed."
    An' the mune was shining clearly !

Twa o' them walkin' an' crackin' their lane,
The mornin' licht cam' grey an' plain,
An' the birds they yammert on stick an' stane,
    An' the mune was shinin' clearly.

O years ayont, O years awa',
My lads, ye'll mind whate'er befa'—
My lads, ye'll mind on the bield o' the law,
    When the mune was shinin' clearly.
                R. L. Stevenson.

twine, part   *crackin'*, talking   *their lane*, alone
yammert, chattered   *bield*, shelter

BOOK XVI
PHILOSOPHY

206   THE FULL LIFE

I HAE been blithe wi' comrades dear ;
   I hae been merry drinking ;
I hae been joyfu' gath'rin' gear ;
   I hae been happy thinking :
But a' the pleasures e'er I saw,
   Tho' three times doubl'd fairly,
That happy night was worth them a',
   Amang the rigs o' barley.

Robert Burns.

207   THE SECRET OF HAPPINESS

IT's hardly in a body's pow'r
To keep, at times, frae being sour,
   To see how things are shar'd ;
How best o' chiels are whiles in want,
While coofs on countless thousands rant,
   And ken na how to wair 't ;
But, Davie, lad, ne'er fash your head,
   Tho' we hae little gear,
We're fit to win our daily bread,
   As lang's we're hale and fier :
     " Mair spier na, nor fear na,"
       Auld age ne'er mind a feg,
     The last o't, the warst o't,
       Is only but to beg.

chiels, fellows	*coofs*, fools	*wair 't*, spend it
fash, trouble	*fier*, sound	*spier*, ask
	feg, fig	

To lie in kilns and barns at e'en,
When banes are craz'd, and bluid is thin,
  Is, doubtless, great distress !
Yet then content could make us blest ;
Ev'n then, sometimes, we'd snatch a taste
  Of truest happiness.
The honest heart that's free frae a'
  Intended fraud or guile,
However Fortune kick the ba',
  Has aye some cause to smile :
    And mind still, you'll find still,
      A comfort this nae sma' ;
    Nae mair then, we'll care then,
      Nae farther can we fa'.

What tho', like commoners of air,
We wander out we know not where,
  But either house or hal' ?
Yet Nature's charms, the hills and woods,
The sweeping vales, and foaming floods,
  Are free alike to all.
In days when daisies deck the ground,
  And blackbirds whistle clear,
With honest joy our hearts will bound
  To see the coming year :
    On braes when we please, then,
      We'll sit an' sowth a tune :
    Syne rhyme till 't, we'll time till 't,
      And sing 't when we hae done.

It's no in titles nor in rank :
It's no in wealth like Lon'on bank,
  To purchase peace and rest :

But, without   *hal'*, holding   *sowth*, hum

It's no in makin' muckle mair ;
It's no in books, it's no in lear,
   To make us truly blest ;
If happiness hae not her seat
   And centre in the breast,
We may be wise, or rich, or great,
   But never can be blest :
     Nae treasures, nor pleasures,
      Could make us happy lang :
     The heart ay 's the part ay
      That makes us right or wrang.

Robert Burns.

208   ADVICE TO LEESOME MERRINESS

     WHEN I have done consider
      This warldis vanitie,
      Sa brukil and sa slidder,
       Sa full of miserie ;
      Then I remember me
      That here there is no rest ;
       Therefore apparentlie
      To be merrie is best.

     Let us be blyth and glad,
      My friendis all, I pray.
     To be pensive and sad
      Na thing it help us may.
      Therefore put quite away
     All heaviness of thocht :
      Thoch we murne nicht and day
      It will avail us nocht.

Sir Richard Maitland.

muckle mair, much more   *lear*, learning   *leesome*, lawful
brukil, brittle   *slidder*, slippery   *murne*, mourn

209   HERMES THE PHILOSOPHER

" Be mirry and glaid and honest and vertuous,
    For that sufficis to anger the invyous."

BE mirry, man ! and tak nocht far in mynd
    The wavering of this wrechit warld of sorrow ;
To God be humill, and to thy freynd be kynd,
    And with thy nychtbouris glaidly len and borrow ;
    His chance to-nicht it may be thine to-morrow.
Be blyth in hairt for ony aventure,
    For oft with wysmen it hes bene said aforrow :
" Without glaidness availis no tressour."

Mak thee gude cheer of it that God thee sendis,
    For warldis wrak but weilfair nocht availis ;
Na gude is thyne saif only bot thow spendis,
    Remenant al thow brukis bot with bailis ;
    Seek to solace when sadness thee assailis,
In dolour lang thy lyfe may nocht indure ;
    Whairfoir of confort set up all thy sailis :
Without glaidnes availis no tresour.

Follow on pitie, flee truble and debait ;
    With famous folkis hald thy company,
Be charitabill and humill in thyne estait,
    For warldly honour lastis bot a cry ;
    For truble in erd tak no malloncoly ;

aforrow, before   *warldis wrak*, worldly goods
but, without   *bot*, if
remenant, etc., what remains thou enjoyest only with
    sorrow   *erd*, earth

Be rich in patience, gif thow in gudis be puir ;
  Who levis mirry, he levis michtely :
Without glaidnes availis no tresour.

Thou seis thir wrechis set with sorrow and cair,
  To gaddir gudis in all thair lyvis space,
And when their baggis are full, their selfis are bair,
  And of thair richess bot the keping hess ;
  Whill otheris come to spend it that hes grace,
Whilk of the wynning no labour had nor cure ;
  Tak thow example, and spend with mirriness :
Without glaidnes availis no tresour.

Thoch all the werk that evir had levand wicht
  Were only thine, no moir thy pairt dois fall,
Bot meit, drynk, clais, and of the laif a sicht,
  Yit to the juge thow sall gif compt of all ;
  Ane raknyng rycht cumis of ane ragment small :
Be just and joyous, and do to none injure,
  And trewth sall mak thee strang as ony wall :
Without glaidness availis no tresure.
                                    William Dunbar.

210   NON SEMPER IMBRES

It's no aye rainin' on the misty Achils,
  It's no' aye white wi' winter on Nigour ;
The winds are no' sae mony sorrowin' Rachels,
  That grieve, and o' their grief will no' gie owre.

gaddir gudis, gather goods	*cure*, care
werk, property	*levand wicht*, living man
laif, rest	*raknyng*, reckoning
ragment, account, income	*Achils*, Ochils
gie owre, give up	

Dark are Benarty slopes, an' the steep Lomon'
    Flings a lang shadow on the watter plain ;
But fair Lochleven 's no' for ever gloomin',
    An' Devon 's no' aye dark wi' Lammas rain.

The birks tho' bare, an' the sune-naked ashes,
    Not always widow'd of their leaves appear ;
The oaks cry oot beneath November's lashes,
    But not for all the months that mak' the year.

Comes round a time, comes round at last tho' creepin',
    And green and glad again stand buss an' tree ;
E'en tender gowans, thro' the young gress peepin',
    Rise in their weakness, and owre-rin the lea.

Thus Nature sorrows, and forgets her sorrow ;
    And Reason soberly approves her way :
Why should we shut oor een against to-morrow
    Because our sky was clouded yesterday ?

                                        James Logie Robertson.

211   FULL OFT I MUSE AND HAS IN THOCHT

FULL oft I muse and has in thocht
How this fals warld is ay on flocht,
Whair no thing ferme is nor degest ;
And when I haif my mynd all socht,
For to be blyth me think it best.

buss, bush   *owre-rin*, over-run
on flocht, in flight   *degest*, fixed

This warld evir dois flicht and wary,
Fortoun sa fast hir wheill dois cary ;
Na tyme bot turne can tak rest ;
For whois fals change suld none be sary ;
For to be blyth me think it best.

Wald men considdir in mynd richt weill,
Or fortoun on him turn hir wheill,
That erdly honour may nocht lest,
His fall less paneful he suld feill ;
For to be blyth me think it best.

Wha with this warld dois warsill and stryfe,
And dois his dayis in dolour dryfe,
Thoch he in lordschip be possest,
He levis bot ane wrechit lyfe ;
For to be blyth me think it best.

Of warldis gud and grit richess,
What fruct hes man but miriness ?
Thoch he this warld had eist and west,
All wer pouertie but glaidness ;
For to be blyth me think it best.

Who suld for tynsall droup or de
For thyng that is bot vanitie,
Sen to the lyfe that evir dois lest
Heir is bot twynkling of ane Ee ;
For to be blyth me think it best.

---

flicht and wary, fleet and change   *bot turne,* without turning
sary, sorry   *Or,* before   *warsill*, wrestle   *dryfe*, spend
but, without   *tynsall*, loss   *lest*, last

Had I for warldis unkyndness
In hairt tane ony haviness,
Or fro my plesans bene opprest,
I had bene deid langsyne, doutless ;
For to be blyth me think it best.

How evir this warld do change and vary
Lat us in hairt nevir moir be sary,
Bot evir be reddy and addrest
To pass out of this fraudfull fary ;
For to be blyth me think it best.
                    William Dunbar.

212 ALL ERDLY JOY RETURNIS IN PANE

OFF Lentren in the first mornyng,
Airly as did the day upspring,
Thus sang ane bird with voce upplane,
" All erdly joy returnis in pane.

" O man ! haif mynd that thow mon pass ;
Remembir that thow art bot ass,
And sall in ass return agane ;
All erdly joy returnis in pane.

" Haif mynd that eild ay followis youth ;
Deth followis lyfe with gaipand mouth,
Devoring fruct and flowring grane :
All erdly joy returnis in pane.

fary, tumult   *upplane*, unpolished, rustic
ass, ashes   *eild*, old age

" Welth, wardly gloir, and riche array
Ar all bot thornis laid in thy way,
Ourcouerd with flouris laid in ane trane :
All erdly joy returnis in pane.

" Come nevir yit May so fresche and grene,
Bot Januar come als wod and kene ;
Wes nevir sic drouth bot anis come rane :
All erdly joy returnis in pane.

" Evirmair unto this warldis joy
As nerrest air succeidis noy ;
Thairfoir, when joy ma nocht remane,
His verry air succeidis pane.

" Heir helth returnis in seikness
And mirth returnis in haviness,
Toun in desert, forrest in plane :
All erdly joy returnis in pane.

" Fredome returnis in wretchitness,
And trewth returnis in doubilness,
With fenyeit wordis to mak men fane :
All erdly joy returnis in pane.

" Vertew returnis in-to vyce,
And honour in-to avaryce ;
With cuvatyce is consciens slane :
All erdly joy returnis in pane.

trane, snare	*als*, also	*wod*, mad
anis, sometimes	*nerrest air*, next heir	*noy*, trouble
fenyeit, feigned, false	*fane*, glad	*cuvatyce*, covetousness

" Sen erdly joy abydis nevir,
Wirk for the joy that lestis evir ;
For uder joy is all bot vane :
All erdly joy returnis in pane."

William Dunbar.

213　　　LATE IN THE NICHT

LATE in the nicht in bed I lay,
The winds were at their weary play,
An' tirlin' wa's an' skirlin' wae
　　Through Heev'n they battered ;
On-ding o' hail, on-blaff o' spray,
　　The tempest blattered.

The masoned house it dinled through ;
It dung the ship, it cowped the coo ;
The rankit aiks it overthrew,
　　Had braved a' weathers ;
The strang sea-gleds it took an' blew
　　Awa' like feathers.

The thrawes o' fear on a' were shed,
An' the hair rose, an' slumber fled,
An' lichts were lit an' prayers were said
　　Through a' the kintry ;
An' the cauld terror clum in bed
　　Wi' a' an' sindry.

wae, woefully　　　　　*on-ding, on-blaff*, onset
dinled, resounded　　　*dung*, struck
cowped, upset　　　　　*sea-gleds*, sea-gulls
thrawes, throes　　　　*sindry*, sundry

To hear in the pit-mirk on hie
The brangled collieshangie flie,
The warl', they thocht, wi' land an' sea,
    Itsel' wad cowpit ;
An' for auld airn, the smashed débris
    By God be rowpit.

Meanwhile frae far Aldeboran,
To folks wi' talescopes in han',
O' ships that cowpit, winds that ran,
    Nae sign was seen,
But the wee warl' in sunshine span
    As bricht 's a preen.

I, tae, by God's especial grace,
Dwall denty in a bieldy place,
Wi' hosened feet, wi' shaven face,
    Wi' dacent mainners :
A grand example to the race
    O' tautit sinners !

The wind may blaw, the heathen rage,
The deil may start on the rampage ;—
The sick in bed, the thief in cage—
    What's a' to me ?
Cosh in my house, a sober sage,
    I sit an' see.

An' whiles the bluid spangs to my bree,
To lie sae saft, to live sae free,

pit-mirk, black dark	*brangled collieshangie*, confused uproar	
airn, iron	*rowpit*, auctioned	*preen*, pin
denty, dainty	*bieldy*, sheltered	*tautit*, ragged
cosh, snug	*spangs*, leaps	*bree*, brow

While better men maun do an' die
   In unco places.
" *Whaur's God ?* " I cry, an' " *Whae is me*
   To hae sic graces ? "

I mind the fecht the sailors keep,
But fire or can'le, rest or sleep,
In darkness an' the muckle deep ;
   An' mind beside
The herd that on the hills o' sheep
   Has wandered wide.

I mind me on the hoastin' weans—
The penny joes on causey stanes—
The auld folk wi' the crazy banes,
   Baith auld an' puir,
That aye maun thole the winds an' rains
   An' labour sair.

An' whiles I'm kind o' pleased a blink
An' kind o' fleyed forby, to think,
For a' my rowth o' meat an' drink
   An' waste o' crumb,
I'll mebbe have to thole wi' skink
   In Kingdom Come.

For God whan jowes the Judgment bell,
Wi' His ain Hand, His Leevin' Sel',

unco, awful	*But*, without	*hoastin'*, coughing
weans, children	*joes*, sweethearts	*causey*, causeway
thole, endure	*fleyed*, frightened	*rowth*, plenty
skink, short commons	*jowes*, rings	

Sall ryve the guid (as Prophets tell)
    Frae them that had it ;
And in the reamin' pat o' Hell,
    The rich be scaddit.

O Lord, if this indeed be sae,
Let daw that sair an' happy day !
Again' the warl', grawn auld an' grey,
    Up wi' your aixe !
An' let the puir enjoy their play—
    I'll thole my paiks.

                        R. L. Stevenson.

214 THE SPAEWIFE

O ! I WAD like to ken—to the beggar-wife says I—
Why chops are guid to brander and nane sae guid to fry ;
An' siller, that's sae braw to keep, is brawer still to gie ?
—*It's gey an' easy spierin'*, says the beggar-wife to me.

O ! I wad like to ken—to the beggar-wife says I—
Hoo a' things come to be whaur we find them when we
    try,
The lasses in their claes an' the fishes in the sea ?
—*It's gey an' easy spierin'*, says the beggar-wife to me.

O ! I wad like to ken—to the beggar-wife says I—
Why lads are a' to sell an' lasses a' to buy ;
An' naebody for dacency but barely two or three ?
—*It's gey an' easy spierin'*, says the beggar-wife to me.

ryve, take away   *reamin' pat*, bubbling pot
scaddid, scalded   *daw*, dawn   *thole*, endure
paiks, punishment   *spierin'*, asking

O ! I wad like to ken—to the beggar-wife says I—
Gin death's as shure to men as killin' is to kye,
Why God has filled the yearth sae fu' o' tasty things to
    pree ?
—*It's gey an' easy spierin'*, says the beggar-wife to me.

O ! I wad like to ken—to the beggar-wife says I—
The reason o' the cause an' the wherefore o' the why,
Wi' mony anither riddle brings the tear into my e'e ?
—*It's gey an' easy spierin'*, says the beggar-wife to me.
                      R. L. Stevenson.

215   WHAT THE AULD FOWK ARE THINKIN'

The bairns i' their beds, worn oot wi' nae wark,
    Are sleepin', nor ever an eelid winkin' ;
The auld fowk lie still wi' their een starin' stark,
    An' the mirk pang-fou o' the things they are thinkin'.

Whan oot o' ilk corner the bairnies they keek,
    Lauchin' an' daffin', airms loosin' an' linkin',
The auld fowk they watch frae the warm ingle-cheek,
    But the bairns little think what the auld fowk are
    thinkin'.

Whan the auld fowk sit quaiet at the reet o' a stook,
    I' the sunlicht their washt een blinterin' an' blinkin',
Fowk scythin', or bin'in', or shearin' wi' heuk
    Carena a strae what the auld fowk are thinkin'.

kye, cows	*yearth,* earth	*pree,* taste
mirk, darkness	*pang-fou,* thick-filled	*keek,* peer
daffin', playing	*reet,* foot	*stook,* sheaf
	heuk, hook	

At the kirk, whan the minister's dreich an' dry,
  His fardens as gien they war gowd guineas chinkin',
An' the young fowk are noddin', or fidgetin' sly,
  Naebody kens what the auld fowk are thinkin'.

Whan the young fowk are greitin' aboot the bed
  Whaur like water through san' the auld life is sinkin',
An' some wud say the last word was said,
  The auld fowk smile, an' ken what they're thinkin'.
                              George Macdonald.

dreich, dull   *gien*, if   *fardens*, farthings   *greitin'*, weeping

BOOK XVII
DEATH

THIS ae nighte, this ae nighte,
   Every nighte and alle,
Fire, and sleet, and candle-lighte;
   And Christe receive thye saule.

When thou from hence away art paste,
   Every nighte and alle,
To Whinny-muir thou comest at laste;
   And Christe receive thye saule.

If ever thou gavest hosen and shoon,
   Every nighte and alle,
Sit thee down and put them on;
   And Christe receive thye saule.

If hosen and shoon thou ne'er gavest nane,
   Every nighte and alle,
The whinnes sall pricke thee to the bare bane;
   And Christe receive thye saule.

From Whinny-muir when thou mayst passe,
   Every nighte and alle,
To Brig o' Dread thou comest at laste;
   And Christe receive thye saule.

From Brig o' Dread when thou mayst passe
   Every nighte and alle,
To purgatory fire thou comest at laste;
   And Christe receive thye saule.

      shoon, shoes

If ever thou gavest meate or drinke,
Every nighte and alle,
The fire sall never make thee shrinke :
And Christe receive thye saule.

If meate or drinke thou gavest nane,
Every nighte and alle,
The fire will burn thee to the bare bane ;
And Christe receive thye saule.

This ae nighte, this ae nighte,
Every nighte and alle,
Fire, and sleet, and candle-lighte ;
And Christe receive thye saule.

217   EDWARD

" WHY dois your brand sae drap wi' bluid,
                    Edward, Edward ?
Why dois your brand sae drap wi' bluid,
    And why sae sad gang ye O ? "
" O I hae killed my hawk sae guid,
                    Mither, mither ;
O I hae killed my hawk sae guid,
    And I had nae mair bot he O."

" Your hawk's bluid was never sae reid,
                    Edward, Edward ;
Your hawk's bluid was never sae reid,
    My dear son, I tell thee O."
" O I hae killed my reid-roan steed,
                    Mither, mither ;
O I hae killed my reid-roan steed,
    That erst was sae fair and free O."

" Your steed was auld, and ye hae gat mair,
                    Edward, Edward ;
Your steed was auld, and ye hae gat mair,
    Some other dule ye dree O."
" O I hae killed my fader dear,
                    Mither, mither ;
O I hae killed my fader dear,
    Alas, and wae is me O ! "

" And whatten penance will ye dree for that,
                    Edward, Edward ?
And whatten penance will ye dree for that ?
    My dear son, now tell me O."
" I'll set my feet in yonder boat,
                    Mither, mither ;
I'll set my feet in yonder boat,
    And I'll fare over the sea O."

" And what will ye do wi' your towers and your ha',
                    Edward, Edward ?
And what will ye do wi' your towers and your ha',
    What were sae fair to see O ? "
" I'll let them stand till they down fa',
                    Mither, mither ;
I'll let them stand till they down fa',
    For here never mair maun I be O."

" And what will ye leave to your bairns and your
        wife,
                    Edward, Edward ?
And what will ye leave to your bairns and your wife,
    When ye gang over the sea O ? "

dule, sorrow   *dree*, suffer

" The warldis room, lat them beg thro' life,
        Mither, mither ;
The warldis room, lat them beg thro' life,
    For hame never mair will I see O."

" And what will ye leave to your ain mither dear,
        Edward, Edward ?
And what will ye leave to your ain mither dear ?
    My dear son, now tell me O."
" The curse of hell frae me sall ye bear,
        Mither, mither ;
The curse of hell frae me sall ye bear,
    Sic counsels ye gave to me O."

218   THE TWA CORBIES

    As I was walking all alane,
    I heard twa corbies makin' a mane ;
    The tane unto the t'other say,
    " Where sall we gang and dine the day ? "

    " In ahint yon auld fail dyke,
    I wot there lies a new-slain knight ;
    And naebody kens that he lies there
    But his hawk and his hound and his lady fair.

    " His hound is to the hunting gane,
    His hawk to fetch the wild fowl hame,
    His lady has ta'en another mate,
    Sae we may mak' our denner sweet.

            corbies, ravens   *fail*, turf

" Ye'll sit on his white hause-bane,
And I'll pike out his bonny blue een,
Wi' ae lock o' his gowden hair
We'll theek our nest when it grows bare.

" Mony a ane for him maks mane,
But nane sall ken where he is gane ;
Ower his white banes when they are bare
The wind sall blaw for evermair."

219   LORD RANDAL

" Oh, where have you been, Lord Randal, my son ?
Oh, where have you been, my handsome young man ? "
"I hae been to the wild wood ; mother, mak' my bed soon ;
For I'm weary wi' hunting, and fain wad lie doun."

" Where gat ye your dinner, Lord Randal, my son ?
Where gat ye your dinner, my handsome young man ? "
" I dined wi' my true love ; mother, mak' my bed soon ;
For I'm weary wi' hunting, and fain wad lie doun."

" What gat ye to your dinner, Lord Randal, my son ?
What gat ye to your dinner, my handsome young man ? "
" I gat eels boiled in broo ; mother, mak' my bed soon ;
For I'm weary wi' hunting, and fain wad lie doun."

" What became of your bloodhounds, Lord Randal, my
       son ?
What became of your bloodhounds, my handsome young
       man ? "

hause-bane, neck-bone   *theek*, thatch   *broo*, broth

" Oh, they swelled and they dee'd ; mother, mak' my
    bed soon ;
For I'm weary wi' hunting, and fain wad lie doun."

" Oh, I fear ye are poisoned, Lord Randal, my son !
Oh, I fear ye are poisoned, my handsome young man ! "
" Oh, yes, I am poisoned ; mother, mak' my bed soon ;
For I'm sick at the heart, and fain wad lie doun."

220   YOUTH AND DEATH

O then bespake her little son,
    Sat on the nurse's knee :
Says, " Mither dear, gie owre this house,
    For the reek it smithers me."

" I wad gie a' my gowd, my bairn,
    Sae wad I a' my fee,
For ae blast o' the western wind,
    To blaw the reek frae thee."

O then bespake her dochter dear—
    She was baith jimp and sma' :
" O row me in a pair o' sheets,
    And tow me owre the wa'."

They row'd her in a pair o' sheets,
    And tow'd her owre the wa' ;
But on the point o' Gordon's spear
    She gat a deadly fa.'

jimp, slender   *row*, roll   *tow*, toss

O bonnie, bonnie was her mouth,
    And cherry were her cheeks,
And clear, clear was her yellow hair,
    Whereon the red bluid dreips.

Then wi' his spear he turn'd her owre ;
    O gin her face was wan !
He said, " Ye are the first that e'er
    I wished alive again."

He turn'd her owre and owre again ;
    O gin her skin was white !
" I might hae spared that bonnie face
    To hae been some man's delight.

" Busk and boun, my merry men a',
    For ill dooms I do guess ;
I canna look in that bonnie face
    As it lies on the grass."

221   BONNIE GEORGE CAMPBELL

HIE upon Hielands,
    And laigh upon Tay,
Bonnie George Campbell
    Rode out on a day.

He saddled, he bridled,
    And gallant rode he ;
And hame cam his guid horse,
    But never cam he.

Busk and boun, make ready to go   *laigh,* low

Out cam his mother dear,
  Greetin' fu' sair ;
And out cam his bonnie bride
  Rivin' her hair.

" The meadow lies green,
  The corn is unshorn ;
But bonnie George Campbell
  Will never return."

Saddled and bridled
  And booted rode he,
A plume in his helmet,
  A sword at his knee.

But toom cam his saddle
  All bluidy to see ;
Oh, hame cam his guid horse,
  But never cam he.

222   ELEGY ON THE DEATH OF BERNARD
       STEWART, LORD OF AUBIGNY

O DUILFULL death !   O dragon dolorous !
  Why hes thow done so dulfullie devoir
The prince of knychtheid, nobill and chivilrous,
  The witt of weiris, of armes and honour,
    The crop of curage, the strenth of armes in stour,
The fame of France, the fame of Lumbardy,
    The choiss of chiftanes, most awfull in armour,
The charbunckell, cheif of every chevilrie !

rivin', tearing   *toom*, empty   *devoir*, devour
the witt of weiris, the very wisdom of wars   *crop*, summit
                  charbunckell, carbuncle

Pray now for him, all that him loveit heir !
 And for his saull mak intercessioun
Unto the Lord that hes him bocht so deir,
 To gif him mercie and remissioun,
 And namelie we of Scottis natioun,
Intill his lyff whom most he did affy,
 Foryett we nevir into our orisoun
To pray for him, the flour of chivelrie.

William Dunbar.

223   HELEN OF KIRKCONNEL

I WISH I were where Helen lies,
Where night and day on me she cries ;
Oh that I were where Helen lies,
    On fair Kirkconnel lea !
Oh, Helen fair, beyond compare,
I'll mak' a garland o' thy hair,
Shall bind my heart for evermair,
    Until the day I dee.

Oh, think na ye my heart was sair,
When my love dropt and spoke nae mair ?
She sank, and swoon'd wi' mickle care
    On fair Kirkconnel lee.
Curst be the heart that thocht the thocht,
And curst the hand that shot the shot,
When in my arms burd Helen dropt,
    And died to succour me.

namelie, especially
intill his lyff, etc., in whom he put most trust during his life
        burd, maid

As I went down the water side
None but my foe to be my guide,
None but my foe to be my guide,
　　On fair Kirkconnel lee ;
I lichtit doun, my sword did draw,
I hackit him in pieces sma',
I hackit him in pieces sma',
　　For her sake that died for me.

Oh that I were where Helen lies !
Nicht and day on me she cries,
Out of my bed she bids me rise :
　　" Oh come, my love, to me ! "
Oh, Helen fair ! oh, Helen chaste !
If I were with thee I were blest,
Where thou lies low, and takes thy rest,
　　On fair Kirkconnel lee.

I wish my grave were growin' green,
A windin' sheet drawn ower my een,
And I in Helen's arms lying,
　　On fair Kirkconnel lee.
I wish I were where Helen lies ;
Nicht and day on me she cries ;
I'm sick of all beneath the skies,
　　Since my love died for me.

224　　THE BONNIE EARL OF MORAY

Ye Highlands and ye Lawlands,
　　Oh ! where hae ye been ?
They hae slain the Earl of Moray,
　　And hae laid him on the green.

Now wae be to thee, Huntly,
    And wherefore did you sae ?
I bade you bring him wi' you,
    But forbade you him to slay.

He was a braw gallant,
    And he rid at the ring ;
And the bonnie Earl of Moray,
    Oh ! he might hae been a king.

He was a braw gallant,
    And he play'd at the ba' ;
And the bonnie Earl of Moray
    Was the flower amang them a'.

He was a braw gallant,
    And he play'd at the glove ;
And the bonnie Earl of Moray,
    Oh ! he was the Queen's luve.

Oh ! lang will his lady
    Look owre the castle Doune,
Ere she see the Earl of Moray
    Come sounding thro' the toun.

225   THE LOWLANDS OF HOLLAND

My love he's built a bonnie ship, and set her on the sea,
With seven score guid mariners to bear her companie.
There's three score is sunk, and three score dead at sea ;
And the Lowlands of Holland hae twined my love and
    me.

My love he built another ship, and set her on the main,
And nane but twenty mariners for to bring her hame ;
But the weary wind began to rise, and the sea began to
    rout ;
My love then, and his bonnie ship, turned withershins
    about.

There shall neither coif come on my head, nor kame
    come in my hair ;
There shall neither coal nor candle-licht come in my
    bower mair ;
Nor will I love another man until the day I dee,
For I never loved a love but ane, and he's drown'd in
    the sea.

O haud your tongue, my daughter dear, be still and be
    content ;
There are mair lads in Galloway, ye need na sair lament.
O ! there is nane in Galloway, there's nane at a' for me ;
For I never loved a love but ane, and he's drown'd in
    the sea.

226   THE LAMENT OF THE BORDER WIDOW

My love he built me a bonnie bower,
And clad it a' wi' lilye flower ;
A brawer bower ye ne'er did see
Than my true love he built for me.

There came a man, by middle day,
He spied his sport, and went away ;
And brought the king that very night,
Who brake my bower, and slew my knight.

rout, roar   *withershins*, upside down

He slew my knight, to me sae dear ;
He slew my knight, and poin'd his gear.
My servants all for life did flee,
And left me in extremitie.

I sewed his sheet, making my maen ;
I watched the corpse, myself alane ;
I watched his body night and day ;
No living creature came that way.

I took his body on my back,
And whiles I gaed, and whiles I sat ;
I digg'd a grave and laid him in,
And happ'd him with the sod sae green.

But think na ye my heart was sair
When I laid the moul' on his yellow hair ?
O think na ye my heart was wae
When I turn'd about, awa' to gae ?

Nae living man I'll love again,
Since that my lovely knight is slain.
Wi' ae lock of his yellow hair
I'll chain my heart for evermair.

227 DROWNED IN YARROW

WILLY's rare, and Willy's fair,
   And Willy's wondrous bonny ;
And Willy hecht to marry me
   Gin e'er he married ony.

poin'd, confiscated   *moul',* mould   *hecht,* promised

Yestreen I made my bed fu' braid,
　This night I'll make it narrow ;
For a' the live-lang winter night
　I lie twin'd of my marrow.

O came you by yon water-side,
　Pou'd you the rose or lily ?
Or came you by yon meadow green ?
　Or saw you my sweet Willy ?

She sought him east, she sought him west,
　She sought him braid and narrow ;
Syne in the cleaving of a craig
　She found him drown'd in Yarrow.

228　BESSIE BELL AND MARY GRAY

O BESSIE BELL and Mary Gray,
　They war twa bonnie lasses ;
They bigget a bower on yon burn-brae,
　And theekit it ower wi' rashes.

They theekit it ower wi' rashes green,
　They theekit it ower wi' heather ;
But the pest cam frae the burrows-toun,
　And slew them baith thegither.

twin'd, bereft		*marrow*, mate	
craig, rock		*bigget*, built	
theekit, thatched		*rashes*, rushes	
	burrows-toun, burgh-town		

They thought to lie in Methven kirkyard,
   Amang their noble kin ;
But they maun lie in Stronach haugh
   To biek forenent the sin.

And Bessie Bell and Mary Gray
   They war twa bonnie lasses ;
They bigget a bower on yon burn-brae,
   And theekit it ower wi' rashes.

229   MACPHERSON'S FAREWELL

FAREWELL, ye dungeons dark and strong,
   The wretch's destinie !
Macpherson's time will not be long
   On yonder gallows-tree.
     Sae rantingly, sae wantonly,
      Sae dauntingly gaed he ;
     He play'd a spring, and danc'd it round,
      Below the gallows-tree.

Oh ! what is death but parting breath ?
   On mony a bloody plain
I've dar'd his face, and in this place
   I scorn him yet again !

Untie these bands from off my hands,
   And bring to me my sword !
And there's no a man in all Scotland
   But I'll brave him at a word.

   biek forenent the sin, bake in the sun

I've lived a life of sturt and strife ;
  I die by treacherie :
It burns my heart I must depart,
  And not avengèd be.

Now farewell light—thou sunshine bright,
  And all beneath the sky !
May coward shame distain his name,
  The wretch that dares not die !

                              Robert Burns.

230   KIRKBRIDE

BURY me in Kirkbride,
  Where the Lord's redeemed anes lie !
The auld kirkyaird on the grey hillside
    Under the open sky ;
    Under the open sky,
  On the briest o' the brae sae steep,
And side by side wi' the banes that lie
  Streikt there in their hinmaist sleep.
This puir dune body maun sune be dust,
  But it thrills wi' a stoun' o' pride
To ken it may mix with the great and just
  That slumber in thee, Kirkbride. . . . .

Wheesht ! did the saft win' speak ?
  Or a yaumerin' nicht bird cry ?
Did I dream that a warm haun touch't my cheek,
  And a winsome face gaed by ?

sturt, violence   *streikt*, stretched   *hinmaist*, last
dune, worn-out   *stoun'*, spasm   *yaumerin'*, babbling

And a winsome face gaed by,
  Wi' a far-aff licht in its een—
A licht that bude come frae the dazzlin' sky,
  For it spak' o' the starnies' sheen.
Age may be donart, and dazed, and blin',
  But I'se warrant, whate'er betide,
A true heart there made tryst wi' my ain,
  And the tryst-word seem'd " Kirkbride."

Hark ! frae the far hilltaps,
  And laich frae the lanesome glen,
Some sweet psalm tune, like a late dew, draps
    Its wild notes doun the win' ;
    Its wild notes doun the win',
  Wi' a kent soun' owre my min',
For we sang't on the muir, a wheen huntit men,
  Wi' oor lives in oor haun langsyne ;
But never a voice can disturb this sang,
  Were it Claver'se in a' his pride,
For it's raised by the Lord's ain ransomed thrang
  Forgethered abune Kirkbride.

I hear May Moril's tongue
  That I wistna to hear again,
And there—'twas the Black M'Michael's rung
    Clear in the closin' strain ;
    Clear in the closin' strain,
  Frae his big heart bauld and true ;
It stirs my saul as in days bygane,
  When his guid braidsword he drew ;

          bude, must have   *starnies*, stars
                  donart, confused

I needs be aff to the muirs ance mair,
  For he'll miss me by his side ;
I' the thrang o' the battle I aye was there,
  And sae maun it be in Kirkbride.

Rax me my staff and plaid,
  That in readiness I may be,
And dinna forget that The Book be laid
    Open across my knee ;
    Open across my knee,
  And a text close by my thoom.
And tell me true, for I scarce can see,
  That the words are, " Lo ! I come ; "
Then carry me through at the Cample ford,
  And up by the lang hillside,
And I'll wait for the comin' o' God the Lord
  In a neuk o' auld Kirkbride.

                              Robert Reid.

231 THE WAN MOON IS SETTING BEHIND
            THE WHITE WAVE

O, OPEN the door, some pity to show,
  If love it may na be, O !
Tho' thou hast been false, I'll ever prove true,
  O, open the door to me, O !

Cauld is the blast upon my pale cheek,
  But caulder thy love for me, O !
The frost that freezes the life at my heart
  Is naught to my pains frae thee, O !

        Rax, reach   *neuk*, corner

The wan moon is setting behind the white wave,
    And Time is setting with me, O !
False friends, false love, farewell ! for mair
    I'll ne'er trouble them nor thee, O !

She has open'd the door, she has open'd it wide ;
    She sees the pale corse on the plain, O !
My true love ! she cried, and sank down by his side
    Never to rise again, O !

Robert Burns.

232   ## THE FA' O' THE YEAR

AFORE the Lammas tide
    Had dun'd the birken tree,
In a' our water-side
    Nae wife was blest like me ;
A kind gudeman, and twa
    Sweet bairns were round me here,
But they're a' ta'en awa'
    Sin' the fa' o' the year.

Sair trouble cam' our gate,
    And made me, when it cam',
A bird without a mate,
    A ewe without a lamb.
Our hay was yet to maw,
    And our corn was to shear,
When they a' dwined awa'
    In the fa' o' the year.

gate, way   *maw,* mow   *dwined,* faded

I downa look a-field,
　　For aye I trow I see
The form that was a bield
　　To my wee bairns and me ;
But wind, and weet, and snaw,
　　They never mair can fear,
Sin' they a' got the ca'
　　In the fa' o' the year.

Aft on the hills at e'ens
　　I see him 'mang the ferns,
The lover o' my teens,
　　The father o' my bairns :
For there his plaid I saw
　　As gloamin' aye drew near—
But my a's now awa'
　　Sin' the fa' o' the year.

Our bonnie rigs theirsel',
　　Reca' my waes to mind,
Our puir dumb beasties tell
　　O' a' that I have tined ;
For wha our wheat will saw,
　　And wha our sheep will shear,
Sin' my a' gaed awa'
　　In the fa' o' the year ?

My heart is growing cauld,
　　And will be caulder still ;
And sair, sair in the fauld
　　Will be the winter's chill ;

downa, cannot　　　　　　　　　*bield,* shelter
　　　　　　tined, lost

For peats were yet to ca',
  Our sheep they were to smear,
When my a' passed awa'
  In the fa' o' the year.

I ettle whiles to spin,
  But wee, wee patterin' feet
Come rinnin' out and in,
  And then I just maun greet :
I ken it's fancy a',
  And faster rowes the tear,
That my a' dwined awa'
  In the fa' o' the year.

Be kind, O Heaven abune !
  To ane sae wae and lane,
An' tak' her hamewards sune,
  In pity o' her maen ;
Long ere the March winds blaw,
  May she, far, far frae here,
Meet them a' that's awa'
  Sin' the fa' o' the year.

Thomas Smibert.

233   THE LAST O' THE TINKLER

LAY me in yon place, lad,
  The gloamin's thick wi' nicht ;
I canna' see yer face, lad,
  For my een's no richt.

ca', drive	*ettle*, mean
greet, weep	*rowes*, rolls

But it's ower late for leein',
An' I ken fine I'm deein',
Like an auld craw fleein'
   To the last o' the licht.

The kye gang to the byre, lad,
   An' the sheep to the fauld,
Ye'll mak' a spunk o' fire, lad,
   For my he'rt's turned cauld ;
An' whaur the trees are meetin',
There's a sound like waters beatin',
An' the bird seems near to greetin',
   That was aye singin' bauld.

There's jist the tent to leave, lad,
   I've gaithered little gear,
There's jist yersel' to grieve, lad,
   An' the auld dog here ;
An' when the morn comes creepin'
An' the wauk'nin' birds are cheipin',
It'll find me lyin' sleepin'
   As I've slept saxty year.

Ye'll rise to meet the sun, lad,
   An' baith be traiv'lin west,
But me that's auld an' done, lad,
   I'll bide an' tak' my rest ;
For the grey heid is bendin',
An' the auld shune's needin' mendin',
But the traiv'lin's near its' endin',
   And the end's aye the best.

                              Violet Jacob.

   kye, cows   *shune,* shoes

234 THE GREEN GRASS

THE dead spake together last night,
  And one to the other said :
  " Why are we dead ? "

They turned them face to face about
  In the place where they were laid :
  " Why are we dead ? "

" This is the sweet, sweet month o' May,
  And the grass is green o'erhead—
  Why are we dead ?

" The grass grows green on the long, long tracks
  That I shall never tread—
  Why are we dead ?

" The lamp shines like the glow-worm spark,
  From the bield where I was bred—
  Why am I dead ? "

The other spake : " I've wife and weans,
  Yet I lie in this waesome bed—
  Why am I dead ?

" O, I hae wife and weans at hame,
  And they clamour loud for bread—
  Why am I dead ? "

Quoth the first : " I have a sweet, sweet heart,
  And this night we should hae wed—
  Why am I dead ?

bield, shelter   *weans*, children   *waesome*, woeful

" And I can see another man
    Will mate her in my stead,
    Now I am dead."

They turned them back to back about
    In the grave where they were laid—
    " Why are we dead ? "

" I mind o' a field, a foughten field,
    Where the bluid ran routh and red—
    Now I am dead."

" I mind o' a field, a stricken field,
    And a waeful wound that bled—
    Now I am dead."

They turned them on their backs again,
    As when their souls had sped,
    And nothing further said.

The dead spake together last night,
    And each to the other said,
    " *Why are we dead ?* "

                                    Joseph Lee.

235   THE SEASON FOR DEATH

(1)

MONY a year, mony a year,
    Hae I seen the snaw awa',
    Hae I seen the primrose blaw
And the bud upon the brier.

        routh, plentiful

Mony a year, mony a year,
  Yule has brocht the thocht anew,
  If my strength wad bear me through,
If the spring wad see me here.

Aft, when winter trailed awa'
  And the flowers were round my feet,
  Stood I 'tween the lauch and greet,
Half believin' a' I saw.

Aft, when bare was blawn the tree,
  And the flowers were a' laid by,
  Hae I braced mysel' to sigh,
" Ay, it's by wi' flowers for me ! "

Then I wad been blithe to gang ;
  But I canna think to sleep
  When I hear at mornin' peep
Some bit mavie at his sang.

Walter Wingate.

(2)

GANE were but the winter cauld,
  And gane were but the snaw,
I could sleep in the wild woods
  Where the primroses blaw.

Allan Cunningham.

236

ANE BY ANE

ANE by ane they gang awa',
The Gatherer gathers great an' sma',
Ane by ane mak's ane an' a'.

  by, past   *mavie*, thrush

Aye when ane sets doun the cup,
Ane ahint maun tak' it up,
Yet thegither they will sup.

Golden-heided, ripe an' strang,
Shorn will be the hairst ere lang,
Syne begins a better sang !

George Macdonald.

237   THE LAND O' THE LEAL

I'M wearin' awa', John,
Like snaw-wreaths in thaw, John ;
I'm wearin' awa'
    To the land o' the leal.
There's nae sorrow there, John,
There's neither cauld nor care, John :
The day is aye fair
    In the land o' the leal.

Our bonnie bairn's there, John,
She was baith gude and fair, John ;
And oh ! we grudged her sair
    To the land o' the leal.
But sorrow's sel' wears past, John,
And joy 's a-comin' fast, John—
The joy that's aye to last
    In the land o' the leal.

Sae dear 's that joy was bought, John,
Sae free the battle fought, John,
That sinfu' man e'er brought
    To the land o' the leal.

hairst, harvest   *leal*, loyal, true

Death

Oh, dry your glist'ning e'e, J
My saul langs to be free, Joh
And angels beckon me
  To the land o' the leal.

Oh, haud ye leal and true, Jo
Your day it's wearin' thro', J
And I'll welcome you
  To the land o' the leal.
Now fare ye weel, my ain John,
This warld's cares are vain, John ;
We'll meet, and we'll be fain
  In the land o' the leal.

              Lady Nairne.

238   O HAPPIE DEATH

O HAPPIE death, to life the readie way,
  The ende of greefe, and salve of sorrowes all ;
O pleasant sleepe, thy paines they are bot play ;
  Thy coup is sweete, although it taste of gall.
  Thou brings the bound and wretched out of thrall
Within the port sure from the stormie blast,
  For after death na mischiefe may befall,
But wo, wan-chance, and perrels all are past.
Of kindelie death nane suld affraied be
But sich as hope for na felicitie.

              Alexander Hume.

    haud, keep   *fain,* fond
      wan-chance, misfortune

My soul langs to be free, John;
And I'll welcome you
This warld's cares are vain, John;
We'll meet, and we'll be rich

Lady Nairne.

238   O HAPPIE DEATH

O happie death, to life the readie way,
The ende of greefe, and salve of sorrowes all;
O pleasant sleepe, thy paines they are bot play;
Thy coup is sweete, although it taste of gall.
Thou brings the bound and wretched out of thrall
Within the port sure from the stormie blast.
For after death na mischiefe may befall,
But sich as hope for na felicitie.

Alexander Hume.

BOOK XVIII
DIVINE PHILOSOPHY

BOOK XVIII
DIVINE PHILOSOPHY

RORATE CELI DESUPER

RORATE celi desuper !
  Heavens distil your balmy schouris,
For now is risen the bricht day ster
    Fro the rose Mary, flour of flouris ;
    The clear Sin, whom no clud devouris,
Surmounting Phœbus in the east,
    Is comen of his heavenly touris ;
Et nobis Puer natus est.

Archangellis, angellis, and dompnationis,
  Tronis, potestatis, and martyris seir,
And all ye heavenly operationis,
    Ster, planet, firmament, and sphere,
    Fire, erd, air, and water clear,
To him gife loving, most and lest,
    That come in-to so meek manner ;
Et nobis Puer natus est.

Sinneris be glaid and penance do,
  And thank your Maker hairtfully ;
For he that ye micht nocht come to,
    To you is comen full humly,
    Your saulis with his blude to buy,
And louse you of the Fiendis arrest,
    And only of his awn mercy ;
Pro nobis Puer natus est.

comen of, arrived from   seir, various
  in-to, in   humly, humbly   awn, own

All clergy do to him incline,
　　And bow unto that bairn bening,
And do your observance divine
　　To him that is of kingis King ;
　　Ensence his altar, read, and sing
In haly kirk, with mind degest,
　　Him honouring attour all thing,
Qui nobis Puer natus est.

Celestial fowlis in the air,
　　Sing with your notis upon hicht ;
In firthis and in forestis fair
　　Be mirthful now, at all your micht,
　　For passit is your dully nicht ;
Aurora has the cludis pierc'd,
　　The sun is risen with glaidsome licht,
Et nobis Puer natus est.

Now spring up flouris fra the root,
　　Revert you upward naturally,
In honour of the blissit fruit
　　That raise up fro the rose Mary ;
　　Lay out your leaves lustily,
Fro dede tak life now at the lest
　　In worship of that Prince worthy,
Qui nobis Puer natus est.

Sing heaven imperiall, most of hicht,
　　Regions of air mak harmony ;
All fish in flood and fowl of flicht,
　　Be mirthful and mak melody ;

ensence, burn incense before　　*degest*, grave
attour, above　　　　　　　　*at the lest*, at last

All GLORIA IN EXCELSIS cry,
Heaven, erd, sea, man, bird, and beast,
 He that is crownit abune the sky
Pro nobis Puer natus est.

William Dunbar.

240   THE SOUL TO ITS REDEEMER

ALL my Lufe, leif me not,
 Leif me not, leif me not !
All my lufe, leif me not,
 Thus myne alone ;
With ane burden on my back,
I may not beir it I am sa waik,
Lufe, this burden from me tak,
 Or ellis I am gone.

With sinnis I am ladin soir,
 Leif me not, leif me not.
With sinnis I am ladin soir,
 Leif me not alone !
I pray thee, Lord, thairfoir,
Keip not my sinnis in stoir,
Lowse me, or I be forloir,
 And hear my mone.

With thy handis thou hes me wrocht,
 Leif me not, leif me not !
With thy handis thou hes me wrocht,
 Leif me not alone !

Lowse, loose

I was sauld, and thou me bocht,
With thy blude thou hes me coft,
Now am I hidder socht
    To thee, Lord, alone.

I cry and I call to thee
    To leif me not, to leif me not,
I cry and I call to thee
    To leif me not alone.
All they that laden be,
Thou biddis thame come to thee ;
Then sall they savit be
    Throw thy mercy alone. . . .

Faith, Hope, and Charitie,
    Leif me not, leif me not !
Faith, Hope, and Charitie,
    Leif me not alone !
I pray thee, Lord, grant me
Thir godly giftis thrie,
Then sall I savit be,
    Dout have I none. . . .

241   ANE BALLAT OF OUR LADY

HAIL, sterne superne !   Hail, in eterne,
    In Godis sicht to shyne !
Lucerne in derne, for to discerne
    By glory and grace devyne ;

> *sauld*, sold   *coft*, bought
> *lucerne in derne*, lamp in darkness

Hodiern, modern, sempitern,
  Angelicall regyne !
Our tern inferne for to dispern
  Help rialest rosyne.
    Ave Maria, gratia plena !
  Hail, fresh flower femynyne !
Yerne us, guberne, virgin matern,
  Of reuth baith rute and ryne.

Hail, young, benyng, fresh flurising !
  Hail, Alphais habitakle !
The dyng ofspring made us to syng
  Before his tabernakle ;
All thing maling we doun thring
  Be sicht of his signakle ;
Whilk king us bring unto his ryng
  Fro Dethe's derk umbrakle.
    Ave Maria, gratia plena !
  Hail, moder and maid but makle !
Bricht sign, gladyng our languissing,
  Be micht of the mirakle.

Hail, bricht be sicht, in Hevyn on hicht,
  Hail, day sterne orientale !
Our licht most richt, in clud of nycht,
  Our dirknes for to scale :

Hodiern, modern, sempitern, of to-day, now, and for ever
tern, trouble   *dispern*, disperse   *rosyne*, rose
Yerne, influence   *virgin matern*, virgin mother   *reuth*, pity
ryne, stem   *habitakle*, habitation   *dyng*, worthy
doun thring, crush down   *signakle*, sign   *ryng*, kingdom
umbrakle, shadow   *but makle*, without blemish
be sicht, to see   *scale*, scatter

Hail, wicht in sicht, putter to flicht
    Of fendis in battale !
Hail plicht, but sicht, hail mekle of mycht !
    Hail, glorious Virgin, hail !
      Ave Maria, gratia plena !
    Hail, gentill nychttingale !
Way stricht, cler dicht to wilsome wicht,
    That irke bene in travale.

Hail, queen serene !   Hail, most amene !
    Hail, Hevinlie hie empryss !
Hail schene, unseyne with carnal eyne,
    Hail, rose of paradyss !
Hail, clene, bedene, ay till conteyne !
    Hail, fair fresh flour-de-lyce !
Hail, grene daseyne !   Hail, fro the splene
    Of Jesu genetrice !
      Ave Maria, gratia plena !
    Thou bair the prince of pryss ;
Our teyne to meyne, and ga betweyne,
    Ane hevinle oratrice.

Hail, more decore than of before,
    And swetar be sic sevyne,
Our glore forlore for to restore,
    Sen thou art quene of hevyne !

---

wicht, strong   *plicht, but sicht*, anchor unseen
way stricht, etc., way straight, clear shown to wilful man
irke bene, is weary *amene*, gentle *schene*, beautiful one
eyne, eyes   *clene, bedene, etc.*, pure, and always to continue
daseyne, daisy   *teyne to meyne*, misery to pity
decore, becoming   *be sic sevyne*, sevenfold

Memore of sore, stern in Aurore,
  Lovit with angellis stevyne,
Implore, adore, thou indeflore,
  To mak our oddis evyne.
    Ave Maria, gratia plena !
With lovingis loud ellevyn,
Whyll store and hore my youth devore
  Thy name I sall ay nevyne.

Empryce of pryss, imperatrice,
  Brycht polist precious stane ;
Victryce of vyce, hie genetrice
  Of Jesu, lord soverayne :
Our wyss pavysse fra enemyss,
  Agayne the Feindis trayne ;
Oratrice, mediatrice, salvatrice,
  To God gret suffragane !
    Ave Maria, gratia plena !
  Hail, stern meridiane !
Spyce, flour-de-lice of paradyse,
  That bair the gloryuss grayne.

Imperiall wall, place palestrall,
  Or peirless pulcritud ;
Tryumphale hall, hie tour royal
  Of Godis celsitud ;

    memore of sore, remembering pain
stern in Aurore, star of the morning   *stevyne*, voices
indeflore, undefiled   *ellevyn*, extolled   *whyll*, till
store, trouble   *hore*, old age   *nevyne*, honour
wyss pavysse, wise shield   *trayne*, snare
palestrall, like a palace   *celsitud*, might

Hospital riall, the lord of all
Thy closet did include ;
Bricht ball cristall rose virginall
Fulfillit of angell fude !
Ave Maria, gratia plena !
Thy birth has with his blude
Fra fall mortall originall
Us raunsound on the rude.

William Dunbar.

242   THE LORD IS MY SHEPHERD

I'm a puir man, I grant,
But I am weel neiboured ;
And nane shall me daunt,
Though a puir man, I grant ;
For I shall not want—
The Lord is my Shepherd !
I'm a puir man I grant,
But I am weel neiboured !

George Macdonald.

243   IN FORMA PAUPERIS

Who is at my windo ?   Who, who ?
Go from my windo, go, go !
Who callis thair, sa lyke a strangeir ?
Go from my windo, go !

Hospital riall, royal guest-house
raunsound, ransomed   *rude*, cross

Lord, I am hair, ane wretchit mortall,
That for thy mercy dois cry and call
Unto the, my lord celestiall.
   Se who is at my windo, who ? . . .

With richt humbill hart, lord, the I pray,
Thy comfort and grace obtain I may :
Schew me the path and reddy way
   In at thy dure for to go . . .

Lord, I pray the with all my hart,
Of thy greit mercy remuve my smart,
Let ane drop of thy grace be my part,
   That in at thy dure I may go . . .

Remember thy sin, and als thy smart,
And als for the what was my part :
Remember the speir that thirlit my hart,
   And in at my dure thou sall go . . .

I ask na thing of the thairfoir,
But lufe for lufe, to lay in stoir :
Gif me thy hart, I ask no moir,
   And in at my dure thow sall go. . . .

Who is at my windo ?   Who ?
Go from my windo, go !
Cry na mair thair, lyke ane stranger
   But in at my dure thow go.

244   THE ABBAY WALK

ALONE as I went up and doun
    In ane Abbay was fair to se,
Thinkand what consolatioun
    Was best into adversitie ;
On caiss I kest on side mine e'e,
    And saw this written upoun a wall :
" Of what estate, Man, that thou be,
    Obey and thank thy God of all."

Thy kingdom and thy grit empire,
    Thy ryaltie, nor rich array,
Sall nocht endure at thy desire,
    Bot, as the wind, will wend away ;
Thy gold, and all thy gudis gay,
    When fortoun list will fra thee fall :
Sen thou sic sampillis seis ilk day,
    Obey, and thank thy God of all.

Job was moist rich, in Writ we find,
    Thobè moist full of cheritie,
Job waxed pure, and Thobè blind
    Baith tempit with adversitie.
Sen blindness wes infirmitie,
    And poverty wes natural ;
Rycht patiently baith he and he
    Obeyit, and thankit God of all.

Thoch thou be blind, or haif ane halt,
    Or in thy face deformit ill,

On caiss, by chance   *sampillis*, instances
                    pure, poor

Divine Philosophy

Sa it cum nocht through thy default,
    Na man suld thee repreif by skill,
Blame nocht thy Lord, sa is his will ;
    Spurn nocht thy foot aganis the wall ;
Bot with meik hairt and prayer still
    Obey, and thank thy God of all.

God of his justice maun correct,
    And of his mercy pitie haif ;
He is ane Judge, to nane suspect,
    To puneis sinful man and saif.
Thoch thou be lord attour the laif,
    And eftirwart made bound and thrall,
Ane pure beggar, with skrip and staiff :
    Obey, and thank thy God of all.

This changeing and grit variance
    Off erdly staitis up and doun
Is nocht bot casualty and chance,
    Sa some men sayis, without ressoun,
Bot be the grit provisioun
    Of God aboif that rewll thee sall ;
Thairfoir ever thou mak thee boun
    To obey, and thank thy God of all.

In wealth be meik, heich not thyself ;
    Be glaid in wilful povertie ;
Thy power and thy warldis pelf
    Is nocht but very vanitie.
Remember him that deit on tree,
    For thy sake taistit the bitter gall,

saif, save	*laif*, rest	*erdly*, earthly
be, by	*boun*, ready	*heich*, exalt

Wha heis law hairtis, and lawis he :
Obey, and thank thy God of all.
                    Robert Henryson.

245   THE MERLE AND THE NIGHTINGALE

In May as that Aurora did upspring,
    With cristall ene chasing the cluddis sable,
I herd a merle with mirry notis sing
    A sang of lufe, with voice rycht confortable,
    Agane the orient bemis amiable,
Upone a blisful brench of lawryr grene ;
    This wes hir sentens sweit and delectable,
A lusty lyfe in luvis service bene.

Undir this brench ran doun a revir bricht,
    Of balmy liquour, cristallyne of hew,
Agane the hevinly aisur skyis licht,
    Whair did, upone the othair syd, persew
    A nychtingall, with sugarit notis new,
Whois angell fetheris as the peacok schone ;
    This wes hir song, and of a sentens trew,
All luve is lost bot upone God allone.

With notis glaid and glorious harmony,
    This joyfull merle so salust scho the day,
Whill rong the wooddis of hir melody,
    Saying, " Awake, ye luvaris, O, this May.
    Lo, fresche Flora hes flurest every spray,

wha heis law hairtis, etc., who raises low hearts and
                    humbles the high
    lawryr, laurel   *salust*, saluted

As natur hes hir taucht, the noble quene,
  The feild bene clothit in a new array ;
A lusty lyfe in luvis service bene.

Nevir sweter noys wes hard with levand man,
  Na maid this mirry gentill nychtingaill,
Hir sound went with the revir as it ran,
  Outthrow the fresche and flureist lusty vaill.
  " O merle," quod scho, " O fule, stynt of thy taill,
For in thy song gud sentens is thair none,
  For boith is tynt the tyme and the travaill
Of every luve bot upone God allone."

" Seiss," quod the merle, " thy preching, nychtingale.
  Sall folk thair yewth spend in-to holiness ?
Of yung sanctis growis auld feyndis but fable ;
  Fy, ypocreit, in yeiris tendirness,
  Agane the law of kynd thow gois express,
That crukit aige makis one with yewth serene,
  Whome natur of conditionis maid dyverss :
A lusty life in luvis service bene."

The nychtingaill said, " Fule, remembir the,
  That both in yewth and eild, and every hour,
The luve of God most deir to man suld be,
  That him of nocht wrocht lyk his awin figour,
  And deit him self fro deid him to succour.
O, whithir wes kythit thair trew lufe or none ?
  He is most trew and steidfast paramour ;
All luve is lost bot upone him allone."

flureist, blossoming   *stynt of*, check   *tynt*, lost
but fable, in truth   *eild*, old age   *of nocht*, out of nothing
awin, own   *deit*, died   *deid*, death   *kythit*, shown

The merle said, " Why put God so grit bewty
  In ladeis, with sic womanly having,
Bot gife he wald that thay suld luvit be ?
  To luve eik natur gaif thame inclynnyng ;
  And He, of natur that wirker wes and king,
Wald no thing frustir put, nor lat be sene,
  In to his creature of his awin making :
A lusty lyfe in luvis service bene."

The nychtingall said, " Nocht to that behufe
  Put God sic bewty in a ladeis face,
That scho suld haif the thanks thairfoir or lufe,
  Bot He, the wirker, that put in hir sic grace,
  Off bewty, bontie, richess, tyme or space.
And every gudness that bene to cum or gone ;
  The thanks redoundis to him in every place ;
All luve is lost bot upone God allone."

" O nychtingall, it wer a story nyce,
  That luve suld nocht depend on cherite,
And gife that vertew contrair be to vyce,
  Then luve mon be a vertew, as thinkis me ;
  For ay to lufe envy maun contrair be :
God bad eik lufe thy nychtbour fro the splene,
  And who than ladeis sweter nychbouris be ?
A lusty lyfe in luvis service bene."

The nychtingaill said, " Bird, why dois thow raif ?
  Man may tak in his lady sic delyt,
Him to forget that hir sic vertew gaif,

bewty, beauty	*having*, behaviour	*bot gife*, unless
eik, also	*wirker*, creator	*frustir*, uselessly
behufe, purpose	*fro the splene*, from the heart	*raif*, rave

And for his hevin rassaif hir cullour whyt ;
  Hir goldin tressit hairis redomyt,
Lyk to Appollois bemis thoch thay schone,
  Suld nocht him blind fro lufe that is perfyt ;
All lufe is lost bot upone God allone."

The merle said, " Lufe is causs of honour ay,
  Luve makis cowardis manheid to purchass,
Luve makis knychtis hardy at assey,
  Luve makis wrechis full of lergeness,
  Luve makis sueir folkis full of bissiness,
Luve makis sluggirdis fresche and weill besene,
  Luve changis vyce in vertewis nobilness ;
A lusty lyfe in luvis service bene."

The nychtingaill said, " Trew is the contrary ;
  Sic frustir luve, it blindis men so far,
In-to thair myndis it makis thame to vary ;
  In fals vane glory thai so drunkin ar,
  Thair wit is went, of wo thai ar nocht war,
Whill that all wirchip away be fro thame gone,
  Fame, guddis and strenth ; whairfoir weill say I dar,
All luve is lost bot upone God allone."

Than said the merle, " Myn errour I confess ;
  This frustir luve all is bot vanite ;
Blind ignorance me gaif sic hardiness,
  To argone so agane the verite ;

rassaif, receive	*redomyt*, beautiful	*sueir*, unwilling
frustir, vain	*war*, aware	*whill*, till
	argone, argue	

Whairfoir I counsall every man, that he
With lufe nocht in the feindis net be tone,
 Bot luve the luve that did for his lufe dee ;
All lufe is lost bot upone God allone."

Than sang they both with voicis lowd and cleir ;
 The merle sang, " Man, lufe God that hes the wrocht ; "
The nychtingall sang, " Man, lufe the Lord most deir,
 That the and all this warld maid of nocht."
 The merle said, " Luve him that thy lufe hes socht
Fra hevin to erd, and heir tuk flesche and bone : "
 The nychtingall sang, " And with his deid the bocht ;
All lufe is lost bot upone him allone."

Thane flaw thir birdis our the bewis schene,
 Singing of lufe amang the levis small,
Whois ythand pleid yit maid my thochtis grene,
 Bothe sleping, walking, in rest and in travall ;
 Me to reconfort most it dois awaill
Agane for lufe, when lufe I can find none,
 To think how sang this merle and nychtingaill,
All lufe is lost bot upone God allone.

William Dunbar.

tone, taken *our the bewis schene*, over the bough's sheen
     ythand pleid, earnest contest

COMMENTARY

COMMENTARY

BOOK I

YOUTH AND SPRING

SPRING is a laggard in the North. In April the land is still wintry, the meadows are more yellow than green, buds scarcely show on the trees, the birches are as yet a pale vapour. Remains of old drifts lie behind the dykes, and there are patches of snow on the high tops. You may get an odd day of sun, when the full streams are caught with silver and the clear light sharpens the contours of the hills ; but my common recollection of upland Aprils is of grey skies, acres of heather blackened with the moor-burning, and a perpetual wailing of curlews—the atmosphere of that line of Edgar's in his madness,—

" Through the sharp hawthorn blows the cold wind."

Then comes a morning in early May when the world grows warm and austerity falls from it ; bird-notes awake, green flushes the face of the earth, and in a week it is the Spring of the poet.

To the Middle Ages the transition from Winter was like the sudden outburst of Northern Spring, a yearly miracle which in an instant thawed the ice on the streams of poetry and set them singing. Consider the utter discomfort of a mediæval winter-time. For the towns :

outside, the narrow vennels choked with snow and frozen offal or ankle-deep in evil-smelling mud ; within, draughts and chills save in the immediate vicinity of the smoky fireplace, arctic sleeping-quarters with the gale howling through the chinks of the unglazed windows ; vile food, mostly half-salted beef and mutton which was putrescent by February, no vegetables or fruits, and at the best an occasional fresh meal from a lean deer sent down from the hills ; nothing to do in the long dark hours between half-past three and bedtime but con his few books (if a man was a scholar) by candle-light, or listen to interminable twice-told tales. Small wonder that the Middle Ages were prolix—there was an infinity of time to kill. In the country it was little better, for there was little winter sport before the day of the match-lock. Miry roads and flooded waters did indeed give some security to the little castles, but peace meant ennui, unexercised limbs, and ill-nourished bodies. Winter was a pall which lay black on a man's spirit, and made him think, like Dunbar, of his latter end. Then, like a recovery from sickness, came the Spring, and the world awoke. Men went out of their dark dwellings, bemused with sunlight, drunken with bird song and greenery, marvelling at the common flowers as if they were celestial visitants. Of such sudden awakenings poetry is born. Spring is to us a marvel by a poetic convention, but to the Middle Ages it was in sober reality a new birth.

In Scots literature we find this high mood of surprise and delight only in and before the sixteenth century. The old poets were all of them scholars after a fashion, and gently and often nobly born ; Montgomerie, for example, was of the family of Eglinton, and Dunbar of

that fantastic house of March which had for its motto,
"*Parmi ceu haut bois conduyrai mamie.*" They were
students, courtiers, soldiers, men of affairs or high in the
Church, and in the draughty courts of palaces and in
icy castle chambers they shivered and cursed the Winter.
In their writings they rarely mention it, and when they
do it is, like Dunbar, penitentially, or, like Gawain
Douglas in his seventh Prologue, with a splendid gusto
of hate. The thing was too hideous for the Muses.
But Spring comes to loose the bonds of their discontent,
and they overflow like brooks in thaw. He is blind
indeed who cannot detect behind their enamelled and
aureate style the rapture of the prisoner set free.

The mood was not to be recovered. When the vernacular was left to the peasant (except as a condescen-
sion on the part of men of letters who thought first of
their English style) there was no chance of that sharply
felt antagonism. The gently born poets of the so-called
Golden Age—Henryson, Dunbar, Montgomerie, Alexander Scott, Lyndsay, down to Hume—excluded Winter
from their verse because they detested it, as a bar both
to their pleasures and their duties. But popular poetry
had never known this ban, and some of the finest of
the ballads have their setting in wintry weather. To
the poor man one season was much like another—he
must get through his day's work in them all ; and indeed
Winter meant to him a time of comparative rest. Cut-
ting and carrying peats in Summer and ploughing lea in
Spring were harder jobs than feeding sheep in fold and
cattle in byre with bog hay during the short December
days. Winter, too, brought its modest festivities—
Hallowe'en, the " blyth Yule night when we were fou,"
Hogmanay, Handsel Monday—the cotter's Saturday

night for the sedate and Poosie Nansie's for the lively. He was used to the elements at all times, and made little of them ; the fine gentleman might grumble at the mud and the dark skies, but the poor man took them placidly, and his hearth-fire shone the more brightly because of the dismal out-of-doors.

Hence in Scots verse of the past two centuries we do not find the mediæval exaltation at the coming of Spring. It is taken as a matter of course. Indeed, it may be argued that the Scots Muse is at her best, as in the Ballads, when engaged with bleakness and storm. The poetry of Spring is there, no doubt, but it is conceived in a lower key. A piece like Stevenson's (No. 2) is a recaptured literary mood, not a lyrical cry; " Hugh Haliburton's " is a Dutch picture, and Lady John Scott's song has no more than a temperate joy. We shall never again see the year as that contrast between misery and ecstasy which made Spring to the Middle Ages a miracle and a revelation.

1

Ed. Scottish Text Society, II. 233-4. Five stanzas omitted.

2

Underwoods, Book II. 3.

3

Horace in Homespun, by Hugh Haliburton. " Hughie marks with delight the return of Spring."

4

Ed. Scottish Text Society, 193-4. This is the most famous of the lyrics of Alexander Montgomerie, the author of *The Cherrie and the Slae*, who lived during the latter half of the sixteenth century. Mr. Walter de la Mare has an English version in his *Come Hither*, page 2, and there is another by Allan Cunningham in his *Songs of Scotland*, I. 274. The bird referred to in the first verse may be the corn-bunting ; another version gives " throstle-cock," which would be the thrush. The tune to which the words are written is " Hey tuttie taittie " —one of the oldest of Scots airs, and the one to which Bruce fought the battle of Bannockburn, and which Burns broadened and flattened into " Scots Wha Hae." There must have been many sets of words before Montgomerie's, for Dunbar refers to it, and Gawain Douglas in the prologue to the thirteenth book of his *Eneados*, 177–182 (see page 289, *supra*). It is also—sure proof of a wide popularity—adapted to the uses of theology in *The Gude and Godlie Ballats*.

5

Ed. Scottish Text Society, II. 1–2—first five stanzas. This is the beautiful opening of " The Golden Targe," Dunbar's allegory of love and wisdom. It is in the poet's stateliest heraldic manner—for example, " powderit," which in heraldry is the strewing of a field with small figures, and " goulis," the heraldic " gules." But the sumptuous language does not obscure his keen observation of nature. The fourth stanza is a wonderful picture of a shallow stream at dawn.

6

From the Bannatyne MS. (collected by George Bannatyne, a burgess of Edinburgh, 1546 ?–1608 ?) ; the last stanza is from the *Aberdeen Cantus*. The piece used to be wrongly attributed to Alexander Scott, who did, indeed, write a May ode, but in a very different manner. It was first printed by Chepman and Myllar in 1508, nearly half a century before Scott's date.

7

Ed. Scottish Text Society, II. 183–4. The opening of " The Thistle and the Rose," which Dunbar wrote in honour of the marriage of James IV. and Margaret Tudor in 1503.

8

Songs and Verses, by Lady John Scott, 1904.

9

The opening stanzas of *The Kingis Quair*, which James I. of Scotland wrote in the last year of his captivity in Windsor Castle to commemorate his love for the Lady Jane Beaufort, whom he made his queen.   It was probably written in 1423 ; the earliest manuscript, which is at Oxford, dates from 1475, thirty-eight years after his death during that tragic Christmastide at Perth.   The best edition is Dr. Skeat's, published by the Scottish Text Society, 1883.

BOOK II

PLAISIR D'AMOUR

There is more love poetry in the world than any other kind, and it is all a variation upon half a dozen simple themes, whether it be put in the mouth of man or woman. There is the regal, magnificent note, when the beloved becomes queen and goddess and is praised with litanies.

Hazlitt has given us the prose of it : " In her sight there was Elysium ; her smile was heaven ; her voice was enchantment ; the air of love waved round her, breathing balm into my heart ; for a little while I had sat with the gods at their golden tables ; I had tasted of all earth's bliss." We find it in Dunbar's praise of Mistress Musgrave, and in anonymous early poems like " My heart is heich abufe " and " Baith gud and fair and womanlie," and " When Flora had ourfret the firth ; " we find it in Burns's " O, my luve is like a red, red rose " and " Mary Morison " and " O wert thou in the cauld blast." But human nature cannot dwell for long on these hill-tops, so presently the goddess becomes woman, and the love-making grows warm and natural. Scots poetry is extraordinarily rich in the freshest and simplest of love lays, whether they be Burns's master-pieces, " My ain kind dearie " and " O' a' the airts," or Ramsay's " My Peggy is a young thing," or Mrs. Jacob's " Tam i' the Kirk," or of unknown authorship like " The Ewe-Bughts." It is the girl who sings in some of the best, like " The Yellow-hair'd Laddie," " To daunton me," " I lo'e nae a laddie but ane," " Saw ye Johnnie coming ? " and " Ca' the yowes to the knowes."

Humour, too, comes in to correct a sweetness which might otherwise cloy. The girl in the story complained that her lover was " senselessly ceevil," but many of the pieces do not err on the side of civility. They are bold and candid, but even in the worst of *The Merry Muses* I see little that is indecent, for ogling and leering are rare. It is a robust affection which can admit the comic without loss of charm, which can be merry and yet gracious. Burns is a master of this type—" O for

ane and twenty, Tam," " O whistle and I'll come to
ye," " Last May a braw wooer ; " and in " The Gowk "
Mrs. Jacob walks in the same path.

Then there are the stock comedies of love, pictures of
its inevitable paradoxes, and so we have Henryson's
" Robine and Makyn," Burns's " Duncan Gray " and
" Tam Glen," Mrs. Jacob's " Change o' Deils," anonymous snatches like " Low doun in the broom," and the
graceless ditty which I have called " Kiss'd Yestreen."
From these it is but a short step to love's pleasing cares
and crosses—the lover at his mistress's window, as in
" Let me in this ae night," and " O are ye sleepin',
Maggie ? " the hopeful severance, as in " For the sake
o' somebody " and " Jockie's ta'en the parting kiss,"
the restoration after long absence, as in " Wandering
Willie " and " Logie o' Buchan." I have concluded
with Montgomerie's " Adieu to his Mistress," where the
confident parting of the lovers is ever so faintly clouded
with shadow.

10

The authorship of this song is uncertain, but I am
inclined to attribute it to Alexander Scott, whose *floruit*
was the middle of the sixteenth century. The matter is
that of Scott's " Up, Helsum Heart," but the measure
has no parallel among his lyrics.

11

Written by Burns for Johnson's *Museum* in 1796.
Almost every line, almost every phrase, is taken from
some clumsy original among the black-letter ballads
and broadsheets, for which the curious may consult the
note in the edition of Henley and Henderson, III.

402–6. Out of this patchwork Burns has shapéd one of the great love songs of our literature.

12

Ed. Scottish Text Society, II. 223. The lady honoured in these verses has been conjectured to be one Mistress Musgrave, an English waiting-woman of Queen Margaret's, for whose sake Dunbar, in his " Of a Dance in the Queenis Chalmer," wished he were " the grytest erle or duik in France."

13

From the Bannatyne MS.

14

Contributed to Thomson's *Select Collection*. Burns worked on an old set of words, and a version by Robert Fergusson had already appeared in Johnson's *Museum*.

15

Written by Burns during his honeymoon shortly after his arrival at Ellisland. Third and fourth stanzas of little merit are sometimes printed, the work of an Edinburgh music-seller called Hamilton, in which the lady is described with profound anti-climax as " aye sae neat and clean."

16

This set of words and the tune (after " Auld Lang Syne " perhaps the best known of Scottish airs) were the work of Lady John Scott. Annie Laurie was the daughter of Laurie of Maxwelltown in Glencairn, and married the neighbouring laird of Craigdarroch. The old version is ascribed by Charles Kirkpatrick Sharpe

(*A Ballad Book*, 1824, page 107) to Douglas of Fing-
land, and is said to have been written about 1680.

> " Maxwellton banks are bonnie
>   Whar early fa's the dew ;
> Whar me and Annie Laurie
>   Made up the promise true.
>   Made up the promise true,
>   And never forget will I ;
> And for bonnie Annie Laurie
>   I'd lay me down and die.
>
> She's backit like the peacock,
>   She's breastit like the swan ;
> She's jimp about the middle,
>   Her waist ye weel micht span.
>   Her waist ye weel micht span,
>   And she has a rolling eye ;
> And for bonnie Annie Laurie
>   I'd lay me down and die."

17

This song was first printed in Allan Ramsay's *Tea-
Table Miscellany*, 1724, and marked as an " old song
with additions." It is a pastoral of the Lowlands, and,
judging from the place-names in certain versions, of
the valleys of Tweed and Ale. See Chambers's *Scottish
Songs*, II. 348.

18

" I'll gang nae mair to yon toun " is an old air, which
is echoed in many vagabond snatches, and by Burns
a second time in " O wat ye wha's in yon town." It
is the undercurrent in William Bell Scott's ballad on
page 349.

19

From *The Gentle Shepherd*.   It is difficult to dissociate
the words from the tune, one of the most beautiful of
the old Border viol airs.

20

Songs of Angus, 1915.

21

The first two stanzas of the version in Ramsay's
Tea-Table Miscellany, 1724.   There is another and much
inferior text in Cunningham's *Songs of Scotland*, III. 155.

22

It is not clear how large a part Burns had in this
adaptation from the Jacobite broadside, which is
found as early as 1750 in a collection of *Loyal Songs*,
and of which there are many versions.   One of these is
given by Chambers, *Scottish Songs*, II. 355, and the best
is in Hogg's *Jacobite Relics*, II. 88.

" To daunton me, to daunton me,
  D'ye ken the thing that wad daunton me ?
  Eighty-eight and eighty-nine,
  And a' the dreary years sinsyne
  With cess and press and Presbyt'ry ;
  Gude faith, this had like to daunton me.

  But to wanton me, to wanton me,
  D'ye ken the thing that wad wanton me ?
  To see gude corn upon the rigs,
  And a gallows high to hang the Whigs,
  And right restored where right should be ;
  O, these are the things that wad wanton me.

But to wanton me, but to wanton me,
And ken ye what maist wad wanton me ?
To see King James at Edinburgh Cross
With fifty thousand foot and horse,
And the Usurper forced to flee :
O, this is what maist wad wanton me."

23

Printed first by Ritson with the initials " I.D."
attached, the version I have given seems to have been
the work of the Rev. John Clunie, the minister of Ewes,
who gave Burns the old words of " Ca' the yowes to the
knowes." The song commonly met with is the work
of Hector Macneill, who borrowed Clunie's first stanza
and added four indifferent ones of his own. My text is
that of Allan Cunningham, *Songs of Scotland*, III. 259.

24

Generally accredited to Joanna Baillie (1762–1851),
the dramatist of the Passions and the friend of Scott ;
but she had an early version to work on which Burns
praised highly, and she did little more than expand in
each stanza the first quatrain. The old words will be
found in Cunningham, II. 168.

25

Burns wrote a second version which he sent to Thomson, and which is printed in Henley's edition, III. 268.
The text here given was based on an older song which
Burns heard from the Rev. John Clunie. There seems
no evidence for Laing's tradition that the old version,
which is given in Stenhouse and in Johnson's *Museum*,
was the work of one Isobel Pagan, the keeper of an

ale-house near Muirkirk.   But whoever the author was, the old copy has some admirable verses, not improved by Burns, such as—

> " Yon yowes and lammies on the plain
> Wi' a' the gear my dad did hain,
> I'se gie thee, if thou'lt be my ain,
> My bonnie dearie."

26

From Cunningham's *Songs of Scotland*, IV. 241.

28

Sent to Thomson in 1793.   Burns wrote an earlier version of eight lines for Johnson in 1788 (Henley, III. 304).   The chorus is old, and is found in the Herd MS.

30

Songs of Angus, 1915.

31

This fragrant old pastoral—in a ballad metre and with no trace of Chaucerian influence—has for its theme the converse of Burns's " Duncan Gray." Henryson lived in the third quarter of the fifteenth century, and is said to have been the schoolmaster of Dunfermline. The poem is in the Bannatyne MS., and was first introduced to the modern world by Ramsay's *Ever Green*.

32

" That kind of lighthorse gallop of an air which precludes sentiment," Burns wrote, in sending the piece to Thomson.   He has another version (Henley, III. 23), and both were based on an unprintable original to be found in the Herd MS. and *The Merry Muses*. The " feast day when we were fou " appears in perhaps the oldest Scots song which has been preserved to us, " The Wowing of Jok and Jynny," in the Bannatyne MS., which Ramsay printed in his *Tea-Table Miscellany*.

33

More Songs of Angus and Others, 1918.

34

Versions, slightly different, will be found in Chambers and Cunningham ; I have omitted the last two stanzas. The song in its present form is said to have been written by Carnegie of Balnamoon, an Angus laird who was out in the '45. The chorus is ancient, and is referred to in *The Complaynt of Scotland*.

35

Cunningham, II. 248. This song of a merry and complaisant lady is a variant which Cunningham quotes of a much inferior ballad, said to be based on an adventure of one of the Argylls. Its scene is seventeenth-century Glasgow.

37

From Cunningham's *Songs of Scotland*, II. 213. I prefer Cunningham's version of a tale and a refrain which belong to the ancientry of folk-song. Something of the kind is imitated in *The Gude and Godlie Ballats* (see page 440, *supra*) ; there is a text in Herd (1769) which Burns remodelled (Henley, III. 274). Burns's other songs on the theme—for example, " Wha is that at my bower door ? " and " Open the door to me O,"

and the piece by Tannahill which follows, are of the
same family.

38

To my mind the best of Tannahill's lyrics. It is based
on a ribald old song which is now lost, but the memory
of which is preserved in the " Sleeping Maggie," which
used to be a popular barn dance in the Lowlands.

39

This famous lyric was sent to Thomson in 1793 by
Burns, who described it as " one of my juvenile works
—not very remarkable either for its merits or its de-
merits." Henley suggests that he borrowed the metrical
scheme of it from the piece printed below—which he
may have seen in *The Ever Green*.

40

The only poem in old Scots which approaches the
rhyme scheme of the French *ballade*. It is from the
Bannatyne MS., and, though sometimes given to Alexander Scott, is probably much earlier. Ramsay, in *The
Ever Green*, attributes it to " Stewart," who may be the
otherwise unknown poet mentioned by Sir David Lyndsay in the Prologue to the *Papynge*.

41

A noble song with a most tragic provenance. It was
written by Burns at Dumfries, during his last illness,
in honour of Jessie Lewars, the sister of a fellow-excise-
man, who helped the struggling household and played
old airs to the dying poet.

42

There are two songs besides that of Burns on " Somebody "—which was perhaps originally a Jacobite toast
—one in Ramsay's *Tea-Table Miscellany* (I. 191) with
the same chorus, and one included in Hogg's *Jacobite
Relics* (II. 47), which is probably by Hogg himself.
This last has a definite Jacobite flavour.

> " If somebody were come again,
> Then somebody maun cross the main,
> And ilka ane will get his ain,
> And I will see my somebody.
>
> *wept*]   O ! I hae grutten mony a day
> For ane that's banish'd far away :
> I canna sing and mauna say
> How sair I grieve for somebody."

44

This is the old version from Herd, which I prefer to
Burns's set (Henley, III. 208). The words are in-
separable from the air, almost the most haunting of
Scots melodies—" the saddest of our country tunes which
sets folk weeping in a tavern " (*The Master of Ballan-
trae*, chapter ix.). Stevenson wrote words to the air,
beginning : " Home no more home to me, whither must
I wander ? " (*Songs of Travel*, XII.).

45

Peter Buchan, not the best of authorities, claimed
this piece for George Halkett, the Jacobite schoolmaster
of Rathen in Aberdeenshire, who died in 1756.

46

Ed. Scottish Text Society, 189. The daisy was Montgomerie's flower, as it was Chaucer's. The pleasant
lilting measure is the same as that of *The Cherrie and
the Slae.*

BOOK III

CHAGRIN D'AMOUR

Montgomerie's tail-piece to the last section leads us
naturally to Alexander Scott's " Farewell," in which
rapture is touched with sorrow, and presently to the
same author's " Roundel of Luve," of which the conclusion is that the price out-weighs the pleasure, and to
" Ay Waukin O," which is all hopeless longing. After
that we are in the midst of love's tragedies—the poor
maid jilted for the well-dowered, the Master of Erskine's
lament for a lost mistress, the woe of the deserted mother
who calls on the Martinmas wind and gentle Death,
and the protest against life's ironies of the girl who has
married to save the household from want and abides
with a noble honesty by her bargain—" I darena think
on Jamie, for that wad be a sin." And so we reach
the great tragic poems of Burns, " Ye Banks and Braes "
and " Ae Fond Kiss." The latter, as austere and poig-
nant as a verse of Sappho, is followed by the sonnet in
which Mark Boyd, like some lyrist of the Greek Anthology, turns his back for good and all upon Venus, the

> " wife ingenrit of the sea,
> And lichter nor a dauphin with her fin."

The section is small because, though ready enough to
make love songs, the poets of Scotland have been not-

ably free from any obsession of sex, and are not inclined
to devote themselves to its pathology, or, overmuch, to
its sorrows. They have usually been of the mind of
Dr. Johnson, who declared that poetry was seldom worse
employed than to celebrate the ravings of a love-sick
girl, and of Shakespeare, in whose greatest tragedies
sex plays but a small part. They are ribald enough,
but they are free from the solemn sententious lewdness
of certain moderns. They can imagine far worse misfortunes for a man than being crossed in love. The loss
of a wife or a child, a friend or a cause, seems to these
heretics more tragic than the loss of a mistress or a
lover. This will be ascribed to good sense or to obtuse-
ness, according to the reader's philosophy.

47

Scott wrote a pendant to this, a song of a disillusioned
lover, of which the following in the first verse :—

' Returne thee hamewart, hairt, agane,
  And bide whair thou was want to be ;
  Thou art ane fule to suffer bane,
  For luve of her that luvis not thee.
  My hairt, lat be sic fantasie,
  Luve nane bot as they mak' thee cause,
  And lat her seik ane hairt for thee,
falls to get] For feind a crum of thee scho fawis.''

48

Scott was familiar with the work of Wyatt and Surrey,
and this piece, as Mr. T. F. Henderson has pointed out,
is a condensed and improved version of Wyatt's " Absent
Lover."

49

I give the version which I have always heard sung. In the main it is Burns's, but one verse belongs to the text printed by Robert Chambers (*Scottish Songs*, I. 126), though Chambers's last verse is omitted. The first stanza and the chorus are old, and are found in the Herd MS. It is permissible to quote Dr. John Brown (*Horæ Subsecivæ*, third series, 305) :—

" A ploughman or shepherd—for I hold that it is a man's song—comes in ' wat, wat ' after a hard day's work among the furrows or on the hill. The *watness* of wat, wat, is as much wetter than wet as a Scotch mist is more of a mist than an English one ; and he is not only wat, wat, but ' weary,' longing for a dry skin and a warm bed and rest ; but no sooner said and felt, than, by the law of contrast, he thinks on ' Mysie ' or ' Ailie,' his Genevieve ; and then ' all thoughts, all passions, all delights ' begin to stir him, and ' fain wad I rise and rin ' (what a swiftness beyond ' run ' is ' rin ' !). Love now makes him a poet ; the true imaginative power enters and takes possession of him. By this time his clothes are off, and he is snug in bed ; not a wink can he sleep ; that ' fain ' is domineering over him— and he breaks out into what is as genuine passion and poetry as anything from Sappho to Tennyson—abrupt, vivid, heedless of syntax. ' Simmer's a pleasant time.' Would any of our greatest geniuses, being limited to one word, have done better than take ' pleasant ' ? and then the fine vagueness of ' time ' ! ' Flowers o' every colour ;' he gets a glimpse of ' herself a fairer flower,' and is off in pursuit. ' The water rins over the heugh ' (a steep precipice) ; flinging itself wildly, passionately over, and so do I long for my true lover. Nothing can be simpler and finer than

When I sleep, I dream ;
When I wauk, I'm eerie.'

' Lanely nicht : ' how much richer and more touching than
' darksome.'   ' Feather beds are saft ; '   ' pentit rooms are
bonnie ; '   I would infer from this, that his ' dearie,' his
' true love,' was a lass up at ' the big house '—a dapper
Abigail possibly—at Sir William's at the Castle."

50

First printed in the *Tea-Table Miscellany* and *Orpheus
Caledonius*.   Lady Grizel Baillie (1665–1746) was the
heroic daughter of the Covenanting Earl of Marchmont,
and married George Baillie of Jerviswood, the son of her
father's friend.   Her story may be read in the Memoir
by her daughter, Lady Murray of Stanhope, 1822.   The
refrain is almost certainly much earlier.

51

From the Bannatyne MS.   The Master of Erskine,
who was the lover of the Queen Regent, fell in 1547 at
the Battle of Pinkie.

52

This, the noblest of all the anonymous songs of Scotland, is strangely obscure in its origins.   Several stanzas
of it were transferred to the late ballad of " Jamie
Douglas " (No. 204 in Professor Child's collection), and
consequently the song has been sometimes entitled
" The Marchioness of Douglas's Lament," but it has
no proven relation to the incident in the ballad.   It
first appeared in the *Tea-Table Miscellany*, and then in
the second edition of *Orpheus Caledonius*, where an additional verse was printed—

> " When cockle shells turn siller bells,
>   And mussels grow on every tree :
> When frost and snaw shall warm us a'
>   Then shall my love prove true to me "—

a verse which is found in a slightly different form in
the ballad. " Waly, waly " may be Shakespeare's
" Willow, willow." According to Mr. T. F. Henderson,
the song is in the Percy Folio MS. of 1650, and a parody
occurs in a MS. which may be as early as 1620.

53

Lady Anne Barnard (1750–1825) was Lady Anne
Lindsay, a daughter of the Earl of Balcarres. " Auld
Robin Gray " is, apart from Burns's work and " Annie
Laurie," perhaps the most popular of Scottish songs,
and it is in its own way a masterpiece, for it moves with
sure step on the very brink of a sentiment which might
easily become mawkish. That, I suppose, is the defi-
nition of a popular piece which is also literature.

55

The second and third quatrains are omitted—the
latter surely the worst verse ever written by a poet.
The four remaining stanzas seem to me to be the greatest
of Burns's songs, and, along with one or two from Shakespeare and Shelley and Catullus, among the greatest in
all literature. " At moments," Matthew Arnold wrote,
" he touches it (that is, high seriousness) in a profound
and passionate melancholy, as in those four immortal
lines taken by Byron as the motto for " The Bride of
Abydos," but which have in them a depth of poetic
quality such as resides in no verse of Byron's own—
' Had we never loved sae kindly,' etc." The germ is
to be found in some doggerel by Robert Dodsley, beginning, " One fond kiss before we part."

56

Mark Alexander Boyd (1563–1601), of the Ayrshire family of the Boyds of Penkill, was scholar, wanderer, and soldier of fortune, and a writer of admirable Latin verse, for which see Arthur Johnston, *Deliciae Poetarum Scotorum*, 1637.

BOOK IV

THE HEARTH

In the poetry of a poor and clannish people, living a life of toil in a climate mainly inclement, the hearth and all that it connotes must play a major part. The family is a man's private sanctuary, in which he is barricaded against the " fierce confederate storm " of the outer world. Domestic sentiment has produced some of the worst of Scots verse, and some of the best. The sense of cosiness and security belongs to the " but-and-ben " rather than to the castle ; the " Saturday night " is for the cotter and not for the noble, and no baron's hall could give the snugness of Fergusson's " Farmer's Ingle." But I have tried to make the collection representative of all sides of Scots life, for, happily, family love is not the prerogative of a class. We have the expectant bride in Burns's defiant song, and in the romantic stanzas of the ballad. The perfect housewife is portrayed in Henryson's stately manner as well as in the homely verse of " My wife's a winsome wee thing." The whole range of fireside content will be found in " Bessie at her Spinning-Wheel " and the famous lines from " The Epistle to Dr. Blacklock," and in those perfect pictures of the fisher wife, " There's nae luck about the house " and " Oh, weel may the boatie row." There are cradle songs for the beginning of things, and " John Anderson, my jo " for the end. There is the other side, too—the slattern and the randy, the lady who demands a side-saddle, gold rings, and serving-men ; the feckless gossip of Fergusson's lines, the deplorable spouse of Willie Wastle, and the gently-born wife who has to be taught housewifery by stern methods. I have added two famous domestic comedies, " Get up and bar the door," and " Tak' your auld cloak about ye," the latter of which has been sung at both Scots and English firesides for four hundred years.

58

The opening verse of " The Lass of Lochryan " (Child, No. 76). There are thirteen versions extant, and the comb in the tenth line is given variously as " haw bayberry " (which may be laurel-wood), " red river " (which is perhaps red ivory), and " new-made silver," which explains itself. I incline to " haw bayberry " for the beauty and mystery of its sound, and refuse to believe that it is merely a corruption of " braw ivory."

59

From the Bannatyne MS.

60

From " The Epistle to Dr. Blacklock," Henley, II. 130.

61

The refrain appears in a song in the Percy Folio MS.,

dating from about 1560, satirizing the Church sacraments :—

> " John Anderson, my jo, cum in as ye gae by,
> And ye sall get a sheip's heid weel baken in a pye—
> Weel baken in a pye, and a haggis in a pat ;
> John Anderson, my jo, cum in and ye'se get that."

In Burns's day there was also current another and most Rabelaisian version, which is printed in *The Merry Muses.*

63

First printed in a slightly different form in Johnson's *Museum.*

64

Written by Robert Jamieson (1780–1844) to the old tune, " My wife's a wanton wee thing," and published in his *Popular Songs and Ballads*, 1806, II. 328.

65

Five stanzas omitted. This vigorous piece was in all likelihood the inspiration of Burns's " Cotter's Saturday Night."

66

This is in substance the version printed in Herd with Mickle's rearrangement, but without his added stanzas and without the additions of James Beattie. A copy exists in Mickle's handwriting, but I cannot think that that most anglified of Scots, with his slender and genteel talent, had much to do with its composition ; nor can we credit it to Jean Adam, the Greenock schoolmistress. Burns said that it " came fresh on the streets as a ballad about 1771 or 1772," and with Mr. Henderson, I suspect a Jacobite original.

68

From Johnson's *Museum*. Burns attributed the song to one John Ewen, an Aberdeen merchant (1741–1821), but the chorus is certainly much older.

69

This brisk ditty is the converse of the preceding— the confession of the undomestic fishwife. The text is in Chambers and in Cunningham, and was taken by them from Kirkpatrick Sharpe's *Ballad Book*, published in Edinburgh in 1824.

70

From *An Eclogue : Willie and Sandy*.

71

Willie Wastle himself belongs to the oldest strata of Scots nursery rhyme. Linkumdoddie is on the Tweed, three miles below Tweedsmuir. Willie wove his customers own wool and stole it ("stown a clue").

72

This is Herd's version. There are three others, which may be found in Child, No. 275.

73

This ballad story is very old in popular poetry, and Child has seven versions. The one I have chosen is the chapbook text given in the second series of Mr. Robert Ford's *Vagabond Songs and Ballads of Scotland*, 1901. In two of Child's versions the refrain is "Hollin Green Hollin" and "Bend your Bow, Robin." The song is akin to the "Wee Cooper o' Fife," which possesses a most complicated and rollicking refrain. A variant of the Fife song is quoted by Jamieson, *Popular Ballads and Songs*, I. 324 :—

> There lives a landart laird in Fife,
> And he has married a dandily wife ;
> She wadna shape nor yet wad she sew,
> *gossips*]   But sat wi' her cummers and filled hersel' fou.
>
> She wadna spin nor yet wad she card,
> But she wad sit and crack wi' the laird.
> He is down to his sheep-fauld
> *shoulder*]   And cleekit a wether by the back spauld.
>
> He's whirled aff the gude wether's skin,
> And wrappit the dandily lady therein.
> ' I darena pay ye for your dandily kin,
> But weel may I skelp my wether's skin.' "

74

First published in the *Tea-Table Miscellany*, but probably dating from the late sixteenth century. The first part of the fourth stanza is quoted in an English version by Shakespeare in *Othello*.

BOOK V

THE OPEN ROAD

The Scots are, I suppose, along with the Jews, the most far-wandering race on earth ; but, unlike the Jews, they are eternally homesick. In the section of this book which I have called " Lacrimae Rerum " the tears are mainly those of the exile. From the early Middle Ages they travelled Europe, penetrating as pedlars to the extremes of Muscovy, serving as soldiers of fortune

478

Nicol Jarvie with a red-hot cou
the Highlander at Aberfoyle
gretful instinct vanquishes
even the prospect of exi
find the bugles often
their secret work.
burnside, the st
never lose the
off to the
lady lis
chall
th

in ever
in thos
that dr
them at
cannot
for its
or any
which M
that the
missed
to go al
glittering
son has
men :—

" Ther
with its
mountain
less, sour
castled ci

wind squalls, and the salt showers fly and beat. I do not
even know if I desire to live there ; but let me hear, in
some far land, a kindred voice sing out, ' Oh, why left I
my hame ? ' and it seems at once as if no beauty under the
kind heavens, and no society of the wise and good, can
repay me for my absence from my country." [1]

But in their character, besides its prose and practi-
cality, and as deep as its devotion to home, there is an
element of sheer " daftness," a perpetual expectation of
some strange destiny. The Scot, even when like Saul
he is tending his father's asses, has half a hope of stum-
bling upon a kingdom. The most decorous figures have
in them a capacity for surprising flights, as when Bailie

[1] *The Silverado Squatters.*

ter singed the plaid of
. This perpetual half-re-
common sense and obliterates
le. Hence in Scots poetry we
ounding and the pipes of Pan at
The greenwood and the fire by the
range road and the hazards of battle,
ir compelling power. Leezie Lindsay goes
Highlands with her lover; the southron
ens to the wooing of Jock o' Hazeldean ; the
nge of Bonnie Dundee stirs the most whiggish ;
king's young daughter flings away her seam at
the call of Spring; and the mistress of the castle trips
down the stairs at the song of the gipsy.

75

The first two verses of " The King's Dochter Lady
Jean," Child, No. 52.

76

The first line is old—possibly the first quatrain.

77

There are at least seven versions of this song ; I have
chosen the one in Chambers. Burns sent the first verse,
slightly altered, to Johnson. A tradition in the Mearns
says that the lady was a daughter of Lindsay of Edzell.
The song is probably based on the well-known ballad of
" Lizie Lindsay," Child, No. 266.

78

Scott took the first verse from the ballad of " John of
Hazelgreen " in the Kinloch MS., Child, No. 293.

Child, No. 200—twelve versions. The text given is from the *Tea-Table Miscellany*. In the eighteenth century the story came—without foundation—to be connected with the house of Cassilis; and the ballad in C. K. Sharpe's version begins, " The gypsies they came to my lord Cassilis' yett," and ends with the bringing back of the lady. Stevenson (*Essays of Travel*, page 140) follows this legend. He is writing of the old castle of Maybole :—

" A very heavy string-course runs round the upper story, and just above this, facing up the street, the tower carries a small oriel window, fluted and corbelled and carved about with stone heads. It is so ornate it has somewhat the air of a shrine. And it was, indeed, the casket of a very precious jewel, for in the room to which it gave light lay, for long years, the heroine of the sweet old ballad of ' Johnnie Faa '—she who, at the call of the gipsies' songs, ' came tripping down the stair, and all her maids before her.' Some people say the ballad has no basis in fact, and have written, I believe, unanswerable papers to the proof. But in the face of all that, the very look of that high oriel window convinces the imagination, and we enter into all the sorrows of the imprisoned dame. We conceive the burthen of the long, lack-lustre days, when she leaned her sick head against the mullions, and saw the burghers loafing in Maybole High Street, and the children at play, and ruffling gallants riding by from hunt or foray. We conceive the passion of odd moments when the wind threw up to her some snatch of song, and her heart grew hot within her, and her eyes overflowed at the memory of the past. And even if the tale be not true of this or that lady, or this or that old tower, it is true in the essence of all men and women : for all of us, some time or other, hear the gipsies singing ; over all of us is the glamour cast. Some

resist and sit resolutely by the fire.   Most go and are brought
back again, like Lady Cassilis.   A few, of the tribe of War-
ing, go and are seen no more ;   only now and again, at
springtime, when the gipsies' song is afloat in the amethyst
evening, we can catch their voices in the glee."

80

Mr. T. F. Henderson thinks that Scott's model was
one of D'Urfey's songs, which, in turn, was a parody of
an old Scots catch.   Scott's note in his diary for December 22, 1825, on the eve of his catastrophe, runs :—

" The air of ' Bonnie Dundee ' running in my head to-day,
I wrote a few verses to it before dinner, taking the key-
note from the story of Clavers leaving the Scottish Convention of Estates in 1688–9.   I wonder if they are good.
Ah ! poor Will Erskine !   Thou couldst and wouldst have
told me.   I must consult J. B., who is as honest as was
W. E.   But then, though he has good taste too, there is a
little of *Big Bow-wow* about him.   Can't say what has
made me take a frisk so uncommon of late years as to write
verses of free will.   I suppose the same instinct which
makes birds sing when the storm has blown over."

Alas ! it had not.   Adolphus mentions the fire and spirit
with which Scott was wont to recite this ballad of his.

81

From *Ane Pleasant Satyre of the Thrie Estaitis* (c.
1540), Part II.   " Oppressioun " is speaking.   It should
be compared with Sir Richard Maitland's views of
Liddesdale and its habits (page 220, *supra*).

82

From *The Tea-Table Miscellany*.   Bishop Percy was
inclined to attribute the song to James V. of Scotland ;

but there is neither external evidence nor intrinsic probability for the attribution. It is one of a number of ballads about bold beggars, like " The Beggar Laddie " (Child, No. 280) and " The Jolly Beggar," first printed by Herd. The latter has a delightful chorus which was imitated by Byron :—

> " We'll go no more a-roving,
>   A-roving in the night,
> We'll go no more a-roving,
>   Let the moon shine e'er so bright."

84

Poems, 1919. Walter Wingate (1865–1918) was a mathematical master in a Hamilton school, whose verse has been selected and published by Mr. Adam L. Gowans (Glasgow : Gowans and Gray).

BOOK VI

KING AND COMMONWEAL

For a people so tenacious of nationality there was but a small output of patriotic poetry between Barbour's *Bruce* and Burns's " Scots Wha Hae," though since the latter there has been enough and to spare. After Bannockburn the kings were the chief patriots ; the great nobles were at odds with the throne and with each other, and often intriguing with England, and the plain man was only by fits and starts conscious of a national interest—save for the folk of the Borders, who had their own good reasons for perpetual bickering. Hence it is impossible to present the main march of Scots history in quotations from the poets. The ancient *cantus* which

I have put first, the short extracts from Barbour and
Blind Harry (poets who do not readily permit of selection), " Sir Patrick Spens," " Harlaw " (which settled
that Highlands should not rule Lowlands), and the
Reformers' song from *The Gude and Godlie Ballats*,
alone are in the central national tradition. Most of the
ballads treat of private encounters and family feuds ;
even " Otterbourne " is the story rather of a fray between
Douglas and Percy than between Scotland and England.
The great riding ballads are intensely local ; " Kinmont
Willie," which I have chosen, and which seems to me
the best, is the one which brings us nearest to a national
issue. I would fain have added " The Fray of Suport,"
but its joyous barbarity is perhaps too remote from
poetry.

It is the losing cause which pleases the Muses, and
with the downfall of the Stuarts public affairs became
matter for the bard. I have printed one Whig piece,
" Killicrankie," which admirably sets forth the point
of view of the average man who had no stomach for
fighting on either side. The Jacobite poems, whether
by Burns—and one of his greatest, " It was a' for our
rightfu' king," is Jacobite—or by unknown makers,
are the swan-song of that mediæval loyalty which had
to be broken before the country could advance in
modern ways, but which has a sentimental eternity,
since it enshrines the regret of all men in all ages for
vanished hopes and dreams. A cause, which in England
produced only doggerel, was the parent in Scotland of
two of her greatest novels and many of her best songs.
Prince Charlie, his frailties forgotten, became an incar-
nation of youth and quixotry, an ageless figure like
Arthur, *rex quondam rexque futurus.*

Commentary

" In a Highland cottage I heard so
singing a lament for ' Tearlach Og Alu
Charlie ; and when he ceased tears were
that was there, and in his own throat a
later, was his heart really so full of the
he told me that it was not him he was
all the dead men and women of Scotland
his sake, and of Scotland itself, and of
would not come again. I did not ask w   ....ys, for
I knew that in his heart he lamented his own dead hopes
and dreams, and that the Prince was but the image of his
lost youth, and that the world was old and grey because
of his own weariness and his own grief." [1]

The Great War is, I fear, poorly represented. The
truth is that it brought forth a flood of Scots verse, but
mostly in the manner of the penny reciter. " I Canna
See the Sergeant " has fascinated me since I first heard
it, and one of the best of the war poems in any language,
by the same author, will be found in another section,
No. 234.

85

Probably the oldest Scots verse—written after the
death of Alexander III. in 1285. It is from Wyntoun's
Chronicle, 1425.

86

Child, No. 58. This great ballad was first published
in Percy's *Reliques*, and there are some eighteen versions.
Its historical basis is obscure, but it *may* refer to the
voyage of the Princess Margaret of Scotland, who was
married to Prince Eric of Norway in 1281. I have
taken the text given by Scott in the *Minstrelsy of the
Scottish Border*, except for the last verse, which is from
Percy.

[1] Fiona Macleod, *Iona*.

87

The Bruce, Book I. 226–41.

88

Wallace, Book X. 563–76.

89

The ballad of Elspeth of the Craigburnfoot, in *The Antiquary*, chapter xl.

90

Child, No. 161. There are six versions, and I have chosen Scott's text in the second edition of the *Minstrelsy*, based on copies supplied by James Hogg, which seems to me to be poetically the finest. Otterburn was fought on August 19, 1388, at the foot of Redesdale—for an account of which haunted country let the reader consult Mr. G. M. Trevelyan's essay on " The Middle Marches " in his *Clio : A Muse*, 1913.

91

From *Ane Compendious Booke of Godlie Psalmes and Spirituall Sangis*, commonly known as *The Gude and Godlie Ballats*, collected by James, John, and Robert Wedderburn of Dundee. The first known edition is 1567. It was edited by David Laing in 1868, and by Professor Mitchell for the Scottish Text Society in 1897. The ballads are mainly theological adaptations of old hunting songs and love lays. I have omitted five stanzas. Scott, it will be remembered, uses one verse in *The Abbot*, chapter xv.

92

Child, No. 186—from Scott's *Minstrelsy*. Sir Walter confessed that he got the ballad in a mangled state, and had to admit certain conjectural emendations. Verses *remaing emors* 10–12 and 31 seem to betray his hand. On the whole question of Scott's treatment of his originals, see Andrew Lang, *Sir Walter Scott and the Border Minstrelsy*, 1910.

93

There are other Killiecrankie ballads, such as the excellent one in Herd (1776). The one in the text is from Johnson's *Museum*, and may possibly have passed through the hands of Burns. The additional stanza is from Cunningham's version, *Songs of Scotland*, III. 183.

94

William Gordon, 6th Viscount Kenmure, rose in the '15, was taken at Preston, and suffered death on Tower Hill on February 24, 1716. There is little doubt that the whole song is by Burns, though Cromek in his *Remains of Nithsdale and Galloway Song*, 1810, calls it traditional, and prints some very weak supplementary verses.

95

Poetical Works, 1923, I. 51.

96

The chorus is old, and is in the Herd MS. Hogg has a set in his *Jacobite Relics*, I. 76, with additional verses, which are probably his own composition.

✓ associated with Mock Corporation of Walton-le-Dale

486   The Northern Muse

97

The chorus is old, and though the song is mainly his, Burns must have had a North Country original to work on, for John Ross was the ferryman at the Waterside of Birse on the Dee, just above Aboyne (see *The Old Deeside Road*, by G. M. Fraser, 154) ; so Peter Buchan may not have been so far out in his view of the genesis of the song as Mr. Henley thinks. Hogg (*Jacobite Relics*, II. 76) prints an extra verse, presumably his own :—

> " I ance had sons but now hae nane ;
>   I bred them toiling sairly ;
> And I wad bear them a' again,
>   And lose them a' for Chairlie."

98

The last two verses are omitted. Alexander Geddes (1737–1802) was a Roman Catholic chaplain in Aberdeenshire, and Lewie Gordon was Lord Lewis Gordon, a son of the Duke of Gordon, who raised a regiment for Prince Charlie.

99

" Drumossie " is Culloden, where the battle was fought on April 16, 1746. The " cruel lord " of the last verse is the Duke of Cumberland.

("Stinkin Willie")

100

William Glen (1789–1826) was a Glasgow man who appears to have written nothing else. The song is in Hogg's *Jacobite Relics*, II. 192. It is sung to the tune of " The Gypsy Laddie," to which goes also the ballad of " Johnie Faa."

Chambers, I. 125.   The lady was the mother of Francis Keith, Frederick the Great's field-marshal, whose body lies under a proud monument in the Garrison Church of Berlin.

Poetical Works, I. 62.   At Laffen, William, Duke of Cumberland, was defeated and nearly captured by the Scots and Irish in the French service.   Prince Charlie is said to have served there as a volunteer.   This song of Andrew Lang's is the best, I think, of the many on the theme, " Oh, it's hame, hame, hame."   The refrain and the last verse are old—1750 or thereabouts.   When I was a boy in Tweeddale I used to hear a version which I have never met with since, and of which two lines ran :—

" There's an eye that ever weeps and a fair face will be fain
   When I ride through Annan water wi' my bonnie bands
      again."

Allan Cunningham has a set which I transcribe for the sake of the first verse :—

" Hame, hame, hame !   O hame fain wad I be !
  O hame, hame, hame, to my ain countrie !
  When the flower is i' the bud, and the leaf is on the tree,
  The lark shall sing me hame to my ain countrie.
      Hame, hame, hame !   O hame fain wad I be !
      O hame, hame, hame, to my ain countrie !

The green leaf o' loyaltie's begun for to fa' ;
The bonnie white rose it is withering an' a' ;
But we'll water't wi' the blude of usurping tyrannie,
And fresh it shall blaw in my ain countrie.
      Hame, hame, hame !   O hame fain wad I be !
      O hame, hame, hame, to my ain countrie !

O there's naught now frae ruin my country can save,
But the keys o' kind heaven, to open the grave,
That a' the noble martyrs, who died for loyaltie,
May rise again and fight for their ain countrie.
    Hame, hame, hame ! O hame fain wad I be !
    O hame, hame, hame, to my ain countrie !

The great now are gane—a' wha ventured to save ;
The green grass is growing abune their grave ;
Yet the sun thro' the mirk blinks blithe in my e'e :
' I'll shine on ye yet in your ain countrie.'
    Hame, hame, hame ! Hame fain wad I be !
    O hame, hame, hame, to my ain countrie ! ''

103

Ballads of Battle, 1916—a song of the 4th Black Watch.
To appreciate its truth the reader must have a memory
of the trenches in France, and the tune of '' Ho-ro, my
nut-brown maiden,'' running in his head.

104

Poems Scots and English, 1917.

105

Scottish University Verse, 1918–23. I have it.
(was)

"Our Iounis College" No 24
No 24— Limited Edition
of 250.

BOOK VII

THE HUMAN COMEDY

If my book were a thesaurus and not an anthology,
this section would fill many pages. Comedy must be
given a wide interpretation, stretching from the dignity
of '' Auld Lang Syne '' and Burns's philosophy of classes

to something very like broad farce, and including all the
humours and incongruities of men and women in their
social relations. So we get pictures of Hogmanay and
Hallowe'en, of women wooed for money and the hum-
bling of purse-proud lovers, of the tragi-comedy of childhood, as in Mr. Murray's " Whistle," of ungracious
parents and brisk daughters, of amorous old ladies,
of immortal annuitants, of easily beguiled husbands, of
respectability, as in Fergusson's " Braid Claith," seen
through the mocking eyes of the poet. I have omitted
all the " Blythsome Bridals " and such-like, which are
rather for the philologist than for the lover of poetry,
and I have included nothing from the " flytings " and
satires of the early masters, for they would be unin-
telligible in extracts.

106

There are older versions in Watson's collection (1711),
which may be by Francis Sempill, and in the *Tea-
Table Miscellany*, and various Jacobite copies ; but,
except for the chorus, they have no kinship with Burns's
masterpiece, which, throughout the world, has become
the song of re-united friends. I have heard it sung in
Dutch on a Boer farm on the Swaziland border.

107

From " The Twa Dogs."

108

From " The Twa Dogs." This piece and the fore-
going seem to me a far finer statement of human equality
than robust rhetoric like " A man's a man for a' that."

(2,470)   16 a

109

The two first verses are in Herd (1776). Chambers is inclined to attribute the piece to the Rev. Dr. Strachan, the minister of Carnwath, in Lanarkshire, near which is the hill called Tinto, or Tintock. Tintock is celebrated in a local rhyme :—

> " On Tintock tap there is a mist,
>   And in that mist there is a kist,
>   And in that kist there is a caup,
>   And in that caup there is a drap.
>   Take up the caup and drink the drap,
>   And set the caup on Tintock tap."

110

Carolina Oliphant (1766–1845), of the ancient Jacobite house of Gask, married the fifth Lord Nairne—a title which is now held by the Lansdowne family. She was, beyond question, the foremost poet among Scotswomen. " The Laird of Cockpen " is founded, like most of her lyrics, on an older song. The two stanzas, which Miss Ferrier, the author of *Marriage*, wrote to round off the tale, have been omitted.

111

From *Hamewith*, 1909.

112

For the customs connected with Hallowe'en—and Burns's poem is a treasury of curious folk-lore—see the note in Henley, I. 356–60.

113

This cheerful ditty, which goes to a most jovial tune, is much in request at Lowland kirns and country weddings. The work of Alexander Rodger (1784–1846) is to be found in that curious miscellany, *Whistle Binkie*, 1846, where, says Mr. Hepburn Millar, " the vernacular Muse appears at her very worst, oscillating between extravagant sentiment and intoxicated but cheerless mirth."

114

The best, I think, of Fergusson's pictures of the dirty, drunken, picturesque, and incurably snobbish Edinburgh of his day. He anticipates Burns in his mastery of the " Habbie Simson " stave.

115

From *Lyrics Legal and Miscellaneous*. First printed about 1851.

116

Child, No. 274. There are more versions than Professor Child prints, for I have seen at least four. The story is found in the popular literature of many countries, and there is an English ballad on the same subject, " The Merry Cuckold and the Kind Wife." The copy in the text is that which Herd printed in 1769. A later version, included in Ford's *Vagabond Songs and Ballads*, Second Series, page 61, gives the song a Jacobite complexion. The wife in the last verse confesses :—

> " Oh, hooly, hooly, my gudeman,
>   And dinna angry be ;
>   It's but our cousin Macintosh
>   Frae the North Countrie."

118

From Chambers's *Popular Rhymes of Scotland*, 1826.

I have given the extended version which I used to hear as a child.

119

This is substantially the text which Chambers printed " from recitation " (*Scottish Songs*, II. 455), but I have given the queer song as I used to hear it in my youth in Tweeddale. Tam o' the Linn may be Tam Lin of the ballad, but he has grievously changed from the lover of the Queen of Elfland, and become a grotesque, the father of a family and the sport of circumstance. Joanna Baillie wrote a set of stirring verses, in which the old jingle is cleverly imitated—*Poetical Works*, 1851, page 821.

BOOK VIII

BACCHANALIA

On this unedifying section there is need of little commentary. Claret was the old drink of gentlemen in Scotland, and ale, strong or otherwise, of the peasantry, and whisky came into general use in the Lowlands only towards the end of the eighteenth century. There are no better bottle songs than the three masterpieces of Burns, for they have philosophy as well as good fellowship, and there is a rich fescennine humour in those deplorable ditties, " Todlin' Hame " and " Hoolie and Fairly." The moralist may shake his head over " The Orgiasts," but Sir John Falstaff would have approved.

120

Written by Burns to celebrate a meeting at Moffat with Allan Masterton and William Nichol. In the penultimate line " last " seems the better reading, and it is thus quoted in one letter of Burns, but on the whole the texts favour " first." There are suggestions in it of an old song referred to by Shakespeare, " Three Merry Men we be."

121

A parody of, and to be sung to the tune of, " Lumps o' Pudding."

122

From *Lyrics Legal and Miscellaneous*.

123

The refrain is old. The third verse was inscribed by Burns on a window-pane of the Globe Tavern at Dumfries.

124

An old song amended by Burns for Johnson's *Museum*, and printed in other versions by Cromek, Chambers, and Cunningham. I have given Cunningham's text, which is at least as good as Burns's. There is a verse from Cromek worth preserving :—

" I had forty shillings in a clout,
  Gude ale gart me pyke them out.
  That the gear should moule I thought a sin ; [*moulder*
  Gude ale keeps my heart aboon."

125

A song which is not later in date than the seventeenth century. It was printed by Ramsay in the *Tea-Table Miscellany*. Burns thought it " the first bottle song that ever was composed."

126

The first four verses of the song printed under the title of " The Drucken Wife of Galloway " in Yair's *Charmer* in 1751, and then amended for Johnson's *Museum*. In the ordinary version the erring dame is also a Jacobite, and behaves like the wife of the blacksmith of Cairnvreckan in *Waverley*. Joanna Baillie imitated it, *Poetical Works*, 1851, page 819.

127

(1) was first printed by Herd and then by Cunningham, whose version I give. Barbarous joy at the death of an unwanted wife is not unknown in Scottish literature. Compare Burns's—

> " Bitter in dool, I licket my winnins
> O' marrying Bess to gie her a slave ;
> Blest be the hour she cool'd in her linens,
> And blyth be the bird that sings on her grave ! "

(Henley, II. 67.)

(2) from *Chambers's Popular Rhymes of Scotland*, 134. A tailor of Edinburgh, one Adam Crawford, wrote additional verses, but the wild quatrain of tradition is enough for me.

(3) was used by Burns as a verse of " My luve, she's but a lassie yet " ; it is also a verse of a set of " Green grows the rashes O " in Herd, and, according to Henley, II. 341, is derived from a song in an old chap-book, the *Cowgate Garland*, in the Motherwell collection.

128

From *Lyrics Legal and Miscellaneous*.

BOOK IX

CHARACTERS

This section, but for considerations of space, might have been greatly extended, for Scots poetry is rich in racy portraiture. Happily, the best which I have omitted, such as Captain Grose and all the characters in " The Jolly Beggars," are easily accessible in Burns. There is much, too, in Dunbar which I should have liked to include, and in Sir David Lyndsay, and there is the admirable picture of the fifteenth-century *nouveau riche* in " The Thrie Tales of the Thrie Priestis of Peblis," not to speak of the *genre* pieces of Ramsay and Fergusson. As it is, I have tried to give a glimpse of the old world in Dunbar's " John Dog," in Maitland's " Thievis of Liddisdale," and Lyndsay's " Pardoner," as well as the good and bad of a later Scotland. But indeed all may be said to belong to the past ; even Mr. Hamish Hendry's beadle and Mr. Carnie's auctioneer are figures of a bygone age ; only Mr. Logie Robertson's tinklers are still with us, and likely to remain.

129

Ed. Scottish Text Society, II. 195. James Dog, or Doig, was Queen Margaret's Wardrober.

130

Six verses out of fifteen. Sir Richard Maitland (1496–1586) was an eminent judge who fell blind at the age of sixty-five, after which he devoted himself to literature. His poems were published by the Maitland Club in 1830.

His account of the Liddesdale reivers may be compared with that of Bishop Lesley, written about the same time : *Leslaeus de Origine, Moribus et Rebus Gestis Scotorum* in Scott's *Border Antiquities*, Appendix VI.

131

One of the best characters in literature of a country gentleman : " the ae best fellow e'er was born," and one, says Burns, " who held the patent for his honours immediately from Almighty God " (Henley, I. 262–8).

132

(1) first printed in Yair's *Charmer*, 1751. I have used the text given by Chambers.

(2) is a fragment from *Lyrics Legal and Miscellaneous*.

133

From *The Thrie Estaitis*, Part I. The Middle Scots "makars" are unwearying in their gibes at the Highlands, and Celtic folk-lore is a usual ingredient of their broader farce. Compare the spirited passage in " Ane Littell Interlud," which may or may not be Dunbar's (Ed. Scottish Text Society, II. 315) :—

great]	" My foir grandsyre, hecht Fyn Mackcowll,
	That dang the Devill and gart him yowll,
	The skyis rain'd when he wald scowll,
	He trublit all the air ;
	He gat my gudesyre Gog Magog ;
	He when he dansit, the warld wald schog ;
coat]	Ten thousand ellis wyde in his frog
	Of hieland plaids and mair.

> And yet he was of tendir youth ;
> But eftir he grew meikle at fowth   [*size*
> Ellevin myle wyde was his mouth,
>   His teeth was ten myle squair.
> He wald upon his taes upstand,
> And let the starnis doun with his hand,
> And sett them in a gold garland
>   Aboif his wifis hair."

134

This is Cunningham's version, II. 66. Scott in the *Minstrelsy* prints only the first, second, and fourth stanzas. Yellow and green were the liveries of the house of Home. The Selkirk souters, according to tradition, headed by the town clerk, William Brydone, fought gallantly at Flodden, and perished almost to a man, whereas the family of Home was suspected of being half-hearted.

135

Sempill lived through the first half of the seventeenth century. " Habbie Simson " is the parent of a long family ; Fergusson, Burns, and all the later vernacular poets adopted this stanza—an old Troubadour measure, popular in Scotland since the fifteenth century.

136

Burns from Heaven, with Some Other Poems, 1897.

137

William Carnie was born in 1824, and died in 1908. Hirpletillem of the delectable name was a place close to Rubislaw Den, long since covered by the suburban villas of Aberdeen.

138

Seven stanzas omitted, which localize a satire that in essence is as universal as it is matchless and merciless.

139

Horace in Homespun—" A Wet Day : Hughie's Pity for the Tinklers." For " Poussie Nancy" see Burns's " The Jolly Beggars."

BOOK X

LITERATURE

The substance of this section is the theorizing of the poets about their art, their tributes to their predecessors, and that subtler form of tribute which consists in direct translation. Of the first there is nothing but Burns's robust confession of faith, for the poets, wisely, are shy of theory. Of the second, we have Dunbar's eulogy of his master, Chaucer, and his " Lament of the Makaris," surely the noblest threnody in our literature on a singer's fellow-craftsman. It does not belong to the class of great elegies, like the lament of Bion for Moschus, or "Lycidas," or "Adonais," or "Thyrsis," for the personal element is not predominant ; it is rather a meditation on the fragility of life and the tenuity of human hopes, to which, as illustration, enters a pageant of dead poets. It has a curious resemblance to a passage in Gabriel Harvey (not otherwise a poet) which begins—

" Ah, that Sir Humphry Gilbert should be dead." [1]

[1] Gabriel Harvey's *Marginalia*, page 64.

Commentary

In later Scots verse there is an abundance of these tributes. There is an especial plethora of apostrophes to Burns, and Burns himself has acclaimed his predecessors like Ramsay and Fergusson, but the thing was a mere literary convention, and frequently absurd. The worst is Ramsay's " Richy and Sandy," where in amoebean strain two shepherds of these names lament the death of one " Adie that play'd and sang sae sweet," and the reader is aghast at the discovery that the three are meant for Steele, Pope, and Addison ! [1]

The translations are culled from a narrow field. The page of Virgil which Gawain Douglas gave " rude Scotland " was a very rude page, with nothing Virgilian about it, and Douglas's Scots only becomes a fit medium when dealing with the horrors of Avernus. The truth is that the *felicitas* of Scots is not *curiosa,* and demands in translation either a rugged or a homely original. My imitation of the Twenty-first Idyll of Theocritus was the result of a suggestion of Andrew Lang ; and there are other idylls, notably the Seventh, which might go reasonably well into the vernacular. Horace has to be paraphrased, not translated, whether by Mr. Charles Murray or " Hugh Haliburton " ; but the Horatian philosophy accords well with one side of our temperament, and the Sabine farm is not ill represented by the Lowland cottage. The most natural subject of translation into Scots is the song written to be sung. Mr. Gray has shown what can be done with Heine, and there is much in Béranger and Victor Hugo which I should have thought worth a Northern setting.

[1] I owe this instance to Mr. Gregory Smith's *Scottish Literature.*

140

From "The Epistle to J. Lapraik," April 1, 1785.

141

From "The Epistle to William Simpson of Ochiltree,"
May 1785.

142

From "The Golden Targe," Ed. Scottish Text Society,
II. 10.

143

Ed. Scottish Text Society, II. 48. This poem in the
French kyrielle metre is to my mind quite the equal of
François Villon's two *ballades* on the same subject, on
which it may have been modelled. Dunbar wrote it
probably in 1507, when he was some forty-seven years
old, a stage of life which moves a man to reflection.

144

Henley, IV. 13—the two last verses omitted.

145

Poems Scots and English, 1917.

146

Gawain Douglas (1475–1522) was a son of old " Bell-
the-Cat," Archibald, Earl of Angus. He issued his version of the *Aeneid* in 1513, the year of Flodden, and it
was first printed (in London) in 1553. It is most pleas-
antly read in Ruddiman's folio of 1710.

147

Hamewith, 1909.

I have it

148
Songs and Ballads, chiefly from Heine (Grant Richards, 1920). As to (2) the curious may note that Burns's *John Barleycorn* begins with almost the same line.

BOOK XI

Sport

Sport in Scotland, as the word is generally understood, is a thing of modern growth. In old days the chase was limited in the Lowlands to the hunting of the deer in the royal forests and over the lands of the greater nobles, and no one had occasion to sing of it except in the incidental stave of a ballad—

> " Ettrick Forest is a fair forest,
> In it grows many a seemlie tree ;
> The hart, the hynd, the dae, the rae,
> And of a' wyld beastis great plentie."

For the romance of the " dun deer " we must go to Duncan Ban Macintyre and the Gaelic poets, for it never came within the orbit of the vernacular. The shooting of game birds is a recent thing, depending on the development of the gun, and we can show nothing on it except a stanza or two of Burns in " Tam Samson's Elegy," and three verses in the " Elegy on Captain Matthew Henderson," where the wild things of loch and moor are summoned to lament their destroyer. If the poetry of a grouse drive, when the birds come before an autumn gale like bullets, is ever put into words, I am assured that these words will not be Scots, for the thing is alien to the national tradition.

It is curious that the two ancient games of curling and golf should not have found their bards. The first has only a chance verse of Burns, and the second had to wait till Andrew Lang. Games—even the " roaring game "—and sports played, I fear, only a little part in our forefathers' lives, and never rose into the prominence which made them matter for the rhymer. Even poaching, a romantic trade enough, had to wait till our own day for its *vates sacer* in Mr. Menzies. Fishing, which in England has had a literary atmosphere since Dame Juliana Berners, did not acquire one in Scotland till Scott's prose and the songs of Thomas Tod Stoddart and George Outram. So I will supplement my tiny collection with Meg Dods's *apologia*, which every angler should have by heart, and a taste of Zachary Boyd's preposterous ichthyology. The first is from the opening chapter of *St. Ronan's Well*—Meg on the life of the fisherman :—

" Pawky auld carles, that kend whilk side their bread was buttered upon. . . . They were up in the morning— had their parritch, wi' maybe a thimblefull of brandy, and then awa' up into the hills ; eat their bit cauld meat on the heather, and cam' hame at e'en wi' their creel full of caller trouts, and had them to their dinner, and their quiet cogue of ale, and their drap punch, and were set singing their catches and glees, as they ca'd them, till ten o'clock, and then to bed wi' God bless ye—and what for no ? "

The second is from Boyd's " The English Academie," in MS. in the Library of Glasgow University :—

" God's might so peopled hath the sea
    With fish of divers sort,
That men therein may clearly see
    Great things for their comfort.

There is such great varietie,
  Of fishes of all kind,
That it were great impietie
  God's hand there not to find.

The Puffen Torteuse, and Thorneback,
  The Scillop and the Goujeon,
The Shrimpe, the Spit-fish, and the Sprat,
  The Stock-fish, and the Sturgeon ;

The Torteuse, Tench, and Tunnyfish,
  The Sparling and the Trout ;
And Herring, for the poor man's dish,
  Is all the land about ;

The Groundling, Gilt-head, and the Crab,
  The Gurnard, Cockle, Oyster,
The Cramp-fish and als the Sea-Dog,
  The Crefish and the Conger ;

The Periwinkle and Twinfish—
  It's hard to count them all ;
Some are for oyle, some for the dish ;
  The greatest is the Whale ! ''

149

Henley, I. 221–2. Burns wrote : '' When this worthy old sportsman went out last muir-fowl season, he supposed it was to be, in Ossian's phrase, '' the last of his fields,'' and expressed an ardent wish to die and be buried in the muirs.''

150

Poetical Works, 1923, I. 28.

151

Angling Songs, 1889.

152

Poems Scots and English, 1917.

153

I gave this little piscatorial eclogue as I heard it repeated in my youth. I have never seen it in print. The Kips are the Shielgreen Kips to the north-east of Peebles, which look down upon the head of Leithen Water.

154

Provincial Sketches and Other Verses, 1902.

155

Poetical Works, 1923, II. 69.

BOOK XII

NATURE

Books have been written, such as Professor Veitch's, on the attitude of Scots poetry to nature, but I cannot find that it differs from that of poets in any other land. We have already seen the rhapsodies of the early " makars " in May—spiritual exultations rather than natural description, for they are more concerned with their own hearts than with the face of the earth, though Dunbar has a charming picture of a shallow stream at dawn, and Henryson in " The Swallow " describes with vivid realism the sights on a spring morning in the fields around Dunfermline. For the rest we shall find little of the Wordsworthian metaphysic or the " pathetic fallacy " ; the later writers reproduce a landscape or an atmosphere with extreme precision, and, as a rule, with complete objectivity. They are at their best in the pieces which deal with desolate scenes and wild weather, for the Scots tongue is rich in words for every mood of unfriendly nature. We see this in Gawain Douglas on a winter day, and in Burns on a spate in the river Ayr—each phrase is exact and adequate. Throughout the Ballads, too, there is a perpetual echo of " wan water " and " the roaring of the sea " and " the gryming of a new-fa'en snaw." When storms are forgotten the Muse does not dally in the common meadows of pastoral. She seeks recondite effects, as in Gawain Douglas's picture of a northern night in midsummer when the air is tremulous with dawn before the after-glow in the west has faded, or, as in the poems of J. B. Selkirk and Principal Shairp and the stanza from Stevenson, which aim at recapturing the far-away haunted peace of the Border hills.

The half-dozen local rhymes are a small handful from a rich store. Scarcely a Scottish parish but has its own jingle. The trouble is that these jingles, fascinating as they may be to the antiquarian, rarely approach the confines of literature.

156

Ed. Scottish Text Society, 25–33—eleven stanzas omitted. Alexander Hume was of the Polwarth family, and lived during the second half of the sixteenth century. Unlike the head of the family, his branch took the side of the Reformers, and he spent his life as the minister of Logie. Some of the details of the " Day Estivall " may have been a memory of boyish days at Polwarth ; but many are more French than

English, for Hume was much in France in his youth. The " London beer " is pure Chaucer (Prologue to the *Canterbury Tales*, 382). Hume's *Hymns or Sacred Songs wherein the Right Use of Poesie may be Espied* was published in Edinburgh in 1599.

157

From *Hame Content : a Satire*.

158

From the Prologue to the *Eneados*, Book VII.

159

Henley, I. 204–5.

160

Poems by J. B. Selkirk, collected edition, 1905. The author was James B. Brown, a tweed manufacturer of Selkirk, who also wrote English verse of much charm and technical accomplishment.

161

See Veitch's *History and Poetry of the Scottish Border*, II. 349–51. Shairp's verse is in *Kilmahoe, a Highland Pastoral*, 1864, and *Glen Desseray and Other Poems*, 1888.

162

From the Prologue to the XIII. Book of the *Eneados*. " He (Gawain Douglas) is not often quoted for his great discovery in a line or two of the thirteenth Prologue of *Eneados*, when he tells how he watched the midsummer midnight in the North, and finds not only the right word for what he sees, but the right word for his own poetry. . . . He sees a new thing in the life of the world—no poet that I know of (except Homer) had thought of it before—and in naming it he gives the interpretation also, the spirit of poetry: pleasance and half wonder."—W. P. Ker, *The Art of Poetry*, page 26.

163

From " The Counterblast," 1886. *Underwoods*, II. 8.

164

(1) is from Chambers's *Popular Rhymes of Scotland*, 1826.

(2) is in Child, *Fragments*, quoted from Finlay's *Scottish Ballads*, I. 32.

(3) I owe to Mrs. Jacob, who heard it in Angus.

(4) is still remembered in Tweeddale.

(5) is from Chambers. Scott used it as a heading to chapter xxviii. of *Rob Roy*.

(6) is preserved by Hume of Godscroft in his *History of the Houses of Douglas and Angus* (Edinburgh, 1644). The reference is to the murder of William, sixth Earl of Douglas, in 1440, in Edinburgh Castle, when the black bull's head was put on the table.

BOOK XIII

FRIENDLY BEASTS

Country people, who spend their lives among animals, acquire a curious attitude towards the brute creation, speaking as if its members were reasoning creatures, highly individualized in character. The fact is apparent in all folk-lore. In Scotland the habit is most marked, and the best instance is the treatment by the shepherd of his dogs, as may be read in Hogg and Stevenson and Dr. John Brown. In the little world of a moorland parish birds and beasts are more than half the personages. The warmth and intimacy which attends the subject in Scots poetry come largely from the richness of the Scots language in kindly diminutives. The classic examples are Burns's auld mare Maggie and Mailie the ewe ; he is less natural when in " The Mouse " he seeks deliber- ately a peg for moralizing. Pathos, indeed, is scarcely permissible in this sphere, except by an after-thought ; the note should be sententious comedy, as in " The Louse " and " The Twa Dogs," or farcical comedy, as in " Robin Redbreast's Testament."

This section may be found difficult by many readers, for the vernacular, when it treats of familiar beasts, is apt to run riot. But happily the sense of even obscure words may be often gathered from the sound.

165

First printed by Herd, 1769. The song is probably not later than 1621, the year when the bridge of Perth was destroyed by a great flood.

166

The closing stanzas of the ballad of " The Broomfield Hill," Child, No. 43. There are six versions ; the one printed is that given in Scott's *Minstrelsy*.

167

Sung by Elspeth of the Craigburnfoot, *The Antiquary*, chapter xl.

169

In the absence of a treatise on old Scots veterinary lore, I find it impossible to identify the ailments and the points of this extraordinary mare. The song, on the strength of Allan Ramsay's " Elegy on Patie Birnie," is said to have been the work of Patrick Birnie, a fiddler of Kinghorn in Fife, who lived at the close of the seventeenth century. I have given the version in Chambers's *Scottish Songs*, I. 302. There are longer versions in Cunningham, III. 10, and in Ford's *Vagabond Songs and Ballads*, Second Series, I. 43, from the latter of which I take these verses :—

> " The puir man's head's sair
>   Wi greetin' for his gude grey mare ;
> He's like to die himsel' wi' care
>   Aside the green kirkyaird.
> He's thinkin' on the bygane days,
> And a' her douce and canny ways,
> And how his ain gude wife, auld Bess,
>   Micht neist as weel been spared."

171

John Skinner (1721–1807) was Episcopal minister at Longside, Aberdeenshire, and the author of " Tullochgorum," that most rollicking and dance-compelling of measures. The piece is in Chambers, I. 219.

172

The refrain is old. Burns wrote the verse to fit a tune which was sung by an old woman at Mosspaul, where the road goes over from Ewesdale to Teviot.

174

Burns found his model for this delightful threnody in " The Last Dying Words of Bonnie Heck ; a famous greyhound in the shire of Fife," by William Hamilton of Gilbertfield (? 1665–1751), printed in Watson's *Choice Collection,* 1706.

177

From *Lyrics Legal and Miscellaneous.*

BOOK XIV

ENCHANTMENTS

I first called this section " The Twilight World," but I dropped the title because of its manifest ineptness. It is all enchantments, but many of them belong to broad daylight. Burns's, for example ; no hair will stir on the scalp because of Tam o' Shanter's peril, and the poet's conception of the Accuser of the Brethren is not of a fallen angel, but of a humorous, uncomfortable house-goblin. Burns's clear, sharp vision and classic avoidance of indeterminate colours and ragged edges keep him from one special kind of magic ; and the only instance I can recollect where he attains it is in the solitary line—

" The wan moon is setting behind the white wave."

William Nicholson had more of it in his Aiken Drum, who

" tirl'd na lang, but he glided ben
Wi a dreary, dreary hum ; "

but unfortunately " The Brownie of Blednoch " tails off into the commonplace. So, too, many of the Ballads, and these not the least ancient, treat the unearthly in a comic spirit, or at any rate with a precision which has the effect of comedy. " The False Knight upon the Road," " The Wee, Wee Man," " The Waters o' Wearie's Well," even " The Laily Worm " are enchantments for the full noontide. But with " Thomas the Rhymer " and " Tam Lin " we begin to hear the horns of Elfland ; phrases and cadences " tease us out of thought " and lay a spell on the mind,—

> " And they saw neither sun nor moon ;
> But they heard the roaring of the sea."

> " For a' the blude that's shed on earth
> Rins thro' the springs in that countrie."

> " About the middle o' the night,
> She heard the bridles ring."

" The Daemon Lover " has it—

> " I'll show where the white lilies grow
> On the banks o' Italie."

And in " The Wife of Usher's Well " we are in the pale light of the other world, when the sons come home— " their hats were o' the birk "—

> " It neither grew in syke nor ditch,
> Nor yet in ony sheugh ;
> But at the gates o' Paradise
> That birk grows fair eneugh."

It is not easy to define this peculiar magic, but it is unmistakable and tremendous. You will find it in

Keats, in " Kubla Khan," in an image of Shakespeare's,
like that in *Hamlet*—

> " the fat weed
> That roots itself in ease on Lethe wharf."

It is translunary, not of the earth, troubling the mind
with a sense of powers beyond its ken, as if the monitors
of the unseen whispered for a moment in the ear.   In
Scots verse it is found chiefly in the Ballads ;   the
" bogillis and ghaistis " of the "makars" know it not.
William Bell Scott came very near it in his " Witch's
Ballad," and you will find it in a barbarous form in the
receipt for the " witch cake," which Cromek printed
in an appendix to his *Remains of Nithsdale and Galloway
Song*.   Parts of " Kilmeny " have the true glamour, but
the " vile sixpenny planet " which beset James Hogg
drove him to rhetoric and prolixity, and a single inept
word can break its delicate spell.   Sir Walter Scott at
his greatest can compass it—in prose, as when the witch-
wives talk in the churchyard at the close of *The Bride
of Lammermoor*, and in verse, in " Proud Maisie."
That catch sung by a crazy woman brings a sudden
queer crooked shadow from the outer darkness over the
brightness of youth and love.

178

Burns only told one tale in verse, but it is the best
since Chaucer.   For the topographical and traditional
allusions, see the note in Henley, I. 433–41.

180

Child, No. 3.   Motherwell discovered the ballad in
Galloway, and printed it in his *Minstrelsy*, 1827.   The

idea is that the witch or wizard or devil will carry off the traveller who has no talent for repartee. What would Dickie o' Dryhope (see page 145) have done? " Peit " is the peat which school children in Scotland till our fathers' days had to bring each morning for the master's fire.

181

Child, No. 138—seven versions—first published by Herd in 1776. I have followed his text, except for the first and second lines in the last stanza, which are from Allan Cunningham's version.

182

Child, No. 4—nine versions. There is a ballad on this subject in almost every tongue in Europe.

183

Child, No. 37—five versions.

184

Child, No. 39—fifteen versions. The ballad is so ancient that it is mentioned among the tales told by the shepherds in the *Complaynt of Scotland*, 1549. I have used the text printed in Johnson's *Museum*, 1792, and communicated by Robert Burns. Scott's version in the *Minstrelsy* has some additional verses. Miles Cross (Mary's Cross) is said to have once stood in what are now the grounds of Bowhill, and Carterhaugh is still the name of the meadow at the junction of Yarrow and Ettrick.

185

William Bell Scott (1811–90) was best known as an artist, but he published *Poems*, 1875, and dabbled in artistic and literary criticism. For the details of witchcraft in this poem—the mouse, etc.—the reader may consult Miss Margaret Murray's *The Witch-Cult in Western Europe*, 1921.

186

Child, No. 36. There is but the one version, which is found in a collection made by Skene of Rubislaw in the north of Scotland, and called by Scott " The Old Lady's Complete Set of Ballads." " It is pure tradition," says Child, " and has never been retouched by a pen." I have omitted the repetition of the first four verses in the middle of the ballad.

187

Child, No. 243—eight versions. The text I have printed is that given in the *Oxford Book of Ballads*, composed partly from the version in Scott's *Minstrelsy*, taken down by William Laidlaw, and partly from that of the Kinloch MSS. The English ballad on the same subject in the Pepys Collection has the unromantic title of " James Harris."

188

This is Allan Cunningham's re-telling (*Scottish Songs*, I. 329) of an old ballad tale, of which a version is given by Scott in the *Minstrelsy*, communicated by Charles Kirkpatrick Sharpe. Cunningham follows the more charitable interpretation, a false nurse and a mother careless till too late. The piece is a variant of " The Cruel Mother " (Child, No. 20) :—

" She sat down below a thorn,
    Fine flowers in the valley,
And there she has her sweet babe born—
    And the green leaves they grow rarely.

' Smile na sae sweet, my bonny babe,
An' ye smile sae sweet, ye'll smile me dead.'

She's ta'en out her little penknife
And twin'd the sweet babe o' its life.

She's howkit a grave by the light of the mune,
And there she's buried her sweet babe in.

As she was going to the church
She saw her sweet babe in the porch.

' Oh, sweet babe, an' you were mine,
I wad cleed you in the silk sae fine.'

' Oh, mother dear, when I was thine,
Ye didna prove to me sae kind.' "

189

Child, No. 79—four versions. The text is that of Scott's *Minstrelsy*, taken down from the recitation of an old woman in West Lothian.

190

" Kilmeny " appeared first in *The Queen's Wake*, 1813, the tale told by " Drummond from the moors of Ern." The affected archaic spelling has been modernized. The opening and the close are the best things

which Hogg ever wrote. All that comes between seems
to me to be a long, dull, elaborate blunder, and I have
omitted it.

191

From *The Heart of Midlothian*, chapter xl. (Madge
Wildfire's dying song).

BOOK XV

LACRIMAE RERUM

There is regret in other sections of this book—regret
for departed love, for lost causes and kings, and above
all the secular plaint for the dead. Here I confine the
mood to that vaguer melancholy which is expressed
by the Virgilian phrase, the indefinite sorrow for the
" wrongs that time procureth " of which Minstrel Burne
sang, the regret for vanished days, for friends scattered,
for old ways forsaken. I have included " The Flowers
of the Forest," which is far more than a lament for a
lost battle ; it is less the fallen that the singer weeps
than the happy pastoral life which has been shattered.
Stevenson and Mr. Wingate speak of the loosening of
friendship, not in tragic cataclysm but in the common
processes of life. In " Durisdeer " and " Ettrick " the
place remains while the human accompaniment is gone ;
in others the place is lost, though the human ties may
not be broken. It is in these last that the vernacular
genius shines most brightly, for the passionate love of
one corner of the earth is deep in the Scots character,
and the text in Jeremiah is part of its confession of
faith : " Weep not for the dead, neither bemoan him ;

but weep sore for him that goeth away, for he shall
return no more, nor see his native country." Sometimes
the exile is in a far land, the " Irish shore " or " foreign
France," but it may only be England, as in " The Wild
Geese," or even the next parish, as in " Lucy's Flittin'."
It is not length of space that severs, but the changed
orbit of the mind, and " Craigo Woods " is a longing
for return less to a terrestrial spot than to a forgotten
peace of the soul. The simplest expression of this passion of wistfulness is the best ; and I wonder if others
will be haunted, as I have been, by the four bare lines
of " Lammermuir."

192

First published in *The Scottish Chap-book*.

193

Jean Elliot (1727–1803) was the second daughter of
Sir Gilbert Elliot, second baronet of Minto, and the aunt
of the first earl. Scott printed the poem in the *Minstrelsy*, together with another song (in English) on
Flodden by Alison Rutherford of Fairnilee (Mrs. Cockburn), which first appeared in *The Lark*, 1765. The
story of Miss Elliot's composition will be found in
Veitch's *History and Poetry of the Scottish Border*, II.
264, and the details of her life in *The Border Elliots*
(1897), 454. The opening line and the refrain are traditional, and, with the tune, probably date from the time
of Flodden.

194

This beautiful song was put together by Burns from
a medley of old black-letter and broadside copies, and

out of doggerel he produced immortal poetry. See the note on its antecedents in Henley, III. 433. Sir Walter Scott has used the same refrain—indeed, almost the whole of the third verse—in a song in *Rokeby*, probably working from the same originals.

195

Songs and Verses by Lady John Scott, 1904—last stanza omitted.

196

Published first in the *Book of the Glasgow Ballad Club*, 1898.

197

Songs and Verses by Lady John Scott, 1904.

198

This quatrain, which is traditional, is made the first stanza of Lady John Scott's " A Lammermuir Lilt," in her *Songs and Verses*.

199

William Forsyth (1818–79) was an Aberdeen journalist who published *Idylls and Lyrics* in 1872. The lament is on the same theme as " The Canadian Boat Song," though here it is deer and not sheep that the " degenerate lord " boasts of. I have omitted two verses.

200

William Laidlaw (1780–1853), the son of the farmer of Blackhouse in Yarrow, was the friend and amanuensis of Sir Walter Scott ; see Veitch's *History and Poetry of the Scottish Border*, II. 321. The charm of the piece lies in its extreme naturalness and simplicity ; James Hogg, on his own account, added eight more lines, which are neither natural nor simple, and which accordingly I have omitted.

201

Songs of Angus, 1915.

202

Underwoods, Book II. 16.

203

Songs of Angus, 1915.

204

Poems, 1919.

205

Underwoods, Book II. 4.

BOOK XVI

PHILOSOPHY

Philosophy is, perhaps, too large a word for the homely contents of this section. Here is no prying into the causes of things, but the eternal commonplaces of the conduct of life, as old as the Book of Job, and as young as the youngest poet among us, for each generation must discover and re-state them for itself. It is the gnomic wisdom of the ancients, translated into the language of everyday, and made immortal by the skill of the translator. I have set first Burns's credo of the many-sided man with a talent for diverse enjoyment, and next his classic plea that the source of joy must be sought in the heart. For each stage in life there is an appropriate pleasure, and some comfort attends every state, as Metrodorus sang in the Greek Anthology in reply to the pessimism of Posidippus. The young man is bidden rejoice in the days of his youth :—

> " Quhen fair Flora, the goddess of the flowris,
>   Baith firth and feildis freschely had ourfret,
> And perly droppis of the balmy schowris,
>   Thir woddis grene had with thair watter wet ;
>   Musand allone in mornyng myld, I met
> *tell*] A mirry man, that all of mirth cowth mene,
>   Syngand the sang that richt sweitly wes sett,
>   ' O yowth be glaid in to thy flowris grene ! ' " [1]

But Henryson antiphonally presents the view of age, " Oh, youth, thy flowris faidis ferly sone," and indeed the shadow of eld is on all the " makars," and they are eager, as if to convince their doubting hearts, to insist on its consolations. You will find it in Dunbar, in the anonymous " Welcum to Eild " in the Maitland MS., and very whimsically in Sir Richard Maitland's " Solace in Age " :—

> " When young men cumis fra the grene
>   (Playand at the fute-ball had bene),
> *collar-bone*]   With brokin spald,
>   I thank my God I want my ene,
>   And am sa ald."

Then there is the plea for " leesome merriness," the singing heart, as the best gift of the pilgrim ; Maitland gives

[1] Henryson, *The Ressoning betwixt Aige and Youth.*

it us, and Dunbar very nobly, and both had known vicissitudes. We have Mr. Logie Robertson's version of "*Non semper imbres,*" and Dunbar's solemn converse, a warning of the transience of earthly joys as well as of earthly pain.

The last three pieces carry us nearer metaphysic, with Stevenson's reflections upon the inequality of human lots as he lies warm in bed listening to the storm, and his haunting interrogatories in " The Spaewife." These last are the questions of a soul upon whom the shadows have fallen, and make a curious contrast to the joyous speculations of youth as found in " Hallo my Fancy," the song of that strange Covenanter, William Cleland, who died with his Cameronians at Dunkeld. I close with George Macdonald's answer to the riddle, hidden in the thoughts of the old folk, which the old folk never tell.

206

The last verse of " Corn Rigs " (Henley, I. 181). Burns is fond of these swift panoramas of a varied experience, as, for example :—

> " Oh, merry hae I been teethin' a heckle,
>> And merry hae I been shapin' a spoon !
> Oh, merry hae I been cloutin' a kettle,
>> An' kissin' my Katie when a' was done.

and

>> I've been at drucken Writers' feasts,
> Nay, been bitch-fou 'mang godly Priests—
>> Wi' rev'rence be it spoken !—
> I've often join'd the honour'd jorum
> When mighty Squireships o' the Quorum
>> Their hydra dreuth did sloken."

207

From "The Epistle to Davie, a Brother Poet" (Henley, I. 119–20), written, Burns tells us, in the metre of Montgomerie's *The Cherrie and the Slae.*

208

For Maitland, see note on page 495. Besides being the collector of the Maitland MSS. now in the Pepysian Library, Magdalene College, Cambridge, he himself wrote a number of poems which were published by the Maitland Club in 1830.

209

Ed. Scottish Text Society, II. 108. This specimen of Horatian philosophy has many parallels in Scots poetry, from Sir David Lyndsay's "Sum griedie fuill dois fill ane box, Ane uther fuill cummis and breaks the lox," etc. (*Ane Satyre*, II. 448), to Burns's "The owrecome only fashes folk to keep."

210

Horace in Homespun—"Hughie sings to console a brother shepherd."

211

Ed. Scottish Text Society, II. 110.

212

Ed. Scottish Text Society, II. 76.

213

Underwoods, Book II. 13.

214

Underwoods, Book II. 6.

215

Poetical Works, II. 1893.

BOOK XVII

DEATH

The poetry of mortality in all ages and countries tends to fall into two moods : one which protests and laments, and one which welcomes, waiting, as Bacon says, " upon the shore of death." It is at its best, perhaps, when it draws no moral, but records the fact in all its grimness in the noble bare manner of the Ballads. There is no easy consolation in the " Lyke-wake Dirge," in " Edward," or " The Twa Corbies," or " Lord Randal"; there is not even the cry of regret ; the thing is taken as if it were as natural and inevitable as the falling of night. But in most of the pieces there is the voice of lament and passionate longing. The poet mourns the loss of a brilliant figure from the world, the Lord of Aubigny or the Bonnie Earl of Moray ; the lover his dead mistress, slain for his sake on Kirkconnel Lee ; the girl her sweetheart drowned in Yarrow or in the salt sea, or dead at her chamber door ; the widow of the Border reiver, her husband, whose sheet she has sewn and whose grave she has dug ; the shepherd's wife a household left empty in the " fa' o' the year " ; and the dead in Flanders speak to each other, and ask why they are under the sod.

The defiance of death as in " Macpherson's Farewell "
is rare ; there is a sense of αἰδώς which forbids the
poet to speak slightingly of the great enemy.   The
mood of consolation and expectation, too, is not common
in the best Scots verse, though sadly familiar in the
jingles of conventional piety.   But we find it in " Kirkbride," the only poem of a high order which the Covenant inspired, where to the dying Covenanter the grave
is as a bride-chamber ; and " The Land o' the Leal,"
too deeply enshrined in Scots hearts to permit of criticism, has the same confident hope.   There is at any
rate acquiescence in " The Last o' the Tinkler " ; and
the musing of Mr. Wingate and Allan Cunningham
upon the true season for death has something of the
spirit of Sir William Temple's famous sentence : " When
all is done, human life is, at the greatest and the best,
but like a froward child that must be played with and
humoured a little to keep it quiet, till it falls asleep,
and then the care is over."   It was left for Alexander
Hume, about the same time as Sir Walter Raleigh
and in like words, to call death happy and kindly.

216

From Scott's *Minstrelsy*—a dirge of the Borders,
but of which side of them who shall say ?   Scott's
note is :—

" This is a sort of charm, sung by the lower ranks of
Roman Catholics in some parts of the north of England
while watching a dead body previous to interment.   The
tune is doleful and monotonous, and, joined to the mysterious import of the words, has a solemn effect.   The word
' sleet ' in the charm seems to be corrupted from ' selt ' or

salt, a quantity of which, in compliance with the popular superstition, is frequently placed on the breast of a corpse."

217

Child, No. 13—three versions. First printed in Percy's *Reliques*, communicated by Sir David Dalrymple (Lord Hailes), the friend and correspondent of Dr. Johnson.

218

Child, No. 26. From Scott's *Minstrelsy*, communicated from "recitation" by C. K. Sharpe. There is an English version, "The Three Ravens," first printed in 1611.

219

Child, No. 12—twenty-five versions. I give the short version from Scott's *Minstrelsy*, which seems to be the best. In the longer texts there are a number of bequests similar to those in the "Edward" ballad. When sung to children, the young man of this eerie ballad became a child poisoned by a cruel stepmother; hence we get "The Bonnie Wee Croodlin' Doo," which I quote in the version of the Motherwell MS. :—

"' Oh, whare hae ye been all day, my bonnie wee croodlin' doo ?
                               [*cooing dove*
  Oh, whare hae ye been all day, my bonnie wee croodlin' doo ? '
  ' I've been at my stepmother's ; oh, mak' my bed, mammie, noo !
  I've been at my stepmother's ; oh, mak' my bed, mammie, noo ! '

' Oh, what did ye get at your stepmother's, my bonnie
      wee croodlin' doo ? '
' I gat a wee, wee fishie ; oh, mak' my bed, mammie, noo ! '

' Where gat she the wee fishie, my bonnie wee croodlin'
      doo ? '
' In a dub before the door; oh, mak' my bed, mammie, noo!'

' What did she wi' the wee fishie, my bonnie wee croodlin'
      doo ? '
' She boiled it in a wee pannie ; oh, mak' my bed, mammie,
      noo ! ''

' Wha gied ye the banes o' the fishie till, my bonnie wee
      croodlin' doo ? '
' I gied them till a wee doggie ; oh, mak' my bed, mammie,
      noo ! '

' Oh, whare is the little wee doggie, my bonnie wee crood-
      lin' doo ? '
Oh, whare is the little wee doggie, my bonnie wee crood-
      lin' doo ? '
' It shot out its fit and died, and sae maun I die too :
Oh, mak' my bed, mammie, noo ; oh, mak' my bed,
      mammie, noo.' ''

220

From the ballad, " Edom o' Gordon," Child, No. 178
—nine versions. I have followed the text used by
Percy in the *Reliques* from a copy taken down by Lord
Hailes from the recitation of a lady, and printed by
Foulis in Glasgow in 1755.

221

Child, No. 210—four versions.   From Smith's *Scottish
Minstrelsy*, V. 42.

222

Ed. Scottish Text Society, II. 63—the last two stanzas. Bernard Stewart was the grandson of John Stewart of Darnley, and came in 1484 to Scotland as the ambassador of France to renew the ancient league. In 1485 he led the French auxiliaries who fought for Henry VII. at the battle of Bosworth. He was Captain of the Scots Guards in France, and won great glory in the war with Spain, so that Brantôme ranked him among the most illustrious of French captains. He died in Edinburgh in 1508 of an old fever contracted in Calabria. When he was compelled to surrender at Angertola he made it one of the terms that all of his company except himself should be set at liberty. " He sharply reproved," says the chronicler, " two young lords, his kinsmen, for that more faintly than was fit for men— *namely, for their being Scotsmen and of the blood royal*— they did bewail the unfortunate success of the war."

223

From Scott's *Minstrelsy*—the best of many versions.

224

Child, No. 181—two versions. The one in the text appeared in the *Tea-Table Miscellany*. James Stewart of Doune became Earl of Moray by his marriage with the eldest daughter of the Regent. He was murdered near his house of Donibristle in Fife in February 1592 by the Earl of Huntly, who sheltered himself behind the King's command to apprehend Moray, since the latter was supposed to be in communication with Bothwell. Sir James Balfour mentions a rumour that " the

Queen, more rashly than wisely, some few days before, had commended Moray in the King's hearing, with too many epithets of a proper and gallant man."

225

From Herd, 1769. Another curious and beautiful verse is given by Chambers, I. 178 :—

" New Holland is a barren place, in it there grows nae grain
 Nor ony habitation wherein for to remain ;
 But the sugar canes are plenty, and the wine draps frae
  the tree ;
 But the Lowlands of Holland hae twined my love and me."

226

This ballad, first printed in Scott's *Minstrelsy*, is associated by local tradition with the old tower of Henderland at the foot of Megget, near St. Mary's Loch ; but the Piers Cockburn whose story is in Pitcairn's *Criminal Trials* was executed, not at his house door, but in Edinburgh in 1540 (see Veitch's *History and Poetry of the Scottish Border*, II. 18–20, and the note in Chambers, I. 175). Professor Veitch is right, I think, in saying that " lily " in the second line means merely pale yellow. The lily known to the Borders was the daffodil, and the colour of the bent, as in " lily lee " and " lily leven," is often like that of a pale daffodil.

227

Child, No. 2,015—eight versions. I have printed the shortest, and to my mind by far the most beautiful. It appeared in Ramsay's *Tea-Table Miscellany* and *Orpheus Caledonius*.

228

Child, No. 201. The story relates to the visit of the plague to Perth in 1645.

230

Poems, Songs, and Sonnets, 1894. The district is Upper Nithsdale, where an old man on his deathbed said, " Bury me in Kirkbride, for there is much of God's redeemed dust lies there."

232

Thomas Smibert (1810–54), published *Io Anche : Poems chiefly Lyrical,* 1851.

233

More Songs of Angus, and Others, 1918.

234

Ballads of Battle, 1916.

235

(1) The first is from *Poems,* 1919.
(2) The second is a verse of a song by Allan Cunningham in *Songs of Scotland,* IV. 358.

236

Poetical Works, 1893, Vol. II.

238

Ed. Scottish Text Society, 34. A stanza from the poem, " To his sorrofull Saull, Consolatioun."

BOOK XVIII

DIVINE PHILOSOPHY

Scotland has a name for piety, but the repute has been won since the Reformation. In her Catholic days she was as a nation often at enmity with Rome and little troubled by it : the Borders lay for long seasons under the Papal ban, and cared for it not at all. A piece like " The Thrie Tales of the Thrie Priestis of Peblis," which belongs to the late fifteenth century, gives indeed a pleasant picture of the Church, but in things ecclesiastical satire, even in those orthodox times, was commoner than praise. Yet it is to the pre-Reformation poets that we must look for the great Scots devotional poetry, perhaps for the reason that, when the vernacular went out of fashion among the learned, it acquired a tavern atmosphere which made it ill-suited for such high purposes. Henryson and Dunbar are still at the head of our religious poets. Next to them must stand the early Reformers, who set themselves to adapt the love-lays and hunting songs of the people to the uses of piety. *The Gude and Godlie Ballats* are often ridiculous in the extreme, but they have moments of wistfulness and passion and a strange solemnity. With Alexander Hume, the minister of Logie, the great age of Scots devotional poetry comes to an end.

The seventeenth century, when the divines ran riot, produced only prose. The pity is the greater, for it had the stuff of poetry. There was a George Herbert in Bishop Leighton, whose sermons were admired by Coleridge ; there was a Quarles, perhaps, in Samuel

Rutherford, whose amorous divinity can be sufficiently revolting—Patrick Walker says that his *Letters* were the companion of young rakes in their drinking bouts— but who has passages of tenderness and beauty. There was a Thomas Traherne, or somebody like him, in Mr. William Guthrie, who bade his hearers praise God " if you have no more, for this good day and sunshine to the lambs." Their language was English, and it may be questioned if they were not too far from the common speech to handle it in poetry, even if they had had the gift. Zachary Boyd, who preached against Cromwell and was punished by being invited to dinner, in his *Last Battell of the Soule in Death* can write prose which recalls Fuller and Bunyan, but when it comes to versifying the Scriptures, more especially when he descends to a homely idiom, he is merely grotesque.

In the eighteenth century English was so universal that it might have been made the official language of devotion by a decree of the General Assembly. The metrical version of the Psalms in use to-day is the work of a Provost of Eton; that fine collection, the Paraphrases, is English; and Scotland's few respectable contributions to hymnology have been in the same tongue. It is not surprising, perhaps, that the great body of Scots popular verse on which Burns worked should have contained no religious verse, for popular devotional poetry takes usually the form of carols and cradle songs, which took flight, if they ever existed, at the Reformation. But it is a sign of the groove into which the vernacular has sunk that no Scot since Hume has applied it to this purpose. Perhaps the instinct was right. Words and cadences associated with love-making and drinking would have been apt to raise undevout reminiscences,

The Northern Muse

like the prayer of the minister which began with a line
from " Tam o' Shanter," " Kings may be blest, O Lord,
but Thou art glorious." When in the last century the
Rev. Mr. Hately Waddell turned the Psalms into Scots
the result did not make for edification.

My selection is, therefore, with the exception of one
poem by George Macdonald, wholly from the writers
who lived before the seventeenth century. It begins
with Dunbar's great Christmas ode and his " Ballad of
Our Lady," into which he poured all the exuberance of
his diction and the magnificence of his fancy. It in-
cludes two extracts from *The Gude and Godlie Ballats*,
cries of distressed souls which seem to me to have something of a ballad poignancy. Then comes the gentle
Henryson's version of Ecclesiastes, and last, Dunbar's
noble conclusion of the whole matter. This anthology
began with Dunbar in the fervour of spring and youth,
and it closes with him singing as before of May and
Aurora—but with the solemn voice and the grave eyes
of one who has kept watch over man's mortality.

239

Ed. Scottish Text Society, II. 72. The first line is
Isaiah xlv. 8, " Drop down ye heavens from above "—
the verse for Vespers in Advent.

240

From *The Gude and Godlie Ballats*, Laing's edition,
192—two verses omitted.

241

Ed. Scottish Text Society, II. 269. Dunbar's masterpiece in internal rhyming.

Commentary

242

Poetical Works, 1893, Vol. II.

243

From *The Gude and Godly Ballats,* Laing's edition, 116—seven verses out of twenty-two. The air is in Queen Elizabeth's *Virginal Book.*

244

From the Bannatyne MS.

245

Ed. Scottish Text Society, II. 174.

INDEX TO INTRODUCTION
AND COMMENTARY

535

INDEX OF AUTHORS

(The reference is to the number of the poem.)

INDEX TO TITLES AND
FIRST LINES

(The reference is to the page of the volume.)

18

Index to Titles and First Lines 547

PRINTED IN GREAT BRITAIN AT
THE PRESS OF THE PUBLISHERS

ESTABLISHED 1798

T. NELSON
& SONS, Ltd.
PRINTERS AND
PUBLISHERS